AFTER YOU BELIEVE

AFTER YOU BELIEVE

Why Christian Character Matters

N. T. WRIGHT

BISHOP OF DURHAM

HarperOne
An Imprint of HarperCollinsPublishers

HarperOne

FIRST EDITION

Library of Congress Cataloging-in-Publication Data

Wright, N. T. (Nicholas Thomas)
After you believe : why Christian character matters / N. T. Wright. — 1st ed.
    p. cm.
ISBN 978-0-06-173055-9
1. Character—Religious aspects—Christianity.   2. Christian life—Anglican authors.   I. Title.

BV4599.5.C45W75   2010

  241'.4—dc22   2009030504

    11 12 13 14 RRD (H) 10 9 8 7 6 5 4 3 2

for Maggie
with love and gratitude

CONTENTS

PREFACE

This book is a kind of sequel to *Simply Christian* and *Surprised by Hope*. There I set out (among other things) what seems to me a basic principle of early Christianity—namely, that God the creator intends to bring heaven and earth together at last, and that this plan has been decisively inaugurated in Jesus Christ. This vision has radical implications for every aspect of how we think about Christian faith and life. In *Surprised by Hope*, in particular, I argued that the final hope of Christians is not simply "going to heaven," but resurrection into God's new creation, the "new heaven and new earth."

Part of the point of all this is that resurrection and new creation have, according to the first followers of Jesus, already begun to happen, precisely because of what happened to Jesus himself at Easter. I began, in both those earlier books, to point on to some of the ways this might play out in terms of Christian responsibility in and for the world, and not least in terms of Christian behavior. In the present book I seek to develop this theme much further, with particular attention to the notion of Christian "character" and "virtue." The basic point is this: Christian life in the present, with its responsibilities and particular callings, is to be understood and shaped in relation to the final goal for which we have been made and redeemed. The better we understand that goal, the better we shall understand the path toward it.

The result, offered here, is not a full account of "ethics." It is certainly not a set of rules to cover all occasions, which is what some people expect from a book about Christian behavior. As I will explain,

I think that's the wrong way to go about the whole thing. It is, rather, an exploration of how Christian character is formed, as a particular and focused example of how character is formed in general. I have given particular attention to the close reading of some key New Testament texts, which I think are often either misunderstood or toned down when approached from other points of view. And I have tried to bring out in particular the way in which the early Christians thought of questions about "behavior" not as a separate topic, but as one aspect of their larger aims: worship and mission.

I have tried to keep the level of writing accessible to people of all sorts, and have restrained myself from entering into the many fascinating contemporary debates about Christian behavior as a whole and in its particular parts. Those who know their way around these debates will see easily enough where I am following a line taken by this or that particular writer, or distancing myself from someone else's point of view. I have added a note at the end of the book to indicate some of the places where I have found help, and some of the debates to which, I venture to hope, this book may, in small measure, have something to contribute. In particular, I hope to have reminded readers of the New Testament that the great tradition which discusses behavior in terms of virtue has more to offer than they may have thought, and also to have reminded people who have theorized about virtue that the New Testament has more to offer them than they seem to have supposed. But the main point of the book lies elsewhere: to stimulate tomorrow's Christians of whatever sort, and in whichever tradition, to be encouraged and excited by the pursuit of virtue in its specifically Christian form, and to have their character shaped, together and individually, to become the human beings God meant us to be, which means being concerned primarily with worship and mission and with the formation of our own character as the vital means to that double end.

To those coming to a specifically Christian book from the outside, as it were, I would say this. I have written elsewhere about the reasons why I believe that, despite all the skepticisms of today's Western world, there might after all be a God who made the world and who is going to put it right at last. The dreams we have that refuse to die—dreams of freedom and beauty, of order and love, dreams that we can make a real difference in the world—come into their own when we put them within a framework of belief in a God who made the world and is going to sort it out once and for all, and wants to involve human beings in that process. We now approach these same issues from another angle. In a world where so much confusion abounds, how do we know what is "good"? And how do we discover what being human is really all about? This book is meant to offer a double challenge: to Christians, to think through the nature of Christian behavior from a new angle; to anyone and everyone, to think through what it means to be genuinely human. I am proposing that, when we really understand those two challenges, they eventually meet up.

This sort of book is not the place for entering into other controversies. I have assumed, for the present purpose, that Jesus of Nazareth did and said more or less what the four gospels in the New Testament say he did and said. I have written about all that, in debate with those who take radically different viewpoints, in considerable detail elsewhere. Likewise, I have assumed that St. Paul wrote Ephesians and Colossians, something which many scholars in the last century or so have doubted. Actually, the argument of the book doesn't depend on either of these assumptions, and for that reason, in addition to the risk of clogging up the present line of thought, I won't refer to these questions again.

In writing about the life of the church, and the challenges facing Christians in tomorrow's world, I am uncomfortably aware that I really only know the contemporary Western church. I have enormously enjoyed meeting Christians from other parts of the world, and from traditions very different from my own, and I hope to go on learning things from them as well as about them. But I can't presume to speak about them here. Ideally, I should say "modern Western Christians" all the time, to reflect this, but that gets clunky and awkward. I trust that readers, particularly in other parts of the world, will take it for granted that I am speaking from my own limited perspective. I hope they will have not only the goodness to forgive me my parochial viewpoint but the good sense to transpose what I say into their own contexts.

Translations of the Bible are my own. Those from the New Testament are mostly taken from the translation I have provided in the *Everyone* series of New Testament guides (*Matthew for Everyone,* etc.), published by SPCK in London and Westminster John Knox in Louisville, Kentucky.

As always, I am very grateful to my publishers and editors, particularly Mickey Maudlin and Mark Tauber at HarperOne and Simon Kingston and Joanna Moriarty at SPCK, for all their help and encouragement; and to my colleagues in Durham for their continuing support. I have expressed my thanks to various colleagues for their help in the Afterword.

My wife deserves particular gratitude for her tenacious enthusiasm for my writing and her ready willingness to put up with the usual domestic consequences at a time when other unexpected pressures were crowding upon her. One cannot write about virtue without thinking about love, and I cannot think about love without thinking about her. I have dedicated two other books to her, each of which marked a serious turning point in my life and work. This one comes, as ever, with love and gratitude, but with both of those qualities formed, over further years, into a still deeper habit of the heart.

N. T. Wright
Auckland Castle
Spring 2009

1. WHAT AM I HERE FOR?

ONE

James was in his early twenties when it happened. His life had been going along, nothing too dramatic, just the usual ups and downs. Suddenly, out of the blue, he met up with an old friend who was on his way to a meeting at a nearby church. James went too, and that very night, to his complete astonishment, his life was turned upside down and inside out.

"I never knew these things really happened," he told me when I met him some years later ("James" isn't his real name, of course). "When I talk about it, it sounds like I'm some kind of religious nut, but it's the sober truth. I met Jesus! He was as real to me as you are in this room. All the old clichés suddenly came true. I felt cleansed, rinsed out, and more alive than I'd ever been before. It's as though I'd gone into a deep sleep and woken up in a new world, totally refreshed. I never knew what people were talking about with all that God stuff before, but believe me, it all makes sense."

James was telling me this story because he had now run into a puzzle. He had been attending the church where he'd had that wonderful, life-changing experience. He had learned a lot about God and Jesus. He'd learned a lot, too, about himself. He had been taught, quite correctly, that God loved him more than he could ever imagine—indeed, so much that God sent Jesus to die for him. The preachers he had listened to had insisted that nothing we humans do can make us acceptable to God, now or in the ultimate future. Everything is a gift of God's sheer grace and generosity. James had drunk all this in like someone who's walked ten miles on a hot day and is suddenly given a large glass of cold water. It was wonderful news. He was living by it.

But he found himself now staring at a big question mark.

What am I here for?

He put it like this, as we talked. This is how it stacked up:

God loves me; yes.

He's transformed my life so that I find I want to pray, to worship, to read the Bible, to abandon the old self-destructive ways I used to behave. That's great.

Clearly (people at church kept saying this, too) God wants me to tell other people about this good news, so that they can find it for themselves. Fine. It feels a bit strange, and I'm not sure I'm very good at it, but I'm doing the best I can.

And obviously all this comes with the great promise that one day I'll be with God forever. I know I'll die one day, but Jesus has guaranteed that everybody who trusts him will live with him in heaven. That's great too.

But what am I here for *now*? What happens *after you believe*?

The reason James knocked on my door was that he wasn't satisfied with the answers he'd been getting from his friends and from people in the church he was attending. All they could say was that God called some people to particular spheres of Christian service—into full-time pastoral ministry, for instance, or to be teachers or doctors or missionaries or some combination of these and other similar tasks. But James had no sense that any of that was for him. He was finishing his doctorate in computer science and had all sorts of career options opening up before him. Was all that knowledge and opportunity simply irrelevant to the "spiritual" issues? Was he basically going to be hanging around for a few decades, waiting to die and go to heaven, and in the meantime using some of his spare time to persuade other people to do the same? Was that really *it*? Isn't there anything else that happens after you believe and before you finally die and go to heaven?

What's more, James had discovered a puzzle within this question. Many of his new friends lived very strict, self-disciplined lives. They had learned a lot of rules for Christian behavior, primarily from the Bible, and they believed that God wanted them to follow those rules. But James couldn't see how this squared with the basic teaching that God had accepted him as he was, because of Jesus and what *he*'d done, simply on the basis of his faith. If that was so, why should he be bound by all these old rules, some of which seemed frankly bizarre?

I wish I could say, looking back, that I got the answers right. To be honest, I can't remember exactly what I said—though the last time I heard from James he seemed to have got the message anyway. But he is hardly unique in facing the question. A great many Christians in the Western world today have faced exactly this puzzle, and one of the main reasons for writing the present book is to help them answer it.

I was reminded of James when I had an email, just the other day, from a good friend. Many people, he wrote, find it all too easy to get the idea "that one can just believe in Jesus and then really do nothing else." Many Christians have so emphasized the need for conversion, for the opening act of faith and commitment, for the initial statement of that faith ("believing that Jesus died for me" or whatever), that they have a big gap in their vision of what being a Christian is all about. It's as though they were standing on one side of a deep, wide river, looking across to the further bank. On *this* bank you declare your faith. On the *opposite* bank is the ultimate result—final salvation itself. But what are people supposed to do in the meantime? Simply stand here and wait? Is there no bridge between the two? What does this say about faith itself? If we're not careful, wrote my friend, this opening act of belief can become "simply a matter of assent to a proposition (Jesus is Son of God, etc.), with no need for transformation."

Transformation! Now there's an interesting idea. But is it appropriate to think like that? Are Christians supposed to regard their lives in that way? Isn't that suggesting that there's a way across from the present to the future, across that wide river called The Rest of My Life—a bridge put up in the old days when people thought you could use your own moral effort to make yourself good enough for God? But if moral effort doesn't count for anything, what is then the point of being a Christian—other than to go to heaven one day, and perhaps to persuade a few others to go with you? Is there any reason for doing anything much, after you believe, except to keep your nose reasonably clean until the time comes to die and go to be with Jesus forever?

Some people who ponder this also face another concern. Jesus himself, followed by the writers of the New Testament, seems to have made some pretty stringent moral demands on the early disciples. Where does all that fit in? If we are already saved, why does what we do matter? And are the demands realistic in our day and age?

Not all Christians puzzle over these dilemmas. But many do, and I hope this book will show them that the old bridge which they may have ignored, or assumed to be unusable, will carry their weight and join up the two banks of the river in fine style. The bridge in question goes by many names, and we shall discuss them as we move forward. But one of the most obvious names is *character*. That's what this book is about.

TWO

There is a second reason for writing this book. Many people who have never faced the question James faced may well have run into this one. Let me introduce you to two other old friends (also renamed): Jenny and Philip.

Jenny and Philip found themselves arguing one evening across a crowded church meeting. The trouble was that they weren't really arguing about the same thing.

Jenny was quite clear what the scriptural rules said. Jesus himself had insisted that divorcing your spouse and marrying someone else was adultery. Of course people could be forgiven for sinning when they repented and gave it up, but how could remarried people be forgiven when they were now living in this new, and apparently adulterous, relationship and had no intention of giving it up, regarding it rather as the right and God-given thing? In particular, how could the church even think of appointing someone in that position as its pastor? (That, of course, was the reason the church meeting had been called.) How could such a person ever teach young people what was right and wrong? How could he prepare couples for a lifetime of marriage if he himself had disobeyed the rules? When you believe the gospel, Jenny said, you are then given the New Testament as your handbook for life. The rules in it are quite clear. Either you keep them or you don't.

Philip was equally clear. Jesus didn't come to give us a bunch of rules. After all, didn't St. Paul say that "Christ is the end of the Law"? The whole point of Jesus's teaching was that he *included* people, particularly those who were excluded by the self-righteous. (Philip didn't look straight at Jenny as he said this, but everybody got the message.) Jesus came to help us discover who we really are, and sometimes, as with Jesus's first followers, it takes a while for people to figure it out, and they make mistakes as they're doing so—but they'll get there eventually. Didn't Jesus tell a story about a father welcoming a prodigal son while the self-righteous older brother stayed outside? He, Philip, would much rather have someone as a pastor who had been through difficulties himself and discovered that Jesus loved him anyway, instead of someone who would lay down the law from a great height and lock everybody up in a set of rules that half the congregation didn't really keep anyway. That just encourages hypocrisy! Since the Jesus we believe in is the Jesus who accepts us as we are, the life that follows after we believe is the life of celebrating that acceptance, and moving forward from there. That is the way of honesty, of being true to yourself and open about it.

I don't think Jenny and Philip realized it, but the reason they both got angry and frustrated as the conversation went on was that they were starting from quite different places. Jenny said she was "beginning with the Bible," implying that Philip wasn't, but actually things aren't quite that easy. Jenny was looking for rules—perhaps we should say Rules with a capital R, Rules that you have to keep whether you feel like it or not. She wanted a pastor who would teach like that and live like that. Then everyone would know where they stood. Philip, on the other hand, was eager for ways of being authentic, finding out what was deeply true for yourself, how to live without hypocrisy and with a deep, rich, and vulnerable honesty. That's what *he* looked for in a pastor. He would respect and trust someone like that.

It was an uncomfortable meeting. People got hot under the collar (which, as Jenny reflected sadly later on, was itself against the Rules). They said things they didn't really mean (which, as Philip knew as soon as the angry words came out of his mouth, was itself a form of hypocrisy). They weren't simply disagreeing about the answer to the question. They were disagreeing about the question itself. How do Christians make moral decisions? How do any of us, Christian or not, know what is right and wrong? *Are* there such things as "right" and "wrong," or is life more complicated than that? *Are* there capital-R Rules, and how do they relate to real people rather than moral machines? As far as Jenny was concerned, Philip was one of those dangerous relativists who think that there are no black-and-white moral questions, only shades of gray, and that the most important thing is to be true to yourself. All Philip could hear, in listening to Jenny, was a hard, cold legalism which had nothing to do with the Jesus he knew, the Jesus who was the friend of sinners and who told stories about the angels celebrating with a great party when the lost sheep was found.

That larger confrontation between two ways of approaching the whole question of Christian behavior is repeated, week after week and year after year, in church councils, in synods, in assemblies, in conventions, in private conversations—and, often enough, in the silent debates within individual hearts and minds. It is, in fact, the Christian version of the much wider question which all sensible people ask themselves sooner or later: not only, "How should I live?" but "How does one know?"

This is a different Great Divide to the one we saw a moment ago, but the ultimate answer to it is the same. There, in James's puzzle, the Great Divide was between the initial faith which someone has at conversion and the final moment when, after death, that person is promised God's salvation. This book is partly about the question which bridges that divide: What am I supposed to be doing with all that time in between? But it is also about the question which hovered, unspoken, between Jenny and Philip on that uncomfortable evening. How do we make moral decisions? Do we have to choose between a system of Rules (which we then just need to hammer out and agree on) and a system of Finding Out Who I Really Am (and being true to it)? Are there other ways not only of discovering how we should live but of actually living that way? What happens, not only individually but also corporately, *after you believe*?

The same answer applies to both questions; and so this book addresses both, at the same time. Jesus himself, backed up by the early Christian writers, speaks repeatedly about the development of a particular *character*. Character—the transforming, shaping, and marking of a life and its habits—will generate the sort of behavior that rules might have pointed toward but which a "rule-keeping" *mentality* can never achieve. And it will produce the sort of life which will in fact be true to itself—though the "self" to which it will at last be true is the redeemed self, the transformed self, not the merely "discovered" self of popular thought. I hope that this book will help not only the Jameses of this world to find what they are here for, but the Jennys and Philips to have their debate within a larger, more biblical, more satisfying, and actually more Christian framework. In the last analysis, what matters after you believe is neither rules nor spontaneous self-discovery, but character.

THREE

What am I here for? How do we know what's right and wrong? These are questions every human being, and perhaps every human community, asks from time to time, at least by implication. But there is a third set of questions which also points toward the topic of this book, and which goes much wider, out beyond the confines of the church and into a very confused and scary world. Our world.

In the summer of 2008, a volcano which had been rumbling away in the background suddenly erupted with horrific force. It wasn't a literal volcano, but it had a similarly devastating effect. The whole financial system of the Western world, which had dominated global culture for several generations, grossly overstretched itself and disintegrated under its own weight. It was like a giant who had climbed a tree to pick and eat all the fruit, and who now, in his excessive greed, was stretching out to other trees all around to get at their fruit too. But his weight was too much, and the tree he'd climbed in the first place couldn't take any more strain. It crashed over, with the giant still greedily clinging to as much fruit as he could.

There are many complex reasons why the financial chaos of 2008 happened, and the reader may be relieved to know I'm not going to discuss them. But in the immediate aftermath, lots of people pointed to the fact that over the previous twenty years all kinds of rules and regulations that had previously been in place to stop the banks and other money-lending institutions from behaving in an irresponsible fashion had quietly been set aside. They were over-restrictive, the politicians had been told. A healthy economy needed to take risks and reward the risk-takers. Everyone went along for the ride, not realizing that they were accelerating toward the edge of a cliff. So now, people have been saying, we need to put all the rules and regulations back in place. It's time to tighten things up.

That fits in with many other aspects of today's culture. Since September 11, 2001, airports have installed complex security checks. Most of us have almost forgotten what it was like to get on a plane without first putting yourself and your belongings through electronic screening. Those of us who regularly visit the United States have become wearily used to being photographed and fingerprinted each time we come through Customs. But almost everywhere you travel, and particularly if you're going to be there for more than a few days, there are forms to fill out, interviews to attend, photographs to be taken, and so on. Millions of people who you can tell at a glance have no intention of blowing up planes have had to waste copious time and money going through official procedures to certify that they're law-abiding citizens (though by the time they've queued for hours and then been sent back again to complete yet another trivial form, they may not feel so law-abiding). In my own country, the United Kingdom, anyone who volunteers to do anything in the community that may involve children has to go through complex and time-consuming police checks in case there's a hint of bad behavior on their record. This applies even to people in their seventies and eighties who have lived a blameless life and whose friends and family know their character through and through. We don't trust people anymore. Anyone. Writing this, I am aware that some people will think I'm being dangerously irresponsible in even raising any questions about The System as we now have it. (It's getting worse. Yet more official forms are promised. And it doesn't work—except for the lawyers who win whenever anyone gets sued.) The Western world has become law-bound, rule-bound, regulation-bound.

There are deep cultural reasons why we've gone this route. But at the moment we simply need to notice that our culture has lurched between deregulation in all key areas of life—money, sex, and power, to put it crudely—and what you might call *re*regulation. *De*regulation happened because people wanted to do their own thing, to be (as it were) true to themselves and see what happened. But when deregulation results in chaos, whether in banking (money), in human relationships (sex), or in the way we do war and politics and prisons and interrogation and the like (power), people are eager to reintroduce rules that will get us back on track. The problem is that *introducing new regulations doesn't get to the heart of the problem.* Doing your own thing isn't good enough, but rules by themselves won't solve the problem.

This was borne in on me early in 2009 as I was talking to a senior banker I know quite well, who had been near the heart of the financial crash of summer 2008 and was now, when we talked, trying to work out how to rescue what could be rescued and take things back to some kind of sanity.

"Tom," he said, "they can introduce as many new regulations as they like. Yes, we do need some guidelines put back in place; we went too far, giving people freedom to gamble with huge sums of money and do crazy deals. But any banker or mortgage broker can easily hire a smart accountant and lawyer to help them tick all the boxes the government tells them to, and then go around the back of the system and do what they want. What's the point of that?"

"So what's the answer?" I asked.

"Character," he replied. "Keeping rules is all right as far as it goes, but the real problem in the last generation is that we've lost the sense that character matters; that integrity matters. The system is only really healthy when the people who are running it are people you can trust to do the right thing, not because there are rules but because that's the sort of people they are."

This accords with the pragmatic perspective of J. K. Galbraith, who wrote in the early 1950s about the financial crash of the late 1920s. The best way to keep the financial world on an even keel, he suggested, is to listen to the people who were around when the previous crash occurred. In fact, he suggested that financial crashes happen precisely because the people who remember the last one have either died or retired and thus are no longer around, with memories and character formed by that previous experience, to warn people not to be irresponsible.

Since I had that conversation, something else has happened which has been almost equally volcanic in the public life of the UK. People in other countries may look on with some amusement at the fuss, because it has to do with corrupt politicians—in many countries people *assume* that politicians are corrupt and that the citizenry can't do anything about it—but in my country it has shaken our whole system to its foundations. Suddenly it has emerged that some politicians have been claiming "expenses" for all sorts of things which appear to the taxpayer to be ridiculous and fraudulent, such as mortgage payments on nonexistent properties. And the excuse has been that they were all acting "within the rules." Well, maybe; but they made up the rules themselves! When challenged, some of our politicians declared, in effect, that they saw nothing wrong with using public money to further their own wealth. And when, after intense public pressure, the politicians gave in and allowed their expense claims to be made public, they first made sure that all the key elements were blacked out and illegible. People have been a bit suspicious of politicians for years, but this has sent any remaining trust crashing to the ground.

At one level this has been pure farce, albeit expensive and offensive. But the reason for raising the issue here is that it demonstrates another place at which the moral question of the early twenty-first century is raising its head. What happens "after you believe"—in democracy? In the Western financial system? In the public life and global community of tomorrow's world? Can we live on "rules" and "regulations," or will they encourage a box-checking mentality rather than the development of deep, wise, and trustworthy character? Conversely, what happens if we allow people to "be true to themselves" and hope that it'll all work out? Does that work from the start only, or, again, once "character" has been developed so that people will behave in a selfless spirit of public service (as, to their credit, some of our politicians are now seen to have done)?

Yet another walk of life comes up with a similar story. I found myself a couple of years ago sharing a platform with a very distinguished former England rugby star. He was talking about the massive changes that had taken place in the game in the last ten or fifteen years, with the increased professionalization and the enormous pressure on young players to produce "results." The players today, he said, are overcoached. They are taught dozens of "moves"—how to respond to this situation, how to defend against that strategy, how to keep the game under control, how to open it up. But few of them any longer play the game for fun, acquiring as they do so that sixth sense for how things work which would enable them to improvise in totally new situations. As a result, they're lost when something unexpected happens. They haven't been given a set of rules for what to do in those circumstances. What they lack is a deeply formed character which would "read" the game with a kind of second nature and come up with a shrewd and quick solution.

The questions we began with, then, might have seemed to be specific to Christians (rather than the rest of the world), and indeed to a particular type of Christian (those who see things in terms of initial conversion and final salvation without much in between). But they are not. They are actually the same questions that face the whole Western world right now. And, since the Western world has dominated global culture, politics, and economics—and even, in some areas at least, sports—for some while, that means that they face, sooner or later, the entire global community. Our starting point—what happens "after you believe"—looked initially as though it was simply about the individual Christian. But as we have seen, it also concerns the whole church family, the Jennys and the Philips who go round and round the circle of moral puzzles. And it also points outward from the church to the puzzles faced by the whole wider world. How do we not only think clearly and wisely about *what* to do, in our personal lives, our church lives, and our entire public life, but also discover *how* to do it?

We keep coming back to one particular answer: character. Interestingly, this is what Jesus himself challenged his hearers to develop. We must now look at one of his most famous confrontations, which opens up the issue in a sharp and telling way.

FOUR

One of the most haunting scenes in the gospel story is the tale of the rich, bright, eager young man who comes running up to Jesus with an urgent question (Matthew 19.16–30; Mark 10.17–22; Luke 18.18–30). We should perhaps remind ourselves that serious people in the ancient world did not typically run. It was undignified. But this man really wants to meet Jesus, really wants an answer to his question—or he thinks he does. So he forgets his dignity and runs to see him, asking, in effect, "What good thing must I do?" He's out of breath, excited, keen to see what this extraordinary teacher is going to say. Jesus seems to have an inside track on all sorts of things; let's see what he makes of this one.

The eager young man asks the question because it has a future reference. He wants hope, and like almost all humans he believes that present actions have future consequences. Because he is a first-century Jew, he is thinking particularly of God's coming new age, the time when, so people believed, the God who had made the world would bring heaven and earth together at last, flooding all creation with justice, peace, and glory. "What must I do," he blurts out, "*to inherit eternal life?*"

Now before we go any further, we need to clear our minds of the image which immediately appears when we hear those words. When first-century Jews spoke about "eternal life," they weren't thinking of "going to heaven" in the way we normally imagine it. (On all this, see *Surprised by Hope*.) "Eternal life" meant the age to come, the time when God would bring heaven and earth together, the time when God's kingdom would come and his will be done on earth as in heaven. When that happens, the man was asking Jesus, will I be part of it? How can I know? What sort of person must I be in the present if I'm going to be part of the new age, when God rescues this sad old world and does what he's always promised? How can that future reality shape the sort of person I'm becoming right now? If that's my goal, what is the path which leads there?

Although the young man was a first-century Jew, his underlying question is shared by people of all places and times. Often it is posed in terms of "happiness": How can I find true happiness, the deeply satisfying life that I feel in my bones I was made for but that so often seems to slip through my fingers? The United States has, indeed, written this quest into its foundational documents: all people, it is claimed, have a right to "life, liberty, and the pursuit of happiness." This, of course, begs the question, already asked by ancient philosophers: How do we know what genuine happiness is? Since a lot of people seem to be pursuing it without finding it, are we clear what it really is and how best to go in search of it? What must we do in the present if we are to reach the goal of a fully human existence, realize our potential, become the people we know in our bones we were meant to be?

Many people will assume that one of the aims of Christianity is to give answers to the first question ("How should I behave?") while leaving the second ("How can I become truly happy, the person I was meant to be?") to philosophers and the nonreligious. After all, to many people, the question "How ought I to behave?" cuts clean across the question "How can I be truly happy?" since we tend to assume that rules for behavior are designed to *stop* us from being happy—or, to put it the other way around, if we really want happiness, we need to break, or at least bend, the rules.

I think life is more complex and interesting than that. Questions of how to behave, and also of how to be happy, are both seen by authentic Christian faith as offshoots or byproducts of something else. If we can get that "something else" sorted out—and the story of the rich young man who came running up to Jesus points the way to this—we might be able to make headway with the offshoots as well. I hope to show in this book that the biblical vision of what human life is ultimately for will open up a perspective in which questions of behavior on the one hand, and of a fulfilled human life on the other, dovetail together. But it is with the question of behavior, and the biblical roots of the Christian answer to that question, that this book is primarily concerned.

Those with sharp eyes may have spotted that the question "How should I behave?" contains two significantly different questions within it. First, it refers to the *content* of my behavior: *In what way should I behave?* In other words, what specific things ought I to do and not to do? But second, it refers to the *means* or *method* of my behavior: granted that I know what I ought to do and ought not to do, *by what means* will I be able to put these things into practice? One of the oldest and best-known moral puzzles, after all, is that we all know what it's like to do something we knew we should not do, or not to do something we know we should have done. Interestingly, Jesus seems to have given both sides of this question the same answer: "Follow me!" That is both *what* you should do and *how* you should do it.

We return, then, to Jesus's encounter with the eager young man.

The young man, in company with many first-century Jews, was supposing that God's promised new age would be reserved for loyal Jews—and that Jewish loyalty would be defined in terms of obedience to the Law, encapsulated in the famous Ten Commandments. This wasn't (as people sometimes suppose) a straightforward scheme of merit and reward, of "keeping the rules" and thus earning one's passage into the new world, but rather a matter of God's ancient agreement with his people: he had rescued them to be his people, and in the Law he had outlined the terms of the agreement by which they would demonstrate their gratitude to him. But the young man seems to have kept the terms of the agreement—no murder, adultery, theft, false witness, fraud, disrespect to parents—and still to have had a sense that there must be something more.

Jesus agrees with this, but in offering this "something more" he takes the man into new terrain altogether. The commandments listed up to this point comprise the last six of the ten; what about the others? There is no mention of the Sabbath; that's a topic for another time. But the first three commandments take us into a different realm, the realm of avoiding idolatry and of honoring God and his name alone. Jesus doesn't quote those commandments. Instead, he brings them bang up to date in the young man's life. If you want to be "complete," he says, get rid of your possessions. Sell them, and give the money to the poor. Then come and follow me. Somehow, shockingly, following Jesus means putting God first, and vice versa.

Notice what has happened. The young man has come wanting fulfillment. He wants his life to be complete—complete in the present, so it can be complete in the future. He knows he is still "lacking" something, and he is looking for a goal, a completion. Jesus suggests that he needs turning inside out. His life is to become part of a larger, outward-looking purpose: he is to put God's kingdom first, and put his neighbor (especially his poor neighbor) before his own fulfillment and prospects. Here is the real challenge: not just to add one or two more commandments, to set the moral bar a little higher, but to become a different sort of person altogether. Jesus is challenging the young man to *a transformation of character*.

And the young man isn't up for it. He turns and goes away, sad. Here is the gap between theory and reality, between command and performance. Jesus has told him how to behave (in the first sense) but the young man doesn't know how to do it (in the second sense). The question hangs, disturbingly, over the rest of gospel story. What is the path to God's new age, to the new time when God's kingdom will flood the world with justice and peace? How are we to be the sort of people who not only inherit that world but actually join in right now to help make it happen? What are we to do, and why? How are we to do it? Might there be a better vision of God's future that would help us grasp all this?

Before we leave this powerful little story, notice how Mark in particular has framed it, hinting at its deeper meaning. It is part of a small set of scenes in the chapter we know as Mark 10, where Jesus is on the way to Jerusalem but hasn't got there yet.

In the first scene (verses 2–12) some teachers of the Law ask Jesus about the validity of divorce, which was a political hot potato at the time because the then ruler of Galilee, Herod Antipas, had married his brother's wife. Jesus's cryptic but demanding answer goes back to the original divine intention for male-female relationships. Then, in the last scene of the sequence (verses 35–45), before Jesus and his companions begin the final leg of the journey into Jerusalem, two of Jesus's followers, James and John, ask Jesus for the privilege of sitting at his right and his left in his coming kingdom, and Jesus responds once more with a cryptic but demanding answer, this one going back to the original divine intention for how human power ought to work. There we have it, in the space of fewer than fifty verses: sex, money, and power, all recalled to a sense of original purpose, reframed within a different goal, a larger design for what human life is supposed to be like. Jesus is saying neither "Here are all the rules you need to obey" nor "What you need to do is follow your heart, your dream." James and John were wanting to follow their dream, and so was Herod. But Jesus's answer is not "No; dreams are dangerous; follow the rules instead," but something much more interesting, transformative, character-changing.

But how can character be changed, reformed? Woven into Mark's version of the story, pointing to the answer, are two other, shorter scenes. In the first (verses 13–16), Jesus declares that the way into God's kingdom is the way of the child. In the second (verses 32–34), he declares that when he and his followers get to Jerusalem he will be killed, and will rise again. Somehow, these scenes suggest, the big issues of human life are to be resolved by being put into a quite different frame from the normal one. It is the frame we could summarize in Jesus's own agenda—the coming of God's kingdom—and in his words: "Follow me!"

This agenda and this summons issue a call which cuts across the two main options for how human behavior is normally seen. You can divide theories about human behavior into two: either you obey rules imposed from the outside, or you discover the deepest longings of your own heart and try to go with them. Most of us wobble about between the two, obeying at least some of the rules either because we think God wants us to or because of social convention, but reverting to pursuing our own dreams, our own fulfillment, when given the chance. Whole theories have grown up around these two ways of discovering a pathway through life, and we shall look at them more thoroughly in the next chapter.

But what we notice in Mark 10 is something which seems to operate in a different dimension. For a start, it is a call, not to specific acts of behavior, but to a type of *character*. For another thing, it is a call to see oneself as having a role to play within a *story*—and a story where, to join up with the first point, there is one supreme Character whose life is to be followed. And that Character seems to have his eye on a goal, and to be shaping his own life, and those of his followers, in relation to that goal.

All of this suggests that Mark's gospel, with Jesus himself as the great Character who stands behind it, is inviting us to something not so much like rule-keeping on the one hand or following our own dreams on the other, but a way of being human to which philosophers ancient and modern have given a particular name. My contention in this book is that the New Testament invites its readers to learn how to be human in this particular way, which will both inform our moral judgments and form our characters so that we can live by their guidance. The name for this way of being human, this kind of transformation of character, is *virtue*.

Virtue is itself, as we shall see, a complex and many-sided notion. I shall be suggesting in due course that the early Christian development of the idea meant that Jesus's first followers agreed in some respects with the wider world of philosophical inquiry in their day and sharply disagreed in other respects. This, in turn, can provide a model for our own day, where specifically Christian character is both radically different from "the way of the world" and claims to make sense of all human life in a way that nothing else does. But before we get into those details, let's see in sharp focus what virtue might look like in practice. Let us come forward nearly two thousand years from the rich young man running up to Jesus, and witness a somewhat older man with a cooler head and sounder judgment.

FIVE

Thursday, January 15, 2009, was another ordinary day in New York City. Or so it seemed. But by that evening people were talking of a miracle.

They may have been right. But the full explanation is, if anything, even more interesting and exciting. And it strikes just the note we need as we launch out on our exploration of the development of character in general and Christian character in particular.

Flight 1549, a regular US Airways trip from LaGuardia Airport, took off at 15:26 local time, bound for Charlotte, North Carolina. The captain, Chesley Sullenberger III, known as "Sully," did all the usual checks. Everything was fine in the Airbus A320. Fine until, two minutes after takeoff, the aircraft ran straight into a flock of Canada geese. One goose in a jet engine would be serious; a flock was disastrous. (Airports play all sorts of tricks to prevent birds gathering in the flight path, but it still happens occasionally.) Almost at once both the engines were severely damaged and lost their power. The plane was at that point heading north over the Bronx, one of the most densely populated parts of the city.

Captain Sullenberger and his copilot had to make several major decisions instantly if they were going to save the lives of people not only on board but also on the ground. They could see one or two small local airports in the distance, but quickly realized that they couldn't be sure of making it that far. If they attempted it, they might well crash-land in a built-up area on the way. Likewise, the option of putting the plane down on the New Jersey Turnpike, a busy main road leading in and out of the city, would present huge problems and dangers for the plane and its occupants, let alone for cars and their drivers on the road. That left one option: the Hudson River. It's difficult to crash-land on water: one small mistake—catch the nose or one of the wings in the river, say—and the plane will turn over and over like a gymnast before breaking up and sinking.

In the two or three minutes they had before landing, Sullenberger and his copilot had to do the following vital things (along with plenty of other tasks that we amateurs wouldn't understand). They had to shut down the engines. They had to set the right speed so that the plane could glide as long as possible without power. (Fortunately, Sullenberger is also a gliding instructor.) They had to get the nose of the plane down to maintain speed. They had to disconnect the auto-pilot and override the flight management system. They had to activate the "ditch" system, which seals vents and valves, to make the plane as waterproof as possible once it hit the water. Most important of all, they had to fly and then glide the plane in a fast left-hand turn so that it could come down facing south, going with the flow of the river. And—having already turned off the engines—they had to do this using only the battery-operated systems and the emergency generator.

Then they had to straighten the plane up from the tilt of the sharp-left turn so that, on landing, the plane would be exactly level from side to side. Finally, they had to get the nose back up again, but not too far up, and land straight and flat on the water.

And they did it! Everyone got off safely, with Captain Sullenberger himself walking up and down the aisle a couple of times to check that everyone had escaped before leaving himself. Once in the life raft along with other passengers, he went one better: he took off his shirt, in the freezing January afternoon, and gave it to a passenger who was suffering in the cold.

The story has already been told and retold, and will live on in the memory not only of all those involved but of every New Yorker and many further afield. Just over seven years and four months after the horrible devastation of September 11, 2001, New York had an airplane story to *celebrate*.

Now, as I say, many people described the dramatic events as a "miracle." At one level, I wouldn't want to question that. But the really fascinating thing about the whole business is the way it spectacularly illustrates a vital truth—a truth which many today have either forgotten or never known in the first place.

You could call it the power of right habits. You might say it was the result of many years of training and experience. You could call it "character," as we have done so far in this book.

Ancient writers had a word for it: virtue.

Virtue, in this sense, isn't simply another way of saying "goodness." The word has sometimes been flattened out like that (perhaps because we instinctively want to escape its challenge), but that isn't its strict meaning. Virtue, in this strict sense, is what happens when someone has made a thousand small choices, requiring effort and concentration, to do something which is good and right but which doesn't "come naturally"—and then, on the thousand and first time, when it really matters, they find that they do what's required "automatically," as we say. On that thousand and first occasion, it does indeed look as if it "just happens"; but reflection tells us that it doesn't "just happen" as easily as that. If you or I had been flying the Airbus A320 that after-noon, and had done what "comes naturally," or if we'd allowed things just "to happen," we would probably have crashed into the Bronx. (Apologies to any actual pilots reading this: you, I hope, would have done what Captain Sullenberger did.) As this example shows, *virtue* is what happens when wise and courageous choices have become "sec-ond nature." Not "first nature," as though they happened "naturally." Rather, a kind of second-order level of "naturalness." Like an acquired taste, such choices and actions, which started off being practiced with difficulty, ended up being, yes, "second nature."

Sullenberger had not, of course, been born with the ability to fly a plane, let alone with the specific skills he exhibited in those vital three minutes. None of the skills required, and certainly none of the cour-age, restraint, cool judgment, and concern for others which he dis-played, is part of the kit we humans possess from birth. You have to work at mastering that sort of skill set, moving steadily toward that goal. You have to want to do it all, to choose to learn it all, to practice doing it all. Again and again. And then, sometimes, when the moment comes, it happens "automatically," as it did for Sullenberger. The skills and ability ran right through him, top to toe.

Which is just as well. The other options hardly bear thinking about. Supposing they had been novice pilots simply "doing what came natu-rally"? Or supposing they'd had to get hold of a book with detailed instructions for coping with emergencies, look up the relevant pages, and then try to obey what it said? By the time they'd figured it out, the plane would have crashed. No: what was needed was character, formed by the specific strengths, that is, "virtues," of knowing exactly how to fly a plane, and also the more general virtues of courage, restraint, cool judgment, and determination to do the right thing for others.

These four strengths of character—courage, restraint, cool judg-ment, and determination to do the right thing for others—are, in fact, precisely the four qualities which the greatest ancient philosopher who wrote about such matters identified as the keys to genuine human existence. But before we get there, as we will in the next chapter, I want to look at another example of an emergency where a very specific aspect of "virtue" was on heroic display.

SIX

It rains quite a lot in the north of England, where I live, but early September 2008 was exceptional. It had poured for days on end, with as much rain falling on the final day of the spell as you'd normally expect in a month. It wasn't the nicest time to be out for a walk, but one family had decided to brave it. As they were crossing a park in the town of Chester-le-Street, about fifteen miles north of my home, the family dog went to splash in a large puddle, and the three-year-old daughter went to join him. Suddenly, without warning, the little girl simply disappeared. The father, running up, saw the dog disappear as well. He realized in a flash what had happened: a storm drain had burst its cover beneath the puddle, and the girl and the dog had both been sucked down into the drain itself. Thinking quickly, the father, Mark Baxter, realized that a storm drain would most likely spill out into the river, about a hundred yards away. He set off at once at a run. When he got to the river, he spotted the girl's coat floating downstream—with Laura, his daughter, face-down inside it. Immediately he plunged in and rescued her, bruised and battered but alive.

Another miracle? In a sense, yes. All sorts of things might have happened. The little girl could have become stuck somewhere underground. She might already, by the time her father reached her, have inhaled enough water to kill her. But what impressed me most, hearing the story, was what the father said afterward about his frantic run to the riverbank.

"Every time I thought a bad thought," he said, "I forced myself to think of something else."

Therein lies the secret. Mark Baxter wasn't working out, step by step, what he had to do. He had grasped *that* in a flash. But he needed self-discipline to *keep a firm grip on his own thoughts*. All kinds of fears and terrors were, no doubt, rushing into his mind, threatening to make him panic or go to pieces. But he had what we sometimes call the presence of mind to hold those fears at bay. He consciously made the effort to replace the bad thoughts with good ones, and to concentrate on what he had to do. That is, in the technical sense we've been using, "character."

It doesn't come by accident. It comes through the self-discipline required to do anything in life really well—to learn a musical instrument, to mend a tractor, to give a lecture, to run an orphanage. Or, indeed, to live as a wise human being. Again and again, when you're working hard at a difficult or complex task, the mind will try to jump away, to focus instead on something easier or more enticing. And again and again, if you're going to get the job done, you have to force your mind back onto the job and away from the distraction. And the mental muscles you require if you're going to do that have to be trained, just as much as physical muscles do when you're working up for sustained and strenuous exercise. (This, by the way, is one of the underlying reasons why watching television for hours on end can be such a bad habit. Programs are carefully designed to be enticing and undemanding. They offer "training" in avoiding hard work, in "going with the flow." Which is fine for relaxation, but not for learning the mental habits you need for a fully human existence.) As I was rewriting this section, I heard a radio advertisement for a weight-loss regime: "I discovered," said the excited presenter, "that my craving for food was in my head, not in my stomach." Recognizing that is a vital first step. Get the thoughts right, and the behavior will follow.

As it happens, Mark Baxter worked for the British Royal Air Force. Like Chesley Sullenberger, he learned his self-discipline in a field where it is obviously vital at every minute. The ability to size up a situation, figure out what to do, and do it as though by instinct is one thing. The ability to hold at arm's length the thoughts that would terrify and paralyze you as you go about it is another thing, the kind of back-up mental discipline necessary for "virtue" to take full effect. "I forced myself to think of something else." That's not a skill you pick up by accident. It's something you learn. And it's just as well to do so, whatever sphere of life and work you find yourself in. You never know when you might need that discipline; when it might save a life. You won't have time to stop and think. The "character" of mental discipline needs to run right through you.

There's a nice sideline to this story. Little three-year-old Laura had been taking swimming lessons. She had learned to do a "star float," spreading herself out and allowing the water to support her. When she regained consciousness after being rescued, she explained to her father that she'd been trying to do the "star float," but hadn't been able to because the tunnel was too narrow. Even at that age, she had learned enough to know that if you find yourself suddenly in unexpected danger, there are things to do to make yourself safe. And she had learned, somehow, not to panic when strange things suddenly happen.

Now a great deal of life, fortunately, isn't about coping with emergencies. But part of the problem of knowing how to behave in "ordinary" life, as well as in extraordinary moments, is that this kind of "knowing" isn't straightforward. From the moment a young child is told to eat up quickly, or to sit still, or to stop crying, or to go to sleep, let alone told not to steal or bully or tell lies, he or she has entered a confusing world of wants and hopes, of commands and prohibitions, of feelings and assumptions and questions and expectations. Learning to navigate this world wisely, and to grow toward complete and mature human life in and through it all, is the challenge we all face. And the point of this book is to suggest that the dynamic of "virtue," in this sense—practicing the habits of heart and life that point toward the true goal of human existence—lies at the heart of the challenge of Christian behavior, as set out in the New Testament itself. This is what it means to develop "character." This is what we need—and what the Christian faith offers—for the time, whether short or long, "after you believe."

When we approach things from this angle, we are in for some surprises. A great many Christians, in my experience, never think of things this way, and so get themselves in all kinds of confusion. Vir-

tue, to put it bluntly, is a revolutionary idea in today's world—and today's church. But the revolution is one we badly need. And it is right
at the core of the answer to the questions with which we began. After you believe, you need to develop Christian character by practicing
the specifically Christian "virtues." To make wise moral decisions, you
need not just to "know the rules" or "discover who you really are," but
to develop Christian virtue. And to give wise leadership in our wider
society in the confusing and dangerous times we live in, we urgently
need people whose characters have been formed in much the same
way. We've had enough of pragmatists and self-seeking risk-takers. We
need people of character.

So how do these stories of human virtue—of a pilot landing his
plane safely on a river, and a father pushing away "bad thoughts" and
rescuing his daughter—help us when it comes to following Jesus? Isn't
that quite different?

Some of the greatest minds in the history of Christianity have
wrestled with that question, looking at the "natural human" virtue and
the "specifically Christian" virtue, and have come up with a variety of
answers. The key to it all, though, is that the Christian vision of virtue,
of character that has become second nature, is precisely all about discovering what it means to be truly human—human in a way most of
us never imagine. And if that is so, there are bound to be overlaps with
other human visions of virtue, as well as points at which Christianity
issues quite different demands and offers quite different help in meeting them. Part of the claim of the early Christians, in fact, was that in
and through Jesus they had discovered *both* a totally different way of
being human *and* a way which scooped up the best that ancient wisdom had to offer and placed it in a framework where it could, at last,
make sense. The New Testament itself continually points to this.

What might all this say to James, puzzled about what life is supposed to be like between the first expression of Christian faith and
its final fruition after death? What might it say to Jenny and Philip,
still smarting from their angry encounter in the church meeting?
And what might it say to our wider world, reeling from political and

economic earthquakes, lurching to and fro in a state of moral and cultural confusion?

In a sense, the whole of this book is an attempt to answer those questions, or at least to begin to answer them. But there are one or two things we can say right from the start.

As I have already hinted, people tend to go in one of two directions when they think of how to behave. You can live by rules, by a sense of duty, by an obligation imposed on you whether you feel like doing it or not. Or you can declare that you are free from all that sort of thing and able to be yourself, to discover your true identity, to go with your heart, to be authentic and spontaneous. Jenny and Philip were really having that debate, though they didn't realize it. James was bumping into it, too, but he was framing it within a larger and more worrying challenge: What are we here for in the first place? The fundamental answer we shall explore in this book is that what we're "here for" is to become genuine human beings, reflecting the God in whose image we're made, and doing so in worship on the one hand and in mission, in its full and large sense, on the other; and that we do this not least by "following Jesus." The way this works out is that it produces, through the work of the Holy Spirit, a transformation of character. This transformation will mean that we do indeed "keep the rules"—though not out of a sense of externally imposed "duty," but out of the character that has been formed within us. And it will mean that we do indeed "follow our hearts" and live "authentically"—but only when, with that transformed character fully operative (like an airline pilot with a lifetime's experience), the hard work up front bears fruit in spontaneous decisions and actions that reflect what has been formed deep within. And, in the wider world, the challenge we face is to grow and develop a fresh generation of leaders, in all walks of life, whose character has been formed in wisdom and public service, not in greed for money or power.

The heart of it—the central thing that is supposed to happen "after you believe"—is thus *the transformation of character*. This is so important that it will take another chapter to explore in more detail before we can turn to what Jesus and his first followers had to say on the subject.

2. THE TRANSFORMATION OF CHARACTER

ONE

"Character" is the human equivalent of the writing that runs right through a stick of Brighton Rock. Famously, with that kind of seaside candy, the identifying word ("Brighton," or whatever) isn't simply printed on the top, so that after you'd sucked or bitten at the first half-inch you wouldn't be able to see it anymore. No: the word goes all the way through. Wherever you cut the stick, or bite into it, the letters will always be there.

When we use the word "character" in the sense that I'm giving it in this book—the sense which it often is assigned in the New Testament, too—we mean something similar. Human "character," in this sense, is the pattern of thinking and acting which runs right through someone, so that wherever you cut into them (as it were), you see the same person through and through. Its opposite would be superficiality: we all know people who present themselves at first glance as honest, cheerful, patient, or whatever, but when you get to know them better you come to realize that they're only "putting it on," and that when faced with a crisis, or simply when their guard is down, they're as dishonest, grouchy, and impatient as the next person.

The point is this: I don't actually know how Brighton Rock and similar candy treats are manufactured, but an ordinary stick of candy doesn't automatically have writing that goes all the way through. Someone has to put it there. Likewise, the qualities of character which

Jesus and his first followers insist on as the vital signs of healthy Christian life don't come about automatically. You have to develop them. You have to work at them. You have to think about it, to make conscious choices to allow the Holy Spirit to form your character in ways that, to begin with, seem awkward and "unnatural." Only in that way can you become the sort of "character" who will react instantly to sudden challenges with wisdom and good judgment.

You can tell when this has happened—and when it hasn't. A familiar story makes the point. A famous preacher had a friend who was well known for his short temper. One day, at a party, he asked this friend to help him serve some drinks. The preacher himself poured the drinks, deliberately filling several of the glasses a bit too full. He then passed the tray to his friend. As they walked into the room to distribute the drinks, he accidentally-on-purpose bumped into the friend, causing the tray to jiggle and some of the drinks to slosh over the brim and spill. "There you are, you see," said the preacher. "When you're jolted, what spills out is whatever is filling you." When you're suddenly put to the test and don't have time to think about how you're coming across, your real nature will come out. That's why character needs to go all the way through: whatever fills you will spill out. And it's up to you to do something about it.

Another famous story makes a similar point from a different angle. This time the story is a Jewish one. There was once a rabbi who had a phenomenal reputation for thinking logically and clearly in any and all circumstances. To put him to the test, his students took him out one evening and sent him to sleep by plying him with strong drink. Then they carried him to a graveyard and laid him out neatly in front of a tombstone. They kept watch to see what he would say on waking. When the great man came to, his logic didn't falter for a moment. "Point one," he said: "If I am alive, why am I lying in a graveyard? Point two: If I am dead, why do I want to go to the bathroom?" Even in these bizarre circumstances, his head was as clear as ever.

"Character" in this sense is a general human phenomenon, with "Christian character" as a particular variation on it. We talk about "bad characters," people who, wherever you prod, will reveal unpleasant or destructive characteristics that run right through their life, thought, and actions. Similarly, we talk about people being of "good character." Though different people will mean different specific things by that phrase, most of us know what we have in mind. Such a person will be honest, trustworthy, even-tempered, faithful (including within marriage), kind, generous, and so on.

Within Western culture, much of the expectation of what "good character" includes has been shaped, over many centuries, by certain elements of Christian teaching. Even though the general culture has for a long time shown strong signs of trying to abandon its Christian roots, there is still considerable overlap between the formation of "good character" in widely recognized senses and the formation of "Christian character." This overlap is reflected throughout the book. Though we shall be concerned with Christian character in particular in these pages, it is part of the Christian claim that being Christian involves becoming more genuinely human. When we explore what it means to develop Christian character, this will therefore overlap considerably with wider questions about the "character" that our whole society urgently needs to rediscover and develop.

So how then is "character" transformed? What sort of a process is it?

TWO

Character is transformed by three things. First, you have to aim at the right goal. Second, you have to figure out the steps you need to take to get to that goal. Third, those steps have to become habitual, a matter of second nature.

That sounds fine, put simply, but of course it's easier said than done. And since many people have approached the question of Christian behavior from quite different angles, we'd better have a brief look at those alternative routes first before we go any further.

We return to the people we met in the first chapter. For James and others like him, the whole idea of character, and of it being transformed in the way I'm describing, is simply foreign territory. Now that he has come to faith, people in his church expect him to behave in a particular way (and *not* to behave in other particular ways), but this is seen, not in terms of character, but in terms of straightforward obligation. In other words, Christians are *expected* to live by the rules. When they fail, as they will, they are simply to repent and try to do better next time. You either live a Christian life or you don't. Any suggestion of some kind of moral transformation—a long, slow change of deep, heart-level habits—would be suspect. It would look like "justification by works"—that is, trying to *earn* one's way to salvation. Keeping the rules (as Jenny and her friends would also insist) doesn't contribute to your justification or salvation. It's just what you're expected to do. If there is any change of character involved, it happened already at conversion, through the action of the Holy Spirit. If the Holy Spirit really has come to live in someone's heart and life, that person automatically wants to live in accordance with God's will. It shouldn't be a matter of moral effort and struggle. After you believe, keeping the rules ought to come easily. (And if it doesn't, runs the unspoken subtext, you ought to pretend that it does.)

For Philip, however, and many who take a similar line in today's Western church, what matters is "authenticity." Being true to yourself is what counts. God has accepted you as you are; now you must live out of gratitude for that acceptance. Any attempt to force yourself to keep particular moral rules and standards which seem alien to you is a denial both of God's free acceptance of you and of your own authentic existence. After you believe, you should discover who you really are and live in accordance with that, doing spontaneously whatever your heart, at its deepest level, instructs you to do.

The aim of this book is to hold out a vision of Christian living which has superficial similarities with both of these perspectives, but also radical differences. It is a vision which stands in the tradition of ancient reflection about "virtue," but which has allowed itself to be transformed by the remarkable moral challenge of Jesus himself and of the New Testament. I shall spell all this out in more detail presently. For the moment, let me also sketch, in a fuller but still preliminary way, what I mean by the formation of "character" within a Christian context, and, within that, what we might mean by "virtue."

What is the aim, or final goal, of the whole Christian life? Here we need to develop a bit the point I hinted at in discussing Jesus's conversation with the rich young man. Though many Christians in the Western world have imagined that the aim or goal of being a Christian is simply "to go to heaven when you die," the New Testament holds out something much richer and more interesting. Yes, those who belong to Jesus in this life go to be with him once they die—that's a promise made in various places in the New Testament. But that's only the start of it. In the end—after most of us have had a time of rest and refreshment in the presence of Jesus himself—God has promised to give the entire world, the whole created order, a complete makeover. It will be renewed from top to bottom, so that it is filled at last with the presence and glory of God "as the waters cover the sea" (Isaiah 11.9). And what will happen to us then? We will be given new bodies in which to live with delight and power in God's new world. That, as I fully appreciate, is a much bigger and fuller picture of the ultimate future hope than many Christians have cherished, but it's the one the New Testament promises us.

Notice what happens if you contemplate this vision of the ultimate goal of the Christian life and ask yourself, What are the steps which lead to *this* goal, as opposed to some other?

The answer—given again and again, as we shall see, in the New Testament—is that the transformation we are promised at the end of time *has already begun in Jesus*. When God raised him from the dead, he launched his entire project of new creation, and called people of all sorts to be part of that project, already, here and now. And that means that the steps we take toward the ultimate goal—the things which make sense of Christian living in what might otherwise be a long interval between initial faith and final salvation—already partake of that same character of transformation.

How this happens we shall consider later. But the result is that there are steps we can take which lead to this goal, to the resurrection life within the new creation, and which we can take here and now. And these steps are, quite literally, character-transforming. The aim of the Christian life in the present time—the goal you are meant to be aiming at once you have come to faith, the goal which is within reach even in the present life, anticipating the final life to come—is the life of fully formed, fully flourishing Christian character.

The test will be, as with an airline pilot facing a sudden life-or-death challenge, whether your character is so formed that when the challenge comes you can meet it with a second-nature Christian virtue, or whether you will flail around, panic, wonder what on earth you should be doing—and quite possibly fail to act in the way you should have done.

But sudden moral challenges are not, in themselves, the staple diet of Christian living, of the transformed character, any more than hitting a flock of geese is the staple diet of the airline pilot. They are the emergencies, when the character quietly formed over many years rings true, comes into its own. But the character that can face such moments and do the right thing under sudden pressure is the character that has been formed by a much more sustained and positive purpose. That will be the subject of the next chapter.

Before we get there, however, we must put on the table a few issues which are in a sense in the background but which, as often with great paintings, affect the foreground more than one might think at first glance. First, where does all this belong on the famous map of moral thinking, not least thinking about virtue, in the Western world as a whole? Second, how does this talk of character transformation sit with recent studies in the development of the brain and with the question of how we learn other things, such as languages? The answers to both of these questions will come as a surprise to some, and perhaps an encouragement as well.

THREE

What I have proposed, and will develop in the rest of this book, is basically a Christian answer—Jesus's own answer, in fact—to the tradition of moral thinking that goes back to Aristotle. This tradition was well developed in the ancient world, and serious first-century readers who came upon the teaching of Paul and other early followers of Jesus would have had it in mind as they pondered what was being said.

It was Aristotle, about 350 years before the time of Jesus, who developed the threefold pattern of character transformation. As noted earlier, there is first the "goal," the *telos,* the ultimate thing we're aiming at; there are then the steps you take toward that goal, the "strengths" of character which will enable you to arrive at that goal; and there is the process of moral training by which these "strengths" turn into habits, become second nature.

For Aristotle, the goal was the ideal of a fully flourishing human being. Think of someone who has lived up to his or her full potential, displaying a complete, rounded, wise, and thoroughly formed character. This particular goal, for which Aristotle used the word *eudaimonia,* is sometimes called "happiness," but Aristotle meant it in a technical sense that is actually closer to our idea of "flourishing."

The steps toward that goal, for Aristotle and his followers, were the strengths of character which, when developed, contributed toward the gradual making of a flourishing human being. The way to attain *eudaimonia,* Aristotle thought, was by practicing these strengths, just as a soccer player undergoes training for all the different muscles of the body and practices all the various ball skills that will be needed. Working on one or two of them isn't enough; there's no point having superfit legs while the rest of the body is flabby, for example, or being able

to kick a soccer ball long distances but not to dribble past an opponent. In the same way, a complete and flourishing human being needs
all the basic strengths of character, which we shall look at presently.
Aristotle's word for such a strength was *aretē;* later Latin writers used
the word *virtus,* from which of course we get "virtue." The "virtues"
are the different strengths of character which together contribute to
someone becoming a fully flourishing human being.

For Aristotle—and for the tradition which developed after him
and formed the world of moral discourse at the time when early
Christianity was growing, spreading, and teaching a new way of life—
there were four principal virtues: courage, justice, prudence, and temperance. These, Aristotle proposed, were the "hinges" upon which the
great door to human fulfillment and flourishing would swing open.
That is why those four are often called the "cardinal virtues": *cardo* in
Latin means "hinge." (The "cardinals" in the Roman Catholic Church
are the "hinge men," the ones on whose ministry the rest "hinges." The
birds called "cardinals" have nothing to do with hinges, however, but
are simply named for their color, which resembles the scarlet robe of
the hinge-men cardinals. The same is true of the sports teams called
the "Cardinals"—football in Arizona, baseball in St. Louis.)

The "cardinal virtues" are not the only virtues. But, Aristotle proposed, they are the central ones, and all the others depend on them.
Practice these, he said, and you will become a complete, "happy," flourishing human being. That is the goal, the destination of our journey.
The virtues are the road which will get you there. Look at people who
are suddenly hailed as "heroes," and whose actions are described as "mi-
raculous," and the chances are you'll see people whose characters have
been formed in this way. Even in sports this is often true: the player
who, in a great sporting crisis, manages to pull off the apparently im
possible shot is most likely the player who has practiced that shot over
and over in private until it became second nature. I recall the South
African golfer Gary Player responding to a critic who described him
as "lucky." Yes, he said—and I've noticed that the harder I practice, the
luckier I get.

Indeed, I suspect that calling events such as the safe landing of Flight 1549 a "miracle" may be a way in which our culture chooses to ignore the real challenge, the real moral message, of that remarkable sort of event. The virtues *matter*. They matter deeply. When the great door of human nature swings open to reveal its truest secrets, these are the hinges on which it turns.

But these character strengths don't happen all in a rush. You have to work at them. Character is a slowly forming thing. You can no more force character on someone than you can force a tree to produce fruit when it isn't ready to do so. The person has to choose, again and again, to develop the moral muscles and skills which will shape and form the fully flourishing character. And so, just as a long, steady program of physical training will enable you to do all kinds of things—run in a marathon, walk thirty miles in a day, lift heavy objects—which you would previously never have thought possible, so the long, steady program of working on the character strengths, the virtues, will enable you to live in a way you would never have thought possible, avoiding moral traps and pitfalls and exhibiting a genuine, flourishing human life.

Part of the point of all this is that you will then do certain things *automatically* which before you would have struggled to do at all. As with Captain Sullenberger, certain things will then be second nature. Which is just as well, because if you'd had to stop and think what to do in some particular crisis, the moment would have passed and disaster might have struck.

What the New Testament writers are urging, following Jesus himself, is therefore quite like Aristotle's argument in some ways, but in a significantly different mode. The comparison is somewhat like that between a three-dimensional model sitting beside a two-dimensional one—a cube beside a square, say, or a sphere beside a circle: Jesus and his followers are offering the three-dimensional model toward which Aristotle's two-dimensional one points. When you get the sphere, you get the circle thrown in, as it were, but it now means something rather different.

Reflect for a moment on the three stages we have already noted. The point, each time, is the transformation, and how it happens.

1. Aristotle glimpsed a goal of human flourishing; so did Jesus, Paul, and the rest. But Jesus's vision of that goal was larger and richer, taking in the whole world, and putting humans not as lonely individuals developing their own moral status but as glad citizens of God's coming kingdom.

2. Aristotle saw that to get to the goal of a genuinely human life one should develop the moral strengths he called virtues. Jesus and his first followers, not least Paul, said something similar. But their vision of the moral strengths, corresponding to their different vision of the goal, highlighted qualities Aristotle didn't rate highly (love, kindness, forgiveness, and so on) and included at least one—humility—for which the ancient pagan world (and for that matter the modern pagan world) had no use at all.

3. Aristotle saw that the ultimate aim was to become the kind of character who would be able to act in the right way automatically, by the force of long training of habit. Jesus and Paul agreed; but they proposed a very different way by which the relevant habits were to be learned and practiced. We shall explore all this as the book progresses.

There is, of course, far more that could be said about the interesting interplay between the framework of moral thought offered by Aristotle and that offered by Jesus and the early Christians. That isn't the main subject of the book, so I will content myself at the moment with this reflection. I think if we'd asked St. Paul what he thought about Aristotle and his scheme of the virtues, he would have said about it roughly what he said about the Jewish Law: it is fine up to a point and as far as it goes, but it can't actually give what it promises. It's like a signpost pointing in more or less the right direction (though it will need some adjustment), but without a road that actually goes there.

FOUR

We move from ancient philosophy to contemporary brain science. When people consistently make choices about their patterns of behavior, physical changes take place within the brain itself. Some might regard this as common sense, but for many it will come as a fascinating and perhaps frightening reality. There is a great deal of work still to be done in this field. Neuroscience is still in comparative infancy. But already the clear indications are that significant events in your life, including significant choices you make about how you behave, create new information pathways and patterns within your brain. Neuroscientists often use the metaphor of the "wiring" of the brain, which is not inappropriate since, though of course there are no wires as such involved, information is indeed passed here and there within the brain by what are basically electric currents.

It isn't just that new patterns of wiring are being put down all the time, corresponding to the choices we make and the behaviors we adopt—though behavior is of course massively habit-forming. Parts of the brain actually become physically enlarged when an individual's behavior regularly exercises them. For example, violin players develop not only their left hand (I once knew a boy at school whose left hand was several glove sizes larger than his right due to playing the violin incessantly for years), but also the section of the brain that controls the left hand. "These regions [of the brain]," writes John Medina in his fascinating book *Brain Rules,* "are enlarged, swollen and crisscrossed with complex associations." As Medina stresses, "The brain acts like a muscle. The more activity you do, the larger and more complex it can become." What's more, he says, "our brains are so sensitive to external inputs that their physical wiring depends upon the culture in which they find themselves." As a result, "learning results in physical changes in the brain, and these changes are unique to each individual."[1] In other words, as we learn to connect various things in new ways, our brain records those connections. The result is rather like a gardener's discovery that a patch which has been dug over before is much easier to dig a second time. A particular set of associations in the brain, especially if it is connected with intense emotions or physical reactions, whether pleasurable or painful, will make it much easier for those associations to be triggered a second time. Contemporary neuroscience is thus actually able to study and map the way in which lifelong habits come to be formed.

One of the most famous instances of this phenomenon concerns the brain structure of London taxi-drivers. The work of E. A. Maguire and others has revealed some remarkable evidence.[2] London is not only one of the largest cities on the planet; it is also one of the most complex, with more one-way streets, twisting back alleys, curving rivers, and other traffic hazards than it's easy to imagine. Before a cabbie is allowed to start work, he or she has to pass a rigorous examination testing mastery of what's called "The Knowledge," a process that involves memorizing thousands of street names and ways to get to those streets at the different times of day or night as the traffic conditions change. The result is not just that they are the most effective taxi-drivers in the world, hardly ever having to consult a map, but also that *their brains have actually changed.* The part of the brain called the hippocampus, which is where we do spatial reasoning (among a wide variety of other things), is typically much larger in cabbies than in the average person. Like bodybuilders who develop muscles the rest of us don't know we've got, cabbies develop mental muscles most of us seldom have to exercise.

This kind of research, so far as I know, is not normally undertaken with a view to religious or moral issues, but the implications in those areas are enormous. We are all aware that we have strong memories of particular events. Some of us may have reflected on the way in which our imaginations and emotional reactions have been conditioned by particular moments of joy or shock, delight or horror, intense pleasure or intense pain. But the thought that not only these special events but millions of "ordinary" ones as well leave traces in the physical structure and "electrical wiring" of our brains comes as startling and striking news to most of us.

Most people in today's Western world, I suspect, think of their minds as more or less neutral machines that can be turned this way and that. When I drive down the road to London, and then when I drive up the road to Edinburgh, nothing changes in the structure of the car. But supposing the car had a kind of internal memory, recording the journeys I'd made, so that when I set off in the general direction of London—a trip I make often—the car might click into "we're going to London" mode and nudge me to take the London-bound road, even if in fact I had been intending *this* time to go to Birmingham? I would then have to make a more conscious choice to refuse the pathway the car had chosen and to compel it to do things it hadn't expected.

In the same way, supposing a decision to cheat on my tax return leaves an electronic pathway in the brain which makes it easier to cheat on other things—or people—as well? Or supposing the decision to restrain my irritation with a boring neighbor on the train, and to cultivate instead a calm patience, leaves a pathway which makes it easier to be patient when someone subsequently behaves in a truly offensive manner? As I say, the research is nowhere near as fully developed as we might like. But it seems as though the idea of developing "moral muscles," by analogy with people going to the gym to develop physical ones, may be closer than we had imagined.

The process of acquiring habits in any sphere can be illustrated in many ways. Learning a musical instrument is an obvious one (think of those violinists with their left-hand neurons working overtime). Learning a second language (music being, of course, a kind of language) is another.

Many people in the world can speak only their mother tongue. It's the only language they've ever learned, and they learned it without reflecting on how they did it. Even *that* makes the point, because as we learn our mother tongue, whatever it is, we are building up a massive and highly complex network of habits, both mental and physical, which interrelate in multiple ways with different life-situations.

A great deal of first-language learning, to begin with at least, is simply copycat behavior. The child hears parents and siblings saying things and tries to do the same. But even from an early age, surprising originality can creep in, as the child not only masters habits and patterns of speech but begins to create new ones by subtle variations. And at this stage an enormous amount of what the language specialists call grammar—involving *accidence* (the way words happen to be formed) and *syntax* (the way words fit together within sentences)— and of course vocabulary itself, in both directions ("What's the word for that thing, there?" and "What does this word mean?"), is being assimilated, swallowed whole, all the time. Whether a child is severely dyslexic or a poetic prodigy—and the two might actually sometimes coincide—habits are being formed, patterns laid down in the brain, which mean that the language eventually becomes second nature. In most conversations, most of the time, you aren't discussing language, grammar, and vocabulary. Those matters come up only if someone uses a word or a phrase in a way you don't understand. Normally, you aren't even thinking about vocabulary, much less grammar. You're thinking about the subject matter of the conversation.

Learning your mother tongue, then, is a good illustration as far as it goes. But learning a new language, especially as an adult, is better, for two reasons. First, it's a far more conscious activity. Even in an ultramodern language laboratory, where you are imitating the "natural" conditions in which you learned your mother tongue, you still have to *think* about why this word is formed that way and not some other, why these awkward irregular verbs behave in this way when they should really have done the opposite, and so on. You have to master the nuances and metaphors and emphases that make a living language the lovely but difficult thing it is. You will often get it wrong, but it's worth persisting for the goal, the *telos,* of what lies ahead. If you're an English speaker learning German, you must continually remind yourself that the verb comes at the end of the sentence. And, even in a language quite like your own (think of an Italian learning Spanish), there will be a large amount of vocabulary which just has to be memorized. This requires mental effort, the conscious, acted-out intention to imprint these patterns, with their physical outworkings (the contortions of tongue, teeth, lips, and vocal cords), upon the brain, aiming at the point when they will happen without effort and indeed without conscious thought. It is exactly this kind of complex effort, as we shall see, which the early Christians described when they were urging one another to develop the character which anticipated God's new world.

C. S. Lewis describes the transition to understanding a new language in a memorable passage, referring to the time when he was learning ancient Greek:

> Those in whom the Greek word lives only while they are hunting for it in the lexicon, and who then substitute the English word for it, are not reading the Greek at all; they are only solving a puzzle. The very formula, "*Naus* means a ship," is wrong. *Naus* and *ship* both mean a thing, they do not mean one another. Behind *Naus,* as behind *navis* or *naca,* we want to have a picture of a dark, slender mass with sail or oars, climbing the ridges, with no officious English word intruding.[3]

That is the point at which a second language gives us the clue to how virtue functions: it becomes second nature. Eventually, all being well, you pass beyond the stilted, forced stage to an entirely new sort of "naturalness."

One warning note comes in here. It is possible to learn a new language and then forget it. I learned several languages when I was young. One of them, Syriac, gave me special pleasure, with its liquid sounds and wonderful ancient poetry. But I didn't keep it up through my thirties and forties; and when, in my early fifties, I went back to a Syriac Bible to check something, I found to my sorrow that I couldn't even remember how the alphabet worked. Virtue can be like that, too. Someone who genuinely learns generosity as a child can easily find that the habits of adult life squeeze it out. It then has to be learned, with much more difficulty, all over again. There are, sadly, many times when those who have begun to practice the Christian life encounter the same problem. Stop practicing—allow yourself to forget the goal—and you may lose the language altogether.

Another reason why learning a second language is a good illustration of virtue is that often the reason for doing it is that you want to be able to be at home in the place where that language is spoken, or at least in reading and appreciating the literature of that country (or, in the case of ancient languages, that time). Learning the language thus has a goal in view: that of acquiring those habits of brain and body which will enable you to function already, here and now, as a linguistically competent citizen of that country, with an easy familiarity. The greatest compliment you can pay someone who has learned a second language is to mistake him or her for a native. That, again, is the "reward" for the work—not an arbitrary reward, like a child being given a bicycle because she has passed her exam, but a reward which is the true *telos,* the proper goal, of the original activity.

That's how virtue worked for Aristotle, and that's how it works— once we grasp the important differences between Aristotle and Jesus!—within Christian living. Aristotle's goal, as we saw, was *eudaimonia,* human flourishing. The virtues—the four "cardinal" virtues and the other virtues that hang on those "hinges"—were quite simply the grammar and vocabulary of the language of "flourishing" humanness. Nobody really knows that language as their mother tongue. But we can glimpse that country from time to time and pick up hints about how its language works, what patterns of brain and body are needed to enable us to function as linguistically competent citizens. And the more we practice speaking the language—in other words, the more we learn what it means to act with courage, temperance, prudence, and justice—the more we shall be developing an easy familiarity with how the truly flourishing people live. Who knows, one day we might be mistaken for a native.

If learning virtue is like learning a language, it is also like acquiring a taste, or practicing a musical instrument. None of these "comes naturally" to begin with. When you work at them, though, they begin to feel more and more "natural," until that aspect of your "character" is formed so that, at last, you attain the hard-won freedom of fluency in the language, happy familiarity with the taste, competence on the instrument.

If this is what "character" and "virtue" are all about, how does such exploration of the moral landscape sit alongside the two major moral frameworks which most people in the Western world now assume?

FIVE

Come back to the debate—or the attempted debate—between Jenny and Philip. Jenny assumed that the question was about discovering the correct rules and applying them; Philip assumed that what mattered was discovering "who you really are" and being true to it, in line with Jesus's radical welcome to all comers. These two positions represent, more or less, the two frameworks of moral thought between which most people today find themselves choosing, at least by implication. It's easy for both sides to caricature one another, and at a time of moral nervousness on many fronts we should respect the anxieties that many have. However, we should also look more closely at these frameworks themselves. If, as I believe, the development of character, and the habituation of virtue, offers a better perspective from which to understand our moral dilemmas, we need to see what the alternatives are actually all about.

Take the world of rules, for a start. Many people of my age grew up being taught that there are such things as right and wrong, that these are more or less universal and constant, and that you can know them and do them. Indeed, we had all this drilled into us. (Interesting phrase, that. Do you think, when you hear it, of someone drilling a hole in a piece of wood, or rather of a squad of soldiers doing "drill" so that they learn to obey orders instinctively?) Sometimes these rules are simple but profound in their implications, such as "Do as you would be done by" and "People matter more than things."

In many cultures these rules include, at quite a basic level, prohibitions on murder, theft, and adultery—or (to put it positively) a respect for life, property, and marriage. Most societies most of the time have lived by simple rules of this kind, which then get variously codified into law. The Ten Commandments are one classic example, but there are many others. Many of us were taught not only the Ten Commandments but also various derivatives, so that (confusingly for a child) the prohibitions on stealing, killing, lying, and so on seemed to merge into the equally strong commandments about appropriate table manners, writing thank-you letters, being polite to aged aunts, the "proper" pronunciation of words, not wearing muddy shoes inside the house, and so on. But the point is that many of us grew up in a world of rules, a structured and ordered society where the rules were given and, though there might be disputes about particular ones, if you got them mostly right you were all right, and if you didn't, you weren't. Everyone had a duty to keep the rules, whether or not it suited them. And, tellingly, people often suggested, or even simply assumed, that one of the main things Jesus came to do was to tell us more clearly what the rules were and to give us a wonderful example of how to keep them . . .

. . . Which then runs into difficulties, because people quickly discover that they *can't* keep them, and so a different mode breaks in: Jesus came to bring forgiveness for our rule-breaking; but once we've grasped that, we have to go back to rule-*keeping* again. That is the broad framework within which many people in today's Western world have come to think of the gospel of Jesus Christ.

Actually, the framework comes, not from Jesus or the gospels, but from a particular kind of philosophy. Specialists will recognize it as having quite a lot to do, in the modern world, with the eighteenth-century German writer Immanuel Kant. To a people that knew the rules but knew they broke them, the good news was that God would forgive you—but then you had to keep the rules again, because that's what good Christians did. People then got into puzzles about how you could say both of these things together: how you could talk about rules without undermining God's generosity and forgiving grace, and so on. But, in general, people assumed that part of the point of being a Christian was to know what the rules were and to do your best to keep them.

And of course there's a sense in which that is at least part of the truth. Almost nobody supposes that Christian behavior, or for that matter human behavior in general, is entirely a matter of individual choice, with no guidelines whatever. Ironically, those who pour scorn on some of the older rules, not least about sexual behavior, are often those who insist most loudly on some of the newer rules, for instance about caring for the planet and its ecology. And a huge amount of life depends on common recognition of basic rules—about which side of the road to drive the car, for instance. We cannot simply play off "virtue" or "character" against "rules." When Captain Sullenberger made his snap decision about landing the plane on the Hudson River, the point was that he was instinctively doing what the rulebook would have said, had he had time to go and look it all up.

The problem comes, I think, not with rules themselves (though there are problems there too), but with a rule-based mentality: not so much "what to do" but "how to do it." There was a massive reaction against "duty" in the middle and later years of the twentieth century in Western Europe and North America. This was partly, we may suspect, as a reaction to two generations' having been told it was their "duty" to go and die in major wars. The result has been that many people forget the universal importance of rules as providing a framework, a set of solid guidelines, for millions of aspects of daily life, and have come to see rules themselves simply as a problem, cramping one's style, arbitrarily imposing a framework of behavior on people for whom it might well be inappropriate. This is of course unfair to the fundamental idea of "rule," but it is, I think, a reflection of where a fair amount of our world, not least the Western Christian world, now is. It simply won't do merely to reassert, as Jenny did in the previous chapter, that the rules exist and that they must be forced on people whether they like it or not. We must search for the larger framework within which appropriate rules may play their proper, though ultimately subordinate, part. And we must recognize that as we do so we are, in terms of Western culture as a whole, playing the game facing straight into a strong gale.

We meet similar problems if we speak, as many do today, in larger terms about "principles" or "values." The two are not actually the same.

A principle is a general statement of how things should be, from which specific rules might be derived; a value is some aspect of human life which is prized in itself, and from which principles and thereby rules might be generated. You *uphold* a value—say, of the sanctity of life. You *act from* a principle—say, that one should always ("in principle," as we say) preserve life and not destroy it. You *obey* a rule—"Do not commit murder." But of course in ordinary life people often use these words in a much more fluid, almost interchangeable, fashion. And I suspect that some people speak of "values" and "principles" partly at least because the word "rules" sounds, to many, so negative, restrictive, intrusive, and even arbitrary. People know they want to retrieve some kind of "standards." But "rules" will be unpopular, so they turn to "principles" or "values" instead.

Might it help, then, to think in terms of *Christian* "principles" or "values"? It isn't difficult to highlight various general themes from the moral vision of the New Testament and the early Christians: peace, justice, freedom, love, and several others come readily to mind. But what exactly do these big, abstract words mean? Who says? How do you apply them to particular questions and cases? Is it ever possible, having abstracted such themes from their scriptural and historical settings, to play them off against other aspects of the same scriptures? If so, on what grounds? If not, what was the point of abstracting them in the first place? Principles and values may have their place, but that place cannot be central. They are, basically, Big Rules, subject to the same problem as the ordinary little rules. When politicians bang on, as they do, about the need to restore values in our society, this is usually distressingly vague. Whose values? Who says? How are you going to restore them without tackling the underlying causes of why, if they're so important, most people seem to ignore them? Some people will even talk about "Christian values" or "Judeo-Christian values," though those are usually just as difficult to articulate, let alone to impose. And if one of your principles turns out to be "the greatest happiness of the greatest number"—the principle known as utilitarianism, which has been extremely popular for nearly two hundred years now—you run into all sorts of interesting problems, about what happiness really is, what you do when people have a wrong idea of it, how you calculate what will bring about the effect of happiness, and how you cope with the minority who are not going to be happy with a proposed action designed to bring happiness. Utilitarianism really deserves a whole discussion to itself, but this must suffice here.

However, the real difficulty with rules is not only that we don't keep them very well, though that's true. Nor that there always seem to be troubling exceptions: when we've been taught always to tell the truth, what do we say to the would-be murderer who asks where his intended victim is hiding? Nor, yet, is the real problem that systems of rules differ markedly from one another: in some cultures you are under a solemn obligation to kill the person who rapes your daughter, and in others you are under a solemn obligation *not* to do so. These are indeed problems. But the biggest problem lies elsewhere.

The real problem is that rules always appear to be, and are indeed designed to be, restrictive. But we know, deep down, that some of the key things that make us human are being creative, celebrating life and beauty and love and laughter. You can't get those by legislation. Rules matter, but they aren't the center of it all. You can tell people that they must obey the rule always to be generous. But if someone gives you a present merely because he is obeying a rule or doing his duty, the glory of gift-giving has slipped through your fingers. If rules are taken as the main thing, then the *truly* main thing seems to be missing. What happened to *character*?

A striking example of this problem occurred as I was rewriting this chapter. A senior government civil servant was discovered to be sending scurrilous emails to a colleague proposing a "dirty tricks" smear campaign against leading members of the opposition. The prime minister's response was to say that new rules would be brought in to prevent this happening—though in fact there is already a strict code about such things, which the civil servant had flagrantly breached. The leader of the opposition suggested, by contrast, that what was needed was a change of culture. But how that might come about he did not say.

Another example from further back. I still meet, from time to time, the man who was headmaster of my school when I was a teenager. He once told me that early on in his time as head, in the mid-1950s, one of the school administrators came to him with a challenge. The previous headmaster, he said, had written a new school rule in the rulebook every day. Why wasn't the new headmaster keeping up this tradition? Didn't he care how people behaved? His response, in order to shelve the question for the moment, was to think quickly and invent a new rule: "No boy may, at any time . . . ," etc., etc. But that was the last time he did it. Of course there were rules, and they mattered. But what mattered even more was developing the character of pupils so that they would behave with good sense and judgment in the thousands of areas which *weren't* covered by official rules.

The question of morals or ethics is in fact part of the much larger question of what humans are here *for*. Framing an answer in terms of rules, *any* rules, always implies that human life is a bit like a continual preparation for an examination, with a big assessment coming up and grades to be awarded which might get you into a good job, or a graduate program, or wherever else you hope to end up next. But is human life really a kind of continuous-assessment education program? Is it just a matter of "getting through" by keeping the (mostly negative) rules? Or are the rules there as signposts, pointing to a larger purpose and warning us that there are ways of missing that larger purpose? But if that's the case, what is that larger purpose, and how do we find it? And what about the question which looms up continually within Christian discussion, about how human behavior as a whole relates to the overwhelming grace of God?

This is the point at which the story of the rich young man, and the other scenes in Mark 10, seem to be saying, No: what matters isn't simply keeping a bunch of rules; what matters is character. Not just any old sort of character, either, but a particular sort: the sort Jesus was urging and modeling—the character of patience, humility, and above all generous, self-giving love. And the message of Mark at this point seems to be that you don't get that character just by trying. You get it by following Jesus.

SIX

Rules matter, it seems, but character matters more, and provides a framework within which rules, where appropriate, can have their proper effect. But this is by no means how people have understood Jesus and the Christian message in the last two centuries.

If you asked the average Western person, including the average Western Christian, what Jesus stood for in terms of human behavior, they probably wouldn't tell you about the subtle balance of character and rules. Yes, they would say, Jesus opposed self-righteous legalists who tried to impose their morality on others. But when people say this they don't tend to think ". . . so he urged them to develop character instead," but rather that Jesus offered a kind of radical freedom. The position of Philip in our previous chapter is where many Western Christians are today: Jesus accepted people as they were, and urged them to discover their real identity, and to be true to that essence. He encouraged people to throw the old rules into the trashcan and take up the challenge of living spontaneously, authentically, in the freedom of the spirit rather than the slavery of the letter. This viewpoint is so deeply ingrained in many parts of the Western world in general, and the Western church in particular, that you only have to hint at it and you invoke a whole way of looking at the world which many people instinctively feel is right without further argument.

This point of view is so important that we must go into it in a little more detail. If, as I believe, the New Testament offers us the way of virtue, we need to see more clearly what, for many today, is its principal rival. Like many rivals, it is actually a parody, a caricature, of the real thing.

Three of the greatest opinion-forming movements in the last two centuries of Western thought and culture have led people to set aside the desirability or possibility of virtue altogether. Most people are probably not aware of these movements as historical or cultural forces, but simply imbibe from our present culture—the culture these movements created—a general sense which Jesus and his first followers would in fact have challenged head-on.

What were these three movements? A brief and broad-brush summary will suffice. The importance for us is the effect on today's popular imagination rather than details about where they came from.

1. The romantic movement in the nineteenth century reacted against what it saw as cold, rational formalism (here are the rules; keep them; that's your duty; don't ask for more). The romantics stressed the importance of inner feeling and of actions that flowed from that. As one recent writer put it, they advocated "the spontaneous, the unfettered, the subjective, the imaginative and emotional, and the inspirational and heroic" rather than having things imposed on them by someone else, or by a system of philosophy or politics.[4] Don't give us systems; give us life and love and warmth in the soul!

2. The existentialist movement in the early twentieth century highlighted the notion of "authenticity." To live "authentically," said the existentialists, is to take the dangerous and difficult decision to reject structures and systems that constrict and impair our human freedom, and to live in accordance with our true inner being. That is the way to a kind of completeness, of human fulfillment.

3. As a kind of junior but powerful version of romanticism and existentialism combined, the emotivist movement insisted that all moral discourse could be reduced in any case to statements of likes and dislikes. "Murder is wrong" simply means "I don't like murder." "Giving to charity is good" means "I like people giving to charity." From this point of view, following moral rules and following your own inclinations both boil down to pretty much the same thing. Often today people who are discussing moral choices will say that this person "prefers" Option A or that that person "applauds" Option B, as though moral choices were a matter of personal preference or taste. Sometimes they speak of "moral attitudes," as though what a particular person believed about the rights and wrongs of certain actions were simply an "attitude," an innate prejudice which they hadn't bothered to think through.

Whichever of the three you embrace—and in popular culture romanticism, existentialism, and emotivism tend to swirl together in a confused world of impressions and rhetoric—they arrive at the same general position, which many today assume, without more ado, is roughly what Jesus himself taught, and what Christian living ought to be all about. Be yourself; don't let anyone else dictate to you; don't let other people's systems or phobias cramp your style; be honest about what you're really feeling and desiring. Get in touch with the bits of yourself you've been screening out; make friends with them and be true to them. Anything else will result in a diminishing of your true, unique, wonderful self.

This whole way of thinking has become entrenched in many parts of our world, not least in many parts of many churches. Some people mistake it for the gospel itself, supposing that the romantic and existentialist rejection of rules is the same thing as Paul's doctrine of "justification by faith apart from works of the law," or the same thing as what Jesus was advocating when he confronted the law-bound Pharisees.

Shakespeare put all this in a classic phrase, set in the mouth of Polonius, a man he is teaching us to see as a bit shallow and pompous (to be precise, "a foolish prating knave"):

This above all—to thine own self be true,
And it must follow, as the night the day,
Thou canst not then be false to any man.

Hamlet, act 1, scene 3, lines 78–80

Hmmm. Actually, if you are genuinely true to yourself, you will no doubt be aware of many hidden motives within yourself that other people would ignore, and so may be able to make better choices, both moral and otherwise. But supposing the "self" to which you are true is the self that wants to cheat everyone you meet, including friends and family, out of as much money as possible? In the monetary scandals that came to light in the recent financial crash, several of those who were exposed as serial fraudsters had been utterly true to themselves and utterly false to everyone else.

"Well," you might say, "the fraudulent bankers weren't *really* being true to themselves, because they must have known all along that they were doing wrong." To that I reply that it is exactly part of the problem with our late-modern or postmodern world that the imperative to maximize your own (or your firm's) bank balance has, for many, become the deepest level of truth they can imagine. Once you abolish or sideline older, less apparently tangible notions of morality, what else are you left with?

I came across a perfect contemporary example of the popular-level true-to-yourself philosophy the day after I had given a lecture on the theme of this book, in late February 2009. Browsing in a junk shop in Laguna Beach, California, I discovered a jokey little sign which read:

There are times I think I'm doing things on principle,
But mostly I just do what feels good.
But that's a principle, too.

"Doing what feels good": it would be easy to caricature that as a typically Californian attitude, but that would ignore the fact that a vast swath of contemporary Western life has operated on precisely this "principle," and has strongly resisted, in the name of "freedom," any attempt to question or challenge it. To move from Californian popular culture to the sharp analysis of one of the great minds of the twentieth century, listen to this analysis by Arthur M. Schlesinger Jr., writing about the impact that the theologian Reinhold Niebuhr had on him and his generation, and about the way in which Niebuhr's influence waned in the 1960s:

[Niebuhr's] emphasis on sin startled my generation. We had been brought up to believe in human innocence and virtue. The perfectibility of man was less a liberal illusion than an all-American conviction. . . . But nothing in our system prepared us for Hitler and Stalin, for the death camps and the gulags. . . .

[Niebuhr's] influence waned somewhat in the 1960s. The rebel young of those frenzied years, with their guileless confidence in the unalloyed goodness of spontaneous impulses and in the instant solubility of complex problems, had no feeling for Niebuhr.[5]

"Guileless confidence in the unalloyed goodness of spontaneous impulses": that sums up a good deal of the mood that has gripped, and still grips, many in the Western world. We might note that "virtue," in the second line of that quotation, hardly means what it meant in the classical tradition. The whole point of Schlesinger's sharp analysis was that in the America of his youth, and again in the 1960s, there seemed no need for virtue in the sense of a hard-won *second* nature: "doing what came naturally" was quite good enough. Indeed, the refusal to obey "what came naturally," the "spontaneous impulses" whose "unalloyed goodness" could be confidently assumed, has itself often been deemed to be wrong, dangerous, damaging to one's health and well-being. The idea of a goal, an ultimate aim, calling us to a hard road of self-denial—the idea, in other words, that Jesus of Nazareth meant what he said when he spoke of people taking up their cross to follow him!—has been quietly removed from the record, not only of secular Western life but also, extraordinarily, of a fair amount of Christian discourse.

At a less obvious but perhaps still more insidious level, all this goes with that element in cultures both ancient and modern which is generally called "Gnosis" or "Gnosticism." This, loosely, involves the idea that there is a spark of light hidden deep within us—or at least within some of us. This hidden spark (it is supposed) is often buried deep underneath layers of social and cultural conditioning, and even layers of what we ourselves assume to be "who we really are."

Once this spark has been revealed, however, it takes precedence over everything else, trumping every rule, every happiness calculation, and certainly every virtue, classical or otherwise. Whatever we deeply, most truly find within ourselves must be right. My heart is telling me how it is, and I must go with my heart. That is the "guiding light" at the deep center of my true self. *And this, many people today have been taught and seriously believe, is what Jesus of Nazareth came to model and to teach.* That is the message not only of *The Da Vinci Code* and a good many other popular page-turners, but also of many more serious writers and scholars. It is, after all, the message that many people very much want to hear.

In its corporate version, this kind of philosophy has dominated a good deal of our world. Not for nothing did the great intellectual and cultural revolution of the second half of the eighteenth century call itself "the Enlightenment." Western Europe and North America had "discovered who they really were." They were a race set apart, possessing new knowledge, skills, and techniques which not only could be expressed in terms of conquest of those less "enlightened," but positively *demanded* to be so exploited.

That is a subject for another occasion (though, interestingly, it is what Arthur Schlesinger goes on to speak about immediately after the passage I quoted above). But in its individual version, the Gnosticism of the last two centuries has embedded deep within our imaginations the assumption—I was going to say "the thought," but I suspect that most people don't *think* this, they merely *assume* it—that "being true to oneself" is the central human command, the central (even) "religious" imperative, the central goal and task of every human being, the Holy Grail of personal development. That is simply how millions of people today see themselves and the world.

Examples abound to back this up. The poet John Betjeman had the misfortune to have a father who was running a successful family business and expected his son to follow him into it. Or perhaps we should say that old Mr. Betjeman had the misfortune to have a son who knew in his bones that he was not cut out to be a businessman and who really did want to write poetry. Fortunately, the younger man was eventually "true to himself," in this respect at least. Sadly, however, as his candid self-reflections indicate, when it came to his private life, the "self" to which he tried to be true was deeply confused. He followed its various whims, and thereby created a fair amount of moral and human havoc. There is the problem of romanticism, existentialism, emotivism, and neo-Gnosticism in a nutshell.

Since human beings are deeply mysterious creatures, none of this should surprise us. The ancient Greek maxim "Know yourself" is as good advice now as ever it was. The question, though, of what to do with that knowledge once you've acquired it is far more difficult. What if the self I discover, through the deepest introspection of which I am capable, is a self that longs to murder, or steal, or molest children? How can we tell which of our "hidden depths" are to be acknowledged in order then to be neutralized or (if possible) killed off, and which are to be brought out into the light, celebrated, and acted upon? The fact that they are deep within us provides, in itself, no answer.

Things get still more confused, finally, if we bring in another highly contested notion, the appeal to "freedom." Saying, as many do today, "Surely we're meant to be free?"—meaning by that, "Surely you're not going to say I can't do what I want?"—simply begs the question. It isn't just that the freedom of my fist stops where the freedom of your nose begins. It's that everything any of us does creates new situations which may, themselves, be a severe curtailment of freedom in all directions. If I do actually punch you on the nose, we are neither of us free, thereafter, to be the people we might otherwise have been with one another (and perhaps with others, too). Unless all four musicians in the quartet scrupulously obey the rules of staying in time and keeping to the right pitch, none of them will be free to make the music.

All this means that the massive presumption within our culture in favor of "authenticity" or "spontaneity"—"freedom" in that sense— simply won't do as a serious moral proposal. (Or, for that matter, as a serious proposal for how to decide between different courses of action upon which no immediate moral issue appears to hang.) "Measure once, cut twice," begins the old rule I learned in a carpentry lesson, concluding with "measure twice, cut once." Don't assume that first impressions and inclinations are correct. Don't be afraid of "what comes naturally," but do subject it to the same critical scrutiny that you would anything else—or anything done by anyone else.

In particular, let us name and shame, as being totally inadequate, the idea that if something is done spontaneously it carries an automatic validation, whereas if something is done through obeying orders, or after careful reflection, or despite enormous pressure of various kinds to do something else, it is somehow less valuable, or even "hypocritical" because you weren't really "being true to yourself." This is simply the old "romantic fallacy," the idea that genuine artistic inspiration requires no perspiration, sometimes borrowing a bit of energy from Martin Luther's rejection of what he saw as medieval hypocrisy. Ninety-nine percent of artists—musicians, writers, dancers, painters, whatever—will tell you a very different story. Most art requires massively hard work; so does most moral living. The fact that Wordsworth and Coleridge could improvise blank verse off the top of their head (and Coleridge could quite literally make it up in his sleep) is the exception that proves the rule.

And yet. There is something about spontaneity, about authenticity, about the exact fit or match between the person and her actions, which commands some kind of assent—but when *and only when* the actions are, on other grounds, seen to be right. There is, no doubt, a "fit," an "authenticity," about the money-counting of the miser or the philandering of the serial seducer, but nobody in a right mind says, "Oh well, that's all right then." Part of the problem about authenticity is that virtues aren't the only things that are habit-forming: the more someone behaves in a way that is damaging to self or to others, the more "natural" it will both seem and actually be. Spontaneity, left to itself, can begin by excusing bad behavior and end by congratulating vice.

One of the main proposals of this book is, in fact, that this fit between the person and the action, this authenticity, is what you get through the "second nature" of virtue—at which point the problem I just mentioned has been headed off from the start. Romantic ethics, or the existentialism which insists on authenticity or (in that sense) freedom as the only real mark of genuine humanness, or the popular version of all this I have alluded to above, *tries to get in advance, and without paying the true price, what virtue offers further down the road, and at the cost of genuine moral thought, decision, and effort.* That is what I meant by saying that the cult of authenticity or spontaneity was a parody, a caricature, of what virtue would produce when it has its full effect.

"Being true to yourself," then, is important, but it isn't the principal thing. If you take it as a framework or as a starting point, you will be sadly deceived. Over against all these frameworks, which I suspect have conditioned in various ways the thinking and behaving of many of my readers, we urgently need to recapture the New Testament's vision of a genuinely "good" human life as a life of *character formed by God's promised future,* as a life with that future-shaped character *lived within the ongoing story of God's people,* and, with that, a freshly worked notion of virtue. This is what we need if we are to answer the question of what happens after you believe.

SEVEN

There is another problem about recapturing the notion of virtue, of the development of character strengths, within a Christian framework. I referred to this other problem a moment ago. Basically, the whole idea of virtue has been radically out of fashion in much of Western Christianity ever since the sixteenth-century Reformation.

The very mention of virtue, in fact, will make many Christians stiffen in alarm. They have been taught, quite rightly, that we are not justified by our works, but only by faith. They know that they are powerless to make themselves conform to any high and lofty moral code. In many cases, they've tried it, and it didn't work. It simply left them feeling guilty. (In other cases, they found it too hard, and simply gave up the effort.) Then they discovered that God accepted them as they were: "While we were yet sinners," writes St. Paul, "Christ died for us" (Romans 5.8). Phew! So why bother with all this morality? Can't we just sweep away virtue, commandments, and all the rest, and simply bask in the accepting and forgiving love of God?

So the question that the Christian tradition, particularly the Western Protestant tradition, might raise against the whole topic is this: Aren't we then just whistling in the wind, with all this talk of virtue? Yes, maybe airline pilots and other people need to practice their skills and learn to keep a cool head, but does this have any significance beyond a purely pragmatic one, that certain tasks demand that some people develop certain abilities? Is this really relevant in any way to the serious business of living the way God wants us to live? Can it really teach us anything about Christian morality or ethics? If even the God-given Ten Commandments prove impossible to keep, why should the supposedly character-forming virtues be any different? And if developing character by slow, long practice is what it's all about, doesn't that mean that for most of that time we will be acting hypocritically, play-acting, pretending to be virtuous when actually we aren't? And isn't that kind of hypocrisy itself the very opposite of genuine Christian living?

That, in fact, is more or less what Martin Luther declared, thumbing his nose at the long medieval tradition of virtue. The debates about that, as about some of his other striking rejections of earlier theology, rumbled on in popular culture for a long while, and this one emerges, fascinatingly, in Shakespeare's play *Hamlet,* which we have just noted in another connection.

Hamlet studied at Wittenberg, Luther's university, and has now returned home to Denmark. There he has found—against the grain of what he was no doubt taught—that his late father is not lying quietly in his grave but is deeply disturbed, and that he, Hamlet, must put things right. His mother, the queen, has colluded with his uncle in murdering his father so that the uncle could win both throne and queen together. Hamlet's accusation against his mother in act 3, scene 4, is subtle: she has, he implies, decided not to bother about virtue, and indeed to treat it as mere hypocrisy, so that she can go with the flow of what comes naturally—which she is still doing every time she shares the usurper's bed. Your act, declares Hamlet, "calls virtue hypocrite" (line 42); in other words, she is using Luther's charge against "putting on" a virtue you don't yet possess as an excuse for doing what she wanted. Instead, he says, she should now try to "assume a virtue, if you have it not" (line 160): she should resist the new king's advances, and with time the habit of so doing will make it easier. "Putting it on" is appropriate—"apt," in the English which reflects the regular Latin word for "proper, fitting." Custom—the settled practice, the learned habit—can be used to good effect. This is how it works:

> That to the use of actions fair and good
> He likewise gives a frock or livery
> That aptly is put on. (lines 163–65)

"Putting it on" is all right. It isn't hypocrisy, Hamlet is saying. It's the way virtue comes into its own:

> Refrain tonight;
> And that shall lend a kind of easiness
> To the next abstinence; the next more easy;
> For use almost can change the stamp of nature,
> And either curb the devil, or throw him out,
> With wondrous potency. (lines 165–70)

The alternative is to let "custom"—that is, the force of regular behavior which carves a groove in our minds and our behavior patterns—so dictate to us that we cannot see sense (lines 37–38). Instead, such "custom" or "use" should be turned to good effect, helping us to "put on" the virtues which do not come naturally to begin with but which will do so in time (lines 161–65). It is remarkable, he says, what can be achieved by this means. Hamlet is thus firmly rejecting Luther's proposal. Shakespeare, through him, is putting down a marker in a long and complex debate between those who think virtue can be brought on board within Christian teaching and those who see it as a pagan idea which Christians should reject.

This debate involves the massive and complex thought of some of the greatest Christian thinkers—notably, Augustine in the fifth century and Aquinas in the thirteenth. They, and many lesser thinkers, hover in the background of all such discussions. But one thing that is seldom done in such debates is to inquire of the New Testament itself. Is there a sense in which following Jesus and obeying his call to "seek first God's kingdom" (Matthew 6.33) might be approached as a matter of virtue? Or how might "virtue" fit within what St. Paul calls "the gospel of the grace of God" (Acts 20.24)? Isn't it significant that Paul himself, who knew the culture and philosophy of his own day well enough, never uses the word *aretē,* the standard word for "virtue"? But isn't it also significant that at key points he stresses the importance of the careful development and cultivation of Christian character?

Just in case there should be any doubt, before we get near such questions let's be clear. When St. Paul says that "if righteousness came by the Law, the Messiah died in vain" (Galatians 2.21), he was stating a foundational principle. Whatever language or terminology we use to talk about the great gift that the one true God has given to his people in and through Jesus Christ ("salvation," "eternal life," and so on), it remains precisely a *gift*. It is never something we can earn. We can never put God into our debt; we always remain in his. Everything I'm going to say about the moral life, about moral effort, about the conscious shaping of our patterns of behavior, takes place simply and solely within the framework of grace—the grace which was embodied in Jesus and his death and resurrection, the grace which is active in the Spirit-filled preaching of the gospel, the grace which continues to be active by the Spirit in the lives of believers. It is simply not the case that God does some of the work of our salvation and we have to do the rest. It is not the case that we begin by being justified by grace through faith and then have to go to work all by ourselves to complete the job by struggling, unaided, to live a holy life.

What's more, if we try to put God in our debt by trying to make ourselves "good enough for him" (whatever that might mean), we are prone to make matters worse. One of the horrid truths that we are all too aware of in our own day is that some of the nastiest, most callous and brutal deeds are done by people in the name of "religion." The fact that this is often, manifestly, an excuse for violence whose real causes and motivations lie elsewhere simply proves my point. Saying, in effect, "and, by the way, God is on my side," means that all further moral restraint is unnecessary. And even if nobody else is involved, someone who is determinedly trying to show God how good he or she is is likely to become an insufferable prig. We would all prefer to live with people who knew perfectly well that they weren't good enough for God, but were humbly grateful that God loved them anyway, than with people who were convinced that they had made it to God's standard and could look down on the rest of us from a lofty moral mountaintop.

There is much more to the doctrine of "justification by faith" than this, but not less. The radical insight of St. Paul into what it means to be human, and what it means to have the overwhelming love of God take hold of you, corresponds in quite an obvious way to what most people know about what makes someone more or less livable-with. And livable-with-ness, though of course it contains a large subjective element, is not a bad rule of thumb for what it might mean to be truly human.

Equally, St. Paul and the other early Christian writers were absolutely clear that, even though humans could not make themselves fit for God, could not pull themselves up to God's moral standard by their own efforts, it didn't mean they could shrug their shoulders and give up the moral struggle altogether. One of Paul's most striking questions, answered by his famous "Certainly not!" comes at just this point in his letter to the Christians in Rome (6.1–2). Having laid out in glorious detail the heart-stopping truth that God's love has reached down in Jesus Christ and has brought us redemption, justification, reconciliation, salvation, and peace (Romans 3.21–5.21), he faces the question which ought to challenge many people in today's world: All right then, if God loves us that much even when we have done nothing to deserve it, should we not remain in that utterly undeserving state so that God will go on loving us like that? Or, in his clipped, somewhat technical language, "Shall we remain in sin, so that grace may abound?" If God loves rescuing people from the mud and mess they're wallowing in, wouldn't it be a good idea to stay muddy and messy so that God will love us all the more?

When Paul answers "Certainly not!" he is not being illogical. The logic of God's grace goes deeper than the question imagines. And in that logic, we find the notion of virtue reborn—reborn as the means by which we can obey the call to follow Jesus. Another illustration will make the point.

I know a choir director who took on the running of a village church choir which hadn't had much help for years. They had struggled valiantly to sing the hymns, to give the congregation a bit of a lead, and on special occasions to try a simple anthem. But, frankly, the results weren't impressive. When the congregation thanked the singers, it was as much out of sympathy for their apparent hard work as out of any appreciation of a genuinely musical sound. However long they practiced, they didn't seem to get any better; they were probably merely reinforcing their existing bad habits. So when the new choir director arrived and took them on, gently finding out what they could and couldn't do, it was in a sense an act of grace. He didn't tell them they were rubbish, or shout at them to sing in tune. That wouldn't have done any good. It would have been simply depressing. He accepted them as they were and began to work with them. But the point of doing so was not so that they could carry on as before, only now with someone waving his arms in front of them. The point of his taking them on as they were was so that they could . . . really learn to sing! And now, remarkably, they can. A friend of mine who went to that church just a few weeks ago reported that the choir had been transformed. Same people, new sound. Now when they practiced they knew what they were doing, and thus they could learn how to sound better.

That is a picture of how God's grace works. God loves us as we are, as he finds us, which is (more or less) messy, muddy, and singing out of tune. Even when we've tried to be good, we have often only made matters worse, adding (short-lived) pride to our other failures. And the never-ending wonder at the heart of genuine Christian living is that God has come to meet us right there, in our confusion of pride and fear, of mess and muddle and downright rebellion and sin.

That's the point of the Christian gospel, the good news: "This is how much God loved the world—that he sent his only son, Jesus Christ, so that anyone who believes in him will not die, but will have life, the life of the age to come." That summary, in one of the most famous verses in the New Testament (John 3.16), says it all. God's love comes to us where we are in Jesus Christ, and all we have to do is accept it. But when we accept it—when we welcome the new choir director into our ragged and out-of-tune moral singing—we find a new desire to read the music better, to understand what it's all about, to sense the harmonies, to feel the shape of the melody, to get the breathing and voice production right . . . and, bit by bit, to sing in tune.

Out of our desire to become better musicians, we begin to *practice* and to *learn the habits* of how to sing; to *acquire the character* not only of good individual singers but of a good choir; and so to take our place within *the ongoing story* of music—specifically, church music, the tradition going back to Bach and Handel and beyond. There is the sequence: grace, which meets us where we are but is not content to let us remain where we are, followed by direction and guidance to enable us to acquire the right habits to replace the wrong ones.

So how does this work out in terms of Christian living? How does moral transformation take place? Does it mean that we are simply given the Ten Commandments, and perhaps a lot of other ones as well, and told to get on with it? What about the New Testament's trio of "faith, hope, and love"? Where do they fit in? And if there really is a new desire to sing in tune, morally speaking, how does that relate to the virtues? And, above and around and beneath all of this, what happens to this whole picture when we look, not just at the early Christian preaching about Jesus, but at Jesus himself, his life and teaching, his announcement of God's kingdom, and his death and resurrection?

All these questions about what a friend of mine called "how to think about what to do" may make our heads spin. It's like being asked to fly a plane and having to learn, as you go along, what all the different instruments in the cockpit are telling you, and what all the different switches and buttons will do when you operate them. The good news is that the Christian message offers a framework within which it all really does make sense: sense not only for Christians themselves, but sense which can commend itself to the whole world—sense, too, not only for individuals, but for communities and nations.

As our world shudders like a plane suddenly hitting a flock of geese, we badly need people who will learn that sense, and learn it quickly, not simply or even primarily for their own benefit but because our world, God's world, needs people at the helm in whom courage, good judgment, a cool head, and a proper care for people—and, if possible, faith, hope, and love as well—have become second nature.

The rest of this book will explore how this might come about. I believe, as I said before, that this could result in a revolution—a revolution in the way in which Christians approach the whole question of "how to think about what to do," and also, out beyond that, a revolution in the way human beings in general approach the question of what it means to live a fulfilled, genuinely human life.

EIGHT

What then is the Christian "goal" or "end" at which we aim? How can we "anticipate" it here and now?

First, a note about "anticipating." This idea can be somewhat tricky, and we'd better spend a moment trying to make it clear. If I say "I'm anticipating that it will rain later on," I may mean simply that I expect it's going to rain later even though it isn't doing so at the moment. But if I say it to someone who asks me why I'm wearing a raincoat even though the sun is shining, it means something more: it means that I am already dressed in the way that will be appropriate for the later conditions. In the same way, when a fielder in cricket or baseball is told by the coach to "anticipate" which way the ball is going to fly once it's been hit, this doesn't mean just that the fielder should guess in advance what's going to happen. It means he should start to move before the ball is actually struck so that he's in the right position to make the catch.

To "anticipate" in this second, strong sense means, in other words, not only thinking about what may happen but doing something about it in advance. Sometimes the conductor will tell a singer or instrumentalist to "anticipate the beat," meaning actually to sing or play the note a fraction of a second before the written music indicates. If a chess player guesses rightly what move her opponent is likely to play, she may "anticipate" that move by doing something which heads off the challenge and advances one of her own. If a child gets into the party room ahead of the guests, he may "anticipate" the formal opening of the meal by making a private start on the hors d'oeuvres.

All these point toward the reality that Paul and other early Christian writers are getting at, but that none expresses fully. It might be closer to home—"home" being the New Testament announcement of Jesus and his kingdom-bringing work—to think in terms of a rightful king coming secretly to his people and gathering a group to help him overthrow the rulers who have usurped his throne. When he becomes king fully and finally, his followers will of course still obey him. When they obey him in the present time, however—even though he is not yet publicly owned as king—they are genuinely *anticipating* the obedience they will offer him in the future.

Applying all this to Christian faith and life means doing a kind of calculation. Indeed, Paul uses the word for "calculate" at just this point: Jesus Christ has died and been raised, he says, and you are now "in him," so you must "calculate" or "reckon" that you, too, have died and been raised (Romans 6.11). This truth about who you already are, and the moral life which flows from it, *anticipates* your own eventual bodily death and resurrection and the life of the coming new age. The point is this: the full reality is yet to be revealed, but we can genuinely partake in that final reality in advance. We can draw down some of God's future into our own present moment. The rationale for this is that in Jesus that future has already burst into our present time, so that in *anticipating* that which is to come, we are also *implementing* what has already taken place. This is the framework of thought which makes sense of the New Testament's virtue ethics.

So how does this work out? What is the goal, and how can we "anticipate" it here and now?

This is where many people still cling on to the idea of a disembodied heaven, an existence where we spend eternity simply being in God's company. That gives you a moral framework that looks like this:

1. The goal is the final bliss of heaven, away from this life of space, time, and matter.
2. This goal is achieved for us through the death and resurrection of Jesus, which we cling to by faith.
3. Christian living in the present consists of anticipating the disembodied, "eternal" state through the practice of a detached spirituality and the avoidance of "worldly" contamination.

Fortunately, there is enough of the genuine gospel in there for people to live by, but those who take that path will be trying to live "Christianly" with one hand tied behind their back.

There is at least one other would-be Christian vision current in the Western world. It functions like this:

1. The goal is to establish God's kingdom on earth by our own hard work.
2. This goal is demonstrated by Jesus in his public career, starting off the process and showing us how to do it.
3. Christian living in the present consists of anticipating the final kingdom-on-earth by working and campaigning for justice, peace, and the alleviation of poverty and distress.

Here, again, there is plenty of "good news" by which people can live, though the heart of the matter seems to be strangely missing—which is perhaps why the attempts to live by this scheme are never as successful as their proponents hope.

My counterproposal to both of these (and thereby also to Aristotle's scheme of thought, which I outlined briefly above) brings us to the heart of the present book, and with it to the gateway to a fresh reading of the moral thrust of the New Testament. This is how it goes:

1. The goal is the new heaven and new earth, with human beings raised from the dead to be the renewed world's rulers and priests.

2. This goal is achieved through the kingdom-establishing work of Jesus and the Spirit, which we grasp by faith, participate in by baptism, and live out in love.

3. Christian living in the present consists of anticipating this ultimate reality through the Spirit-led, habit-forming, truly human practice of faith, hope, and love, sustaining Christians in their calling to worship God and reflect his glory into the world.

This vision produces, I suggest, a double revolution:

First, most Christians in today's world have never imagined their moral behavior in these terms. They have, rather, struggled both to articulate and to adhere to a set of "Christian rules." Discussions about "Christian ethics" have tended to settle into a discussion of "how you can tell what the rules are," with the assumption being that one then simply gets on and keeps them as best one can (with the Spirit's help, no doubt), as though they were an arbitrary list of instructions that God had invented for reasons best known to himself. Sometimes Christians have justified such rules by pointing to their consequences: "Think how much better the world would be if we all loved and forgave one another." This appeal to consequence carries some force, but it then usually lets you down at the moment when the ethical discussion reaches the tricky part, as the different points of view in the various moral debates each claim that the likely consequences support

their position. We meet a similar problem if, with many recent thinkers, we try to highlight various "principles" from scripture or Christian tradition. It's all very well to say we must aim at justice (say), or
"inclusivity," or "God being on the side of the poor." It's hard to dis-
agree at that level of generality, but this only postpones the problem of
applying these broad, general terms to particular situations.

By contrast, looking at Christian behavior in terms of virtue—
virtue as anticipating-the-life-of-the-age-to-come—does three things.

First, it helps followers of Jesus Christ to understand how Christian behavior "works." That is, it provides a framework within which
one may grasp the organic connection between what we are called to
do and become in the present and what we are promised as full, genuine human life in the future.

As a result, second, it also ought to provide massive encouragement to all those starting to think seriously about following Jesus. Yes,
declares Virtue, this is going to be tough, especially at first. It's an acquired taste. It's a new language with its own alphabet and grammar.
But the more you practice, the more "natural" it will become. This is
particularly important, because many Christians, finding it difficult
(say) to forgive people, just assume, "This is impossible; I'm never going to manage it." Some may even conclude that rules which they find
difficult and "unnatural" don't apply to them, or that those particular rules belong in a bygone age when people saw things differently.
That misses the point. Did you think you could sit down at the piano
and play a Beethoven sonata straight off? Did you think you could
just fly to Moscow, get off the plane, and start speaking fluent Rus-
sian? Did you think, as a "normal" young person growing up in today's
sex-soaked Western world, that you could attain chastity of heart,
mind, and body just through praying one prayer about it? But here are
the lessons; here is how to practice; here is the path to the goal. And
here—to extend the metaphor to correspond to Christian behavior—
the spirit of Beethoven, or the spirit of Russia, will inhabit you and
give you the help you will need.

Third, looking at Christian behavior in this way means that we approach "ethical" questions—particular questions about what to do and what not to do—through the larger category of the divine purpose for the entire human life. "Ethics" tends to provide a very restrictive view of what human life is about. Even those people with a well-developed conscience don't normally spend every minute of every day wrestling with moral questions about what to do the next minute, and the one after that. But when we look at Christian behavior in terms of the whole of life, seen from the perspective of the Creator's purpose for humans, ethics can be seen as contained within, and hopefully shaped by, that larger vision. The question of content, of how to know what to do, is not then confined to particular "ethical" dilemmas, but opens up as a vocation to the whole of one's life.

When we approach things this way, the line of thought I am proposing easily upstages its main rival, the idea of "going to heaven" and the use of that goal to generate a vision of the present life. The old idea that the goal of Christian existence is simply "going to heaven" doesn't, in fact, do very much to stimulate the fully fledged virtue we find advocated in the New Testament. It can coexist comfortably, as it has done often enough over the centuries, with the old rulebook approach to ethics as well as the romantic, emotivist, and existentialist dreams. (Since the gospel offers us peace in our hearts, romantics, for example, might assume that whatever they "feel peaceful about" in the present must be basically all right.) My contention in this book is that the renewed biblical heaven-and-earth vision, for which I have argued elsewhere, sets a framework within which a genuinely Christian vision of virtue stands out as the best way to think about what to do. The practice and habit of virtue, in this sense, is all about learning in advance the language of God's new world.

The first revolution I propose, then—a revolution for many modern Christians, though many in previous generations, and some already in our own, would simply take for granted much of what I've said so far—is that thinking of Christian behavior in terms of virtue, and reframing virtue in terms of the promised new heaven and new earth and the role of humans within it, provides both a framework of meaning for, and a strong impetus toward the path of, the holiness to which Jesus and his first followers would call us.

This points to the second revolution, which is where this proposal not only clarifies and energizes Christian living, but also poses a challenge and a question to the wider non-Christian world. It isn't enough to pursue our own goals in private, precisely because the "goal" we have in view is not an escapist heaven but God's kingdom of restorative justice and healing joy, coming upon the whole creation. But to develop this further evolution we must wait until we have first set out the fundamental Christian vision.

The Christian claim, you see, is that when you go for the Christian goal you get everything that was worthwhile in Aristotle's scheme thrown in as well, whereas it doesn't work the other way around. To begin with, you have to grasp the fact that Christian virtue isn't about *you*—your happiness, your fulfillment, your self-realization. It's about God and God's kingdom, and your discovery of a genuine human existence by the paradoxical route—the route God himself took in Jesus Christ!—of giving yourself away, of generous love which constantly refuses to take center stage. Aristotle's vision of the virtuous person always tended to be that of the "hero," the moral giant striding through the world doing great deeds and gaining applause. The Christian vision of the virtuous person characteristically highlights someone whose loving, generous character wouldn't normally draw attention to itself. The glory of virtue, in the Christian sense, is that the self is not in the center of that picture. God and God's kingdom are in the center. As Jesus himself said, we are to seek first God's kingdom and his justice (we'll say more about the word "justice" later on), and then everything else will fall into place.

This revolutionary vision of virtue thus enables us to shift attention quite drastically away from the idea that Christian behavior in the world is basically about "good works" in the sense of good moral living, keeping the rules, and so on, and toward the idea that Christian behavior is basically about "good works" in the sense of *doing things which bring God's wisdom and glory to birth in the world*. You get the "good moral living" thrown in as well, of course (just in case anyone might worry that this was the thin end of a wedge leading to some kind of moral relativism). But, as Protestants have always rightly insisted, though without always knowing quite why, to concentrate on the good moral works themselves is to put the cart before the horse, to put the self—even the Christian self!—at the center of the picture. Virtue, after all, isn't just about morals in the sense of "knowing the standards to live up to" or "knowing which rules you're supposed to keep." Virtue, as we have already seen, is about the whole of life, not just the specifically "moral" choices. Those who put rules or consequences first sometimes think of vocational choices as a sort of sub-branch of ethics. I prefer to think of it the other way around. We are called to be genuine, image-bearing, God-reflecting human beings. That works out in a million ways, not least in a passion for justice and an eagerness to create and celebrate beauty. The more specific choices we think of as "ethical" are, I suggest, a subset of that wider image-bearing, God-reflecting vocation.

Once we are clear about our own role, as bit-part players in God's great drama, we are free, in a way that we might not have been if we were still struggling to think of ourselves as moral heroes in the making, to see just what an astonishing vocation we actually have, and hence to reflect on how that works out in the present time. In half a dozen remarkable New Testament passages, we are informed that our future role in God's new creation will be to share in God's wise rule over his world, particularly in making the judgments that will put everything to rights; and to share in creation's praise of its generous creator, particularly in bringing that grateful praise into conscious and articulate speech.

These New Testament passages themselves look back to the passage in which humans are given their original vocation, the vocation to which Jesus claimed to be recalling us. In the next chapter we go back to the beginning, to Genesis.

3. PRIESTS AND RULERS

ONE

In Genesis 1, God made humans in his own image, and entrusted them with sovereignty over the rest of creation:

> Then God said, "Let us make Human in our image, according to our likeness; and let Human reign over the fish of the sea, the birds of the sky, the animals, and over all the earth, and over every creeping thing that creeps on the earth. So God created Human in his image; in the image of God he created them; male and female he created them. And God blessed them, and God said to them, "Be fruitful, and multiply, and fill the earth and bring it into order; and reign over the fish in the sea, the birds in the sky, and over every living creature that goes on the ground." (vv. 26–28)

Let them reign. How do you react to that command?

You could write an entire political novel on the basis of how different people respond to the suggestion that humans should be "reigning" over the world. Remember the two ancient philosophers, one of whom, on coming out of his house in the morning, roared with laughter at the world, while the other one burst into tears? In the same way, we divide sharply into two groups at the idea of humans being given sovereignty over the world.

Some of us heave a sigh of relief: *Someone's in charge! Chaos will be averted!* Others of us, meanwhile, groan: *This is tyranny! We don't want anybody reigning over us! We want to be free!* All the great theories about human society and politics have gone to and fro between those reactions, often because of what people have experienced. Anyone

who has known chaos (think of people living in Iraq in the years following the overthrow of Saddam Hussein), and anyone who has lived
under tyranny (think of people living in Albania or Bulgaria in the old
Communist period), will be very wary of ever going near them again.

The negative reaction, in particular ("No thanks; we don't want
people running things—they'll only mess it all up"), has been very
common in our own day. Many people have declared that the reason
our world has been polluted and despoiled, the reason our seas have
been overfished and our skies filled with acid rain, is that we have followed this very command in Genesis. "Subduing the earth" has become, in many people's eyes, an explanation and even an excuse for
careless and destructive greed.

But is that what Genesis meant? What sort of "reign" did it have in
mind? The creation stories in Genesis 1 and 2, some of the most profound and evocative stories ever written, certainly don't envisage humans tyrannizing creation. Try doing that to a garden, forcing it to do
what you want whether the soil will take it or not, and you may well
create a wilderness. And a garden is what we have here in Genesis, a
fruitful and richly varied landscape with the humans commanded to
look after it, to make it fruitful, and (while they're at it) to give names
to the animals. There's no suggestion that the "reign" in question is
anything other than benign. Humans are to enable the garden to flourish, and to speak words which bring articulate order to the wonderful
diversity of God's creation.

Creation, it seems, was not a tableau, a static scene. It was designed
as a *project,* created in order to go somewhere. The creator has a future
in mind for it; and Human—this strange creature, full of mystery and
glory—is the means by which the creator is going to take his project
forward. The garden, and all the living creatures, plants and animals,
within it, are designed to become what they were meant to be through
the work of God's image-bearing creatures in their midst. The point of
the project is that the garden be extended, colonizing the rest of creation; and Human is the creature put in charge of that plan. Human is
thus a kind of midway creature: reflecting God into the world, and re-

flecting the world back to God. That is the basis for the "truly human" vocation. And that, as the New Testament declares, is also the goal for which we are aiming—indeed, the goal of all human existence. In Aristotle's terms, this is the *telos* toward which we aim, though this goal is very different from what Aristotle had in mind. The Christian vision of virtue is the vision of the pathway toward this goal. And just as the goal is different from that of Aristotle, so is the pathway—but the framework, the concept of discerning the pathway in light of the goal, remains the same.

We who live in the shadow of Genesis 3, the rebellion of Human against this God and this project, often fail to see this extraordinary vocation, because all we can see is what happens when God's delegated authority has been abused. We know it only too well: the bullying, tyrannical behavior which defaces human life, animal life, the world's life, whether that tyranny is carried out in the privacy of a home or in the scarily public world of international politics and business. (Who cares about the flourishing of the ecosystem when there's money to be made or a war to win?) We see, too, the ways in which Human so often now scorns the God of the garden, the God who made Human in his image. But the story to which the early Christians looked back, the story of Genesis 1 and 2, insists that this wasn't the intention from the beginning. God placed Human in the garden to reflect his image into the new world he was making—that is, to be the means, present and visible, whereby his own care of the garden and the animals would become a reality. And if Human was going to do this, Human was going to have to keep in tune with God.

The abuse of Human's authority, then, doesn't abolish its proper use. It doesn't cancel out the vocation. That is why, in another Old Testament passage to which the early Christian texts refer on a number of occasions, the vocation is repeated:

O YHWH our Lord! How excellent is your name in all the earth!...
When I look at your heavens, the works of your fingers,
The moon and the stars which you have brought forth—

What is a human being, that you should remember such a one,

Or the child of Human, that you should watch over such a one?

You have made them a little lower than God,

And have crowned them with glory and honor.

You have given them royal dominion over the works of your hands,

And have put all things under their feet:

All sheep and oxen; yes, even the animals in the wild;

The birds of the air and the fish of the sea, and everything that goes in the highways of the sea.

O YHWH our Lord! How excellent is your name in all the earth!

Psalm 8.1, 3–9

This, clearly, is a celebration of the role of human beings as set out in Genesis 1, and forms an important part of the mental furniture of the early Christians as they explored the human vocation in a fresh way in light of the gospel of Jesus. This is the goal of a genuinely human existence. Forget "happiness"; you are called to a *throne*. How will you prepare for it? That is the question of virtue, Christian style.

This wise rule of humans over God's world is, in fact, what "being in God's image" is partly about, as we shall see in more detail later. The "image" does not refer principally to some aspect of human nature or character which is especially like God. As many writers have shown, it points to the belief that, just as ancient rulers might place statues of themselves in far-flung cities to remind subject peoples who was ruling them, so God has placed his own image, human beings, into his world, so that the world can see who its ruler is. Not only *see,* but *experience*. Precisely because God is the God of generous, creative, outflowing love, his way of running things is to share power, to work through his image-bearers, to invite their glad and free collaboration in his project. Yes, it might be easier in some ways if God had decided to run everything himself, without intermediaries. But it wouldn't have been nearly so much in character. And "character" is what virtue is all about: the character, the sense of "yes, that's the sort of person she is," which is what people conclude on the basis of what someone has become, by habitual choices. Virtue is what happens when those habitual choices have been wise. Jewish and Christian writers alike have suggested that such wisdom reflects the wisdom of the creator himself.

TWO

The early Christians believed, on the authority of Jesus himself, that the original vision for creation, and for Human within it, had been re-captured and restored through Jesus's inauguration of God's sovereign rule. What Jesus did and said was designed to give a decisive answer, in deeds as well as words, to the question, What would it look like if God was running things? And, as in Genesis, part of the answer to that question was, It would look like obedient humans, following the Obe-dient Human, acting as stewards over creation, bringing new creation to birth, and gathering up the praises of that creation to present them to its maker. Jesus himself, as the whole New Testament makes clear, acted as the Obedient Human, summing up creation's praises and in-augurating God's saving sovereignty. What is not so often noticed is that this role is immediately shared with his followers.

The early Christians held out a breathtaking, radical vision of the ultimate goal of all things: the new heavens and new earth, the renewal of all things, the new Jerusalem "coming down from heaven to earth" (Revelation 21.2), a world flooded with the joy and justice of the creator God. The question must then be asked: What place, and what role, will human beings have within this new world? Only when we answer that question can we begin to understand the virtues by which, in the pres-ent time, our characters can be formed. What were we made for, and how can we learn that future language here and now?

The Bible opened, as we saw, with God assigning a particular voca-tion to human beings: that they should look after God's creation and make it fruitful and abundant. The Bible closes with a scene in which this has at last come about, only far more so. Forget the vague and wishy-washy piety which speaks of "heaven" simply as a place of rest and adoration. Put to one side, also, even such noble statements of the "chief end" of human beings as we find in the Westminster Confession: "to glorify God and to enjoy him for ever." (This statement is undoubtedly true, but it is not the *full* truth on which scripture insists.) In the new heavens and new earth, there will be new vocations and new tasks, the ultimate fulfillment of those given to Human in the first place. Once we glimpse this, we will be in a position to see how the New Testament's vision of Christian behavior has to do, not with struggling to keep a bunch of ancient and apparently arbitrary rules, nor with "going with the flow" or "doing what comes naturally," but with the learning of the language, in the present, which will equip us to speak it fluently in God's new world.

In the final chapter of the Bible, we find two things highlighted as the central activities of renewed human beings within God's new creation:

> The throne of God, and of the Lamb, will be in [the new city]; and his servants will worship him. They will see his face, and his name will be upon their foreheads. There will be no more night; they will not need the light of a lamp or the light of the sun, because God the Lord will shine his light upon them, and they will reign for ever and ever. (Revelation 22.3–5)

Worshipping and reigning: those are the twin vocations of the new people in the new city. So important is this theme in the final book of the Bible that it is repeated, in one form or another, no fewer than four times in addition to the above-quoted final one:

> To him who loved us and released us from our sins by his own blood, and made us a kingdom, priests to his God and father, to him be glory and power for ever and ever. Amen! (1.5–6)

> The one who conquers—to that one I will grant the right to sit with me on my throne, just as I conquered and sat down with my father on his throne. (3.21)

They sing a new song, saying, "You are worthy to receive the book and open its seals, for you were slaughtered, and you bought for God, with your blood, people from every tribe and language and people and nation, and you made them rulers and priests to our God, and they shall reign on the earth. (5.9–10)

And I saw thrones, with people sitting on them, and judgment was given to them; and the souls of those who had had their heads cut off because of their witness to Jesus, and because of the word of God, and who had not worshipped the beast or his image, and had not received the mark on their foreheads or on their hands. They came to life and reigned with the Messiah for a thousand years. . . . Blessed and holy are those who share in the first resurrection. The second death will have no authority over them, but they will be priests of God and of the Messiah, and they will reign with him for a thousand years. (20.4, 6)

There can be no mistake. The book of Revelation, so often dismissed as merely dark, strange, and violent, holds out a vision not only of all creation renewed and rejoicing, but of human beings within it able at last to sum up the praise which all creation offers to its maker, and to exercise that sovereignty, that dominion, that wise stewardship over the world which God always intended for his image-bearing creatures. They will be priests and rulers, summing up the praises of all creation and exercising authority on behalf of God and the Lamb.

"Priests and rulers"! The phrase has a grand ring to it, reminiscent in many minds of a bygone age of courtly life, royal robes, and grand pageantry. Distance (in this case, distance in time) lends a certain charm— but also, perhaps, a threat. Do we really want to live in a world like that, an olde-worlde costume drama of nobility and formal religion?

Before we recoil from this image, consider the reality to which the phrase intends to point. It goes back, within the biblical frame of reference at least, to the vocation of Israel. After the Exodus, God led his newly liberated people to Mount Sinai, where they were given the

Law. God himself set the scene for that majestic revelation by giving his people a newly defined vocation:

> You have seen what I did to Egypt, and how I carried you on eagles' wings and brought you to myself. So now, if you will pay full attention to my voice, and keep my covenant, you will be my treasured possession from out of all peoples (for all the earth belongs to me). You will be to me *a kingdom of priests, and a holy nation.* (Exodus 19.4–6; see Isaiah 61.6)

A kingdom of priests? Those who are familiar with the biblical story are accustomed, perhaps, to think of ancient Israel as a people who (at a certain stage) *possessed* kings, starting with Saul and David and continuing to the Exile, with a kind of shadow royal house thereafter; and who also possessed priests, the descendents of the patriarch Levi and more particularly of Aaron, Moses's brother. We may not always be so used to thinking of the whole people of Israel itself as being, at least in God's intention, a "kingdom of priests," an entire nation entrusted with the dual role of royalty and priesthood. This vocation often seems to have been submerged or forgotten in the long and frequently murky history which followed. But it lived on somewhere within the corporate memory of the people. And it resurfaces dramatically in the New Testament.

This vocation, too, has its roots in Genesis 1 and 2. If we read those chapters from the point of view of the developed Judaism of the Exile and thereafter—when most scholars think that the bulk of the Old Testament was edited into its present form—then it appears that the role assigned to Human in creation was seen not only as "royal" (ruling over creation, as in the earlier-cited wording from Genesis) but also as "priestly." Human was simultaneously the bearer of God's wise rule into the world and also the creature who would bring the loyalty and praise of that creation for its creator into love, speech, and conscious obedience. The royal and priestly vocation of all human beings, it seems, consists in this: to stand at the interface between God and his creation, bringing God's wise and generous order to the world and giving articulate voice to creation's glad and grateful praise to its maker.

That is exactly what we find in the book of Revelation. And the setting for this royal, priestly vision is very telling.

First, John's vision of the heavenly host worshipping God and the Lamb in chapters 4 and 5 looks very much like a "throne room," the kind of place where an emperor or great monarch would hold court, surrounded by his retinue. Some have suggested that John is deliberately constructing a scene in which the throne room of God dramatically upstages the throne room of Caesar (or any other worldly monarch). This is the true imperial rule, and it is exercised through the Lamb who was slain, and through his followers, who embrace his way of humility and suffering.

Second, the "new Jerusalem" in chapters 21 and 22 is designed, it seems, to be like the Temple. There is no specific Temple in this new city because the city itself *is* a Temple, or rather is *the* true Temple, the reality toward which the Jerusalem Temple had been pointing all along. Its measurements and adornments speak of this, as do the rules for its holiness (21.8, 11–21, 27; 22.3, 15). This, John is saying, will at last be the reality of which the Garden of Eden itself, and then the ancient Jerusalem Temple, were foretastes. This is the place where the living God dwells, the place from which his healing river will flow out to refresh and cleanse the whole world (22.1–2). Kings and priests, set now in a throne room, now in a Temple. That is the goal, the *telos,* of Human.

As we gaze at the description of the new city-which-is-a-Temple in Revelation 21–22, we notice two things in particular. First, this is the place where God puts everything right at last. He will right all wrongs, wiping away tears from all eyes (21.4), and removing everything that destroys and defaces human life (21.8). Second, the city will be a place of exquisite beauty (21.11–21). The description of the jewels and other adornments of the city echoes various biblical passages (including Exodus 26–28, 2 Chronicles 3, and Isaiah 60) in which the glory and beauty of God himself are present in, respectively, the wilderness tabernacle, Solomon's Temple, and the new Temple of the messianic age. There is little reference to "beauty" in the Bible, but such as there is is mostly directly linked to the glorious presence of God, both in the whole of creation and, specifically and sharply, in the "little world" of the Temple and its adornments. These two notes, of God putting everything right and of the unveiling of God's glorious beauty, are of considerable importance in understanding the "goal" toward which, in Christian thought, all human virtue points.

We shouldn't fail to notice that, in the book of Revelation as elsewhere in the New Testament, this ultimate destiny is anticipated in the present time. The vision of Revelation 5 is not a vision of the ultimate end, the *telos,* but of the heavenly dimension of present earthly reality. In that vision we already see the church at worship, bringing to articulate and reasoned speech the praises of all creation. The animal kingdom praises its creator in Revelation 4.6–9; the church, joining in this praise in Revelation 4.10 and onward through chapter 5, adds the key word *because.* God the creator is *worthy* of praise *because* he created all things (4.11); the Lamb is *worthy* to take the scroll and open its seals *because* of what he achieved through his death (5.9).

Here is a vision of the ultimate destiny of redeemed human beings, already anticipated in the present. In the New Testament, the final "goal" of human beings is not simply *eudaimonia,* or some variation on it. It is not a self-centered goal, the completion of a human character which is then able to stand on its own, as it were, in heroic isolation. The early Christians implicitly challenged the philosophical tradition from Aristotle through to their day, not by abandoning the framework of a life shaped by the goal toward which it aims but by providing a different goal. The goal is the fulfillment of the task for which, according to Genesis 1 and 2, humans were made in the first place; the task to which, according to Exodus, Israel was called. It is the task of being the "royal priesthood," the key middle term in the wise rule of creation by its creator and also in the praise that rises to that same creator from creation itself. If we are to understand virtue—if we are to learn in advance the language we shall be called upon to speak in God's new world—these are among its main features. Worship and stewardship, generating justice and beauty: these are the primary vocations of God's redeemed people. And the habits of heart, mind, and life to which we are called are designed to form us, gradually and bit by bit, into people who can, with the hard-won "second nature" that we call virtue, freely and gladly take forward these tasks.

THREE

The other obvious New Testament passage where the same vocation is stated explicitly, in a direct echo of Exodus 19, is 1 Peter 2. In and through God's action in Jesus Christ a new Temple has come to birth, a Temple consisting not of bricks and mortar but of human beings; that is the point made here. But in order to see exactly what this means, we must pause and reflect further on the significance, for the Jewish people, of the Temple in Jerusalem.

Echoes of the Temple can be heard even in the creation stories themselves. Or, to put it the other way around, when the Temple was made (and its antecedent, the wilderness tabernacle), it was designed so as to be a "microcosm," a "little world," a creation-in-miniature. Its dimensions, its furnishings, its ornaments, its priestly robes and activities—all were supposed to reflect and sum up the great cosmos itself. The point of all this was, of course, that the Temple was where Israel's God, the creator, had promised to come and dwell, to live in the midst of his people. The priests in the Temple, when doing their job, were celebrating and enacting the fact that the God who had promised to fill the whole of creation with his presence and glory was doing just that close up, in sharp focus, in one particular place and building. But the priests were not the only ones deeply involved. The Temple was planned, built, dedicated, and later cleansed by Israel's kings. Thus the Temple drew together the priestly and the royal vocations.

The Temple was never supposed to be a retreat away from the world, a safe holy place where one might stay secure in God's presence, shut off from the wickedness outside. The Temple was an advance sign of what God intended to do with and for the whole creation. When God filled the house with his presence, that was a sign and a foretaste of his ultimate intention, which was to flood *the whole world* with his glory, presence, and love. Just as, in Exodus 19, God tells the Israelites that all the world belongs to him before telling them that they are to be a special people with a ministry to that world, so the tabernacle in the wilderness, and the Temple in Jerusalem, are seen as, in some mind-boggling sense, an anticipation of a much larger reality yet to come.

There is thus a to-and-fro in the Old Testament between the presence of God filling, and dwelling in, the Temple, and that same presence eventually filling, and dwelling in, the whole world. The ancient Israelites themselves seem to have realized that the Temple was only, at best, a kind of temporary and inadequate expression of what it signified, since after all the heavens themselves could not contain God. (For this whole theme see the following: Exodus 24.16; 29.42–43; 40.34; Numbers 14.21; 1 Kings 8.10–11, 27; 2 Chronicles 2.6; 5.13–14; 6.18; 7.1; Psalm 72.19; Isaiah 6.3; 11.9; 35.1–2; 40.5; 58.8; 60.1–2; 66.1–2; Jeremiah 23.24; Ezekiel 10.4; Habakkuk 2.14; and see not least for the expectation of the second-Temple period, in the Apocrypha, 2 Maccabees 2.8; 3 Maccabees 2.15–16; Wisdom 1.7; and, in the New Testament, Acts 7.47–50.) Similar things could be said about the promises regarding the Holy Land: the Temple stood at the heart of the land God had promised to Abraham, and the land itself pointed to a much larger reality, the claim of the creator God upon the whole creation. As Paul insists, in line with some other Jewish thinkers of the time, the promises to Abraham were that he should inherit, not just one small strip of territory, but the whole world (Romans 4.13).

Pull back the lens a bit from this dense, tightly packed little picture of ancient Jewish musings about God, the Temple, the Holy Land, and the world, and what do we see? We see a large, slowly developing story: of the good creator God making a wonderful world, and putting Human in charge of it to rule it wisely and to gather up its grateful praise; of Human rebelling and failing in this task, so that the project cannot get off the ground; of the good God calling one family in order that, through them, he might rescue and restart the project, and giving them the vocation which reflected, on a larger scale, the vocation of Human in the first place; of this good God, now in covenant with this chosen people, giving them a particular place and means by which his eventual intention—to fill the whole world with his glorious presence—might be known mysteriously in advance; of the various institutions (rulers, priests) through which, within the life of this people, this symbol might be brought to birth, guarded, enhanced, and made effective; and, not least, of the miserable failures of this people, pointed out relentlessly by the prophets, resulting in the destruction of the Temple itself.

The story of rulers and priests is told extensively in the Old Testament, not least in the parallel tracks of the books of Samuel and Kings on the one hand and Chronicles on the other, the former focusing especially on rulers and the latter on priests. But the story points forward, as it stands in the Old Testament scriptures, with an open question: What is the creator God going to do now? What is now going to happen to Israel and its vocation, and to that of Human? How will the royal, priestly vocation be taken forward, carrying with it the Creator's purpose for the whole creation?

The whole New Testament is written, from a dozen different angles, to answer that question. Central to the answer is the wonderful, mind-blowing, virtue-generating claim: those who belong to Jesus the Messiah are now to be "rulers and priests, serving our God." The Israel project has been accomplished, and as a result the Human project is back on track, with God's people themselves forming the "new Temple":

> As living stones, be built into a spiritual house, to become a holy priesthood, offering spiritual sacrifices acceptable to God through Jesus the Messiah. . . . You are a chosen race, a royal priesthood, a holy nation, a people for God's possession, so that you may publicly declare the strong deeds of the one who called you out of darkness into his marvelous light. (1 Peter 2.5, 9)

Here, in line with many other New Testament passages, Peter takes the basic Israel vocation and declares boldly that it has now become the fulfilled-Israel vocation. "Fulfilled-Israel" means, primarily, Jesus himself, Israel's Messiah, but the vocation then extends to all those who follow and belong to him. Jesus is the one true "living stone," and his followers are the "living stones" by which the true Temple is to be built, bringing the presence of God into the wider world, carrying forward the mission of declaring God's powerful and rescuing acts, and beginning the work of implementing the messianic rule of Jesus in all the world. This is what it means to be a "royal priesthood."

The rest of 1 Peter makes it clear what this does *not* mean. It does not mean that Jesus's followers are at once to set themselves up as "world rulers," or even local rulers, in the ordinary sense. We know of some local government officials who became Christians in the very early period, but that is an unlooked-for mercy at this stage, not something that of itself would be seen as an anticipation of the eventual vocation to be "rulers and priests." Far from it. First Peter is full of warnings about persecution, and instructions to those who find themselves suffering from it. Rather, in some sense which the writer does not explore explicitly, this very status of the early Christians, as people rejected by the world around and yet living lives of holiness and hope, is what the "royal priesthood" should expect to look like. This is how Jesus's messianic rule is brought to bear, in powerful witness, upon the world. The message that Jesus—the crucified Jesus!—is the world's true Lord is to be made known precisely through the church's following in his footsteps (2.21–23).

FOUR

Once we get our heads around the vision and vocation of Revelation, and of 1 Peter 2, we notice one or two other key passages in the New

Testament which express the same idea. The first of these passages comes in the middle of a paragraph so dense that the reader can easily pass over it without realizing what is actually being said.

The passage in question comes at the point where Paul is summing up the first four chapters of the letter to the Romans so that he can thereby construct a platform for the next four chapters—with the first eight chapters then forming a further solid platform for what he wants to say in chapters 9–16. The passage we are looking at, in other words, is not an aside, a throwaway line without reference to the real substance of Paul's thought in general or in this letter. It is central and vital. This is the point where Paul, as it were, climbs a high mountain from whose pinnacle he can survey the entire landscape of God's plan from the first days through to the final result.

Paul does this principally by contrasting Adam, the first man, who was given God's great commands but who disobeyed, with Jesus Christ, who was obedient to God's saving purpose and thus rescued the human race. Paul is declaring, in other words, that our calling as followers of Jesus is *to be genuine human beings at last*. Thus:

> Therefore, just as sin came into the world through one human being, and death through sin, and in that way death spread to all humans, in that all sinned . . . (Sin was in the world, you see, even in the absence of the Law, though sin is not calculated when there is no Law. But death reigned from Adam to Moses, even over the people who did not sin by breaking a command, as Adam had done—Adam, who was an advance prototype of the one who would come.)
>
> But it isn't "as the trespass, so also the gift." For if many died by one person's trespass, how much more has God's grace, and the gift in grace through the one person Jesus the Messiah, abounded to the many. And nor is it "as through the sin of the one, so also the gift." For the judgment which followed the one trespass resulted in a negative verdict, but the free gift which followed many trespasses resulted in a positive verdict. (5.12–16)

And then, two verses later, triumphantly:

So, then, just as, through the trespass of one person, the result was
condemnation for all people, even so, through the upright act of one
person, the result is justification and life for all people. For just as
through the disobedience of one person many received the status of
"sinner," so through the obedience of one person many will receive the
status of "in the right." (18–19)

Dense and complicated; well, yes. But in principle we can, I think,
see what Paul is saying. Here is Adam, called to a great destiny and
losing it by his disobedience. Here is Jesus Christ, called to undo the
resultant mess, to get the human project back on track, and being obedient to that calling and thereby accomplishing it. We can get our
minds around that.

But the contrast Paul is drawing isn't just between Adam and Jesus
Christ. It is between the status and role which humans have as a result of Adam's disobedience and that which they will have as a result
of Jesus Christ's obedience. Most Christians today, I strongly suspect,
have never really thought of their role in those terms, and are probably
not prepared for it. Thus, in the verse we omitted a moment ago, Paul
goes beyond what many might expect him to say, and declares that humans are not only rescued through Jesus Christ but are *placed in authority over God's new world:*

For if, by the trespass of the one, death reigned through that one, how
much more will those who receive the abundance of grace, and of the
gift of covenant membership, of "being in the right"—how much
more will they reign in life through the one man Jesus the Messiah.
(5.17)

How much more will they reign! What is he saying, and why is he saying it?

This, together with Revelation, is the telltale sign that the Christian vision of a genuinely human existence goes way beyond Aristotle's "happiness" and into a different sphere altogether. Aristotle dreamed of a world where humans would learn the virtues so that they might exercise leadership within the political order of the ancient Greek city. Paul speaks of a world where humans will be put in charge of the whole creation. He sends us back, in fact, to the very foundation of what it means to be human. This is where we need to begin if we are to see how "being human" can become an art we can practice, a language we can learn, a goal, a *telos,* toward which we can begin to take some serious steps here and now.

Paul is here drawing on the ancient Jewish tradition which goes all the way back to Genesis 1.26–28. Jesus Christ has put the human project back on track—actually, more than back on track. It was, all along, God's project *through* human beings *for the whole world.* In Jesus the Messiah, God has indeed overcome the problem caused by the eating of the Tree of the Knowledge of Good and Evil; but he has done more than that. He has also led the human race, at last, to taste the Tree of Life. That is what Jesus's resurrection is all about, which is why, back once more in Revelation 22, we find the Tree of Life growing beside the river that flows out of the city (22.1–2). Humans are called, in and through Jesus Christ, to become what they were always made to be. And what they were made for can be summarized in one single word: glory.

"Glory" is a standard biblical way of referring to the wise rule of humans over creation. Glory isn't simply a quality that individuals might or might not possess in and for themselves—a splendor, a status, a condition to be admired. Glory is an *active* quality. It is the glorious human rule through which the world is brought to its intended flourishing state, and through which humans themselves come to their own intended flourishing. It is, in fact, "the glory of God"—the effective rank and status which shows that humans are indeed the God-reflectors, the ones through whom the loving, wise sovereignty of the creator God is brought into powerful, life-giving presence within creation.

This too, what's more, is a "Temple" theme. The glory of YHWH abandoned the Temple at the time of the Exile, and never returned. But the promise of such a return remained in passages such as Isaiah 40.3–5; 52.7–10; Ezekiel 43.1–9; Zechariah 2.10–12; and Malachi 3.1–4, awaiting fulfillment. Yes, says Paul; humans lost "the glory of God" through their sin (3.23); but now, they are promised, it will be restored, as redeemed humans receive "access to grace," like priests allowed to enter the very holy of holies, and in consequence "celebrate the hope of God's glory" (5.2). That is precisely what Romans 5.17 is declaring.

And notice what happens as a result. Romans 5.1–2 introduces one of the passages where it is most clear that Paul is thinking of the future goal as the thing which forms character in the present. We celebrate, he says, in our sufferings, knowing that suffering produces patience, and patience produces a tried and tested character, and character produces hope—hope which does not disappoint us, because the love of God has been poured into our hearts through the Holy Spirit (5.3–5).

This is one of those dense Pauline passages which draw together several large and interlocking worlds of reference. It is about the new Temple, filled with God's own glory and (through the Spirit) presence. It is about the new humanity, called to a life of anticipating the eventual "royal priesthood" status through the development of appropriate character. And it is about the living God, creating this "new Temple" through Jesus Christ and then filling it with his own presence.

Redeemed humans, then, are to share the "reign" of Jesus Christ over the new world. But what will be the result of this "reign"? Nothing short of the renewal of the whole world! The next three chapters of Romans explore the great story (which first emerges from Paul's summary in chapter 5), modeled on the Exodus from Egypt when the "royal priesthood" vocation was first articulated, of how humans are rescued from the state of slavery and enabled to become genuine human beings at last. And when they do, the creation project will at last get back on track. The climax of this is the great statement that when humans are fully restored, the creation itself will then be fully restored, so that instead of the "slavery" of decay and corruption, it will be given "the freedom of the glory of the children of God" (8.21). In other words, when God's children, the redeemed human race, are "glorified," set at last (as was always intended) in obedient authority over the world, then the whole creation will heave a gigantic sigh of relief and become truly what it always had the capacity to become but what, through the failure of humans to govern it with the "glory" God had in mind, it failed to attain. Thus Paul returns, in his concluding summary, to what he said in 5.17 (that those who receive the gift of righteousness will reign): "those he justified, them he also glorified" (8.30). To "glorify" here means, more or less, "to set in glorious authority over the world."

That is the hope. When God redeems the whole creation, redeemed humans will play the key role, resuming the wise, healing sovereignty over the whole world for which God made them in the first place.

Very well. If that is the *telos,* the goal for which we were made (to say it again: notice how different this is already from any kind of Aristotelian "happiness"!—and also how different from so many would-be "Christian" visions of "redeemed bliss"!), then we must ask the question: In what ways is this "glory" anticipated in the present? How do we learn, in the present, the habits of mind and heart which point us in the direction of this eventual "reign"? We shall return to this later in more detail; but let's just notice, within the immediate context of Romans, the two clear answers Paul gives. The ways of anticipating this "glorious rule" in the present are not, as skeptics might imagine, a regime of getting in practice for running things by learning how to throw your weight about, how to be bossy and tyrannical. The two ways he outlines are *holiness* and *prayer.*

First, the path to the glory which he expounds in the passage just referred to is the path of costly self denial—that is, of holiness.

So then, brothers and sisters, we are debtors; but not to the "flesh," to live in accordance with the "flesh." If you live in accordance with the "flesh," you see, you will die; but if, by the Spirit, you put to death the deeds of the body, you will live. For all who are led by God's Spirit are God's children. You didn't receive a spirit of slavery, after all, to make you go back to fear; rather, you received the Spirit of sonship, the one in whom we shout out, "Abba, Father!" When that happens, that very Spirit is bearing witness with our spirit that we are God's children; and, if children, then heirs, heirs of God and joint heirs with the Messiah, provided we suffer with him so that we can also be glorified with him. (8.12–17)

There we have it. The goal is the "glorification" of God's children, which as we have just seen turns out to be their redemptive sovereignty over the whole creation. But the path by which they are to get to that goal is the path of freedom marked out for God's children. Paul is here deliberately echoing the story of the Exodus, the time when Israel—"God's firstborn son"—was rescued from slavery and led by God himself through the wilderness to the promised "inheritance."

Within that story, the people were sometimes tempted to go back to Egypt, to the state of slavery. But they had to resist that temptation. They had to follow God's personal leading all the way to the promised land.

So it is for those who belong to the Messiah, who are in fact his fellow heirs. God had promised the Messiah that he would give him the whole world for his inheritance (Psalm 2.8—another scriptural passage dear to Paul's heart). Now, it appears, this worldwide "inheritance" is to be shared with all the Messiah's people. That is what Romans 8.18–30 is all about. But if they are called to be God's free and freedom-bringing people, then *they must learn to live as God's free people,* giving up the habit of slavery—yes, slavery is as much a habit of mind as a physical state—and learning the art of responsible, free living. To put it another way, if these people are to take redemptive responsibility for the whole of creation, they must anticipate that by taking redemptive responsibility, in the present time, for that one bit of creation over which they have the most obvious control—namely, their own bodies.

Notice Paul's subtle shift of language. For him, "flesh" is always a negative term, indicating either the corruptible and decaying nature of our present state or actual rebellion against God, and sometimes both together. To live "according to the flesh," then, is to live the life of rebellion whose natural end (not an arbitrary punishment, but the fulfillment of the pattern of the life which is being led) is death. But God intends to raise the "body" from death, as in 8.11 ("If the Spirit of the one who raised Jesus from the dead dwells in you, he who raised the Messiah from the dead will also give life to your mortal bodies, through his Spirit who dwells in you"). For this to happen, the things to which the "body" might naturally incline through the pull of the "flesh"—in other words, those actions growing out of the slave instinct of rebellion against God the freedom-giver—must themselves be put to death. This, it seems, is what happens through the suffering in which the Christian is joined with the suffering of the Messiah.

So the *telos,* the "goal" of being "glorified" over the creation, is to be anticipated in the present by replacing the slave-habits of mind, heart, and body with freedom-habits—habits that both share in God's freedom themselves and bring that freedom to the world. That is, more or less, what Paul understands by *holiness* or sanctification, the learning in the present of the habits which anticipate the ultimate future. But that sovereign and redemptive rule of renewed humans over God's world is also anticipated in the present time through *prayer*.

The whole creation, he says, is groaning in labor pains, longing for the birth of the new creation from the womb of the old (8.22). We ourselves, within that creation, find ourselves groaning as we await our own "adoption as sons and daughters, the redemption of our bodies" (8.23). But precisely in that state, as we are longing for and anticipating the final "glorification," the Spirit is also at work within us, "groaning without words," and thus enabling us, even when we don't know what to pray for as we ought, nevertheless to be interceding for the whole world (8.26–27). This essentially priestly vocation, standing before God with his whole creation on our hearts, joins up with the vision of royal sovereignty over creation, and is one of its key aspects. This passage offers one of the strangest but also most moving descriptions in the whole New Testament of what the Christian understands by prayer: the inarticulate groaning in which the pain of the world is felt most keenly at the point where it is also being brought, by the Spirit, into the very presence of God the creator. This is central, in the present time, to the entire human vocation. Learning this language is the second key habit which forms the pathway to the eventual goal, the goal of "royal priesthood."

In other words, the present anticipation of the future glory consists not in lording it over creation, imagining ourselves already its masters, able to tyrannize it and bend it to our will. It consists, rather, in the humble, Christlike, Spirit-led activity of prayer, the prayer in which the love of God is poured into our hearts by the Spirit (5.5) so that the extraordinary and almost unbelievable hope that is set before us is nevertheless firm and secure (5.1–5; 8.28–30). Thus, at the heart of arguably the greatest chapter of certainly his greatest letter, Paul sets out the pattern of *present anticipation of future hope.* This is what virtue is all about. The hope is that all those who are "in Christ" and are indwelt by the Spirit will eventually reign in glory over the whole creation, thereby taking up at long last the role commanded for humans in Genesis 1 and Psalm 8 and sharing the inheritance, and the final rescuing work, of the Messiah himself, as in Psalm 2. And if that is the *telos,* the goal, it is to be anticipated in the present by the settled habits of holiness and prayer.

If this is what Paul means by the final "reign," and its present strange anticipation, we observe that alongside this vision at every point in his writings is his equal emphasis that the Spirit comes to "dwell" in the hearts and lives of believers, inspiring precisely this holiness, this prayer, this love, and this hope. But this theme of the "indwelling" of the Spirit (see Romans 8.5–11; Ephesians 3.17) is nothing other than Paul's vision of the church, Christ's people, as the "new Temple," as in 1 Corinthians 3.10–17, 6.19–20, and Ephesians 2.11–22. Just as Israel's God "dwelt" in the old Temple (and its predecessor, the wilderness tabernacle), leading the people from Egypt to the promised land, so now God's own Spirit dwells within his people, leading them from previous slavery to future ultimate freedom. The Spirit thus enables God's people to be a community of priests, gathering up the worship of creation, just as the Spirit also constitutes God's people as rulers, bringing God's wise, healing order to the world.

And the Spirit, as we shall see, is vital for the quest and practice of virtue. The early Christians did not suppose they were undertaking that quest, and that practice, in their own unaided strength. This is one of the great watersheds in the whole discussion of virtue. Whereas Aristotle's virtuous man was encouraged to take pride in his self-made character, the classic Christian stance is seen in Paul's insistence, "Yet it was not I, but the grace of God that was with me" (1 Corinthians 15.10).

FIVE

Three further New Testament passages fill out this vision of God's intended future and the way in which it is to be anticipated in the present. First, we have another Pauline passage which, I suspect, is so surprising to most modern readers that it is passed over in silence and quickly forgotten:

> One of you even has the nerve to go to court with a neighbor, to be judged before unrighteous people rather than before God's saints! Don't you know that the saints will judge the world? And if the world is to be judged by you, are you unworthy of judging lesser things? Don't you know that we shall judge angels? So why not matters relating to the present life? So if you have ordinary lawsuits, are you going to appear before judges who are, in the eyes of the church, people of no account? I say this to your shame. Is it really the case that you

haven't got anybody among you who is wise, who can judge between one Christian and another? (1 Corinthians 6.1–5)

As often, when Paul says "Don't you know . . . ?" as he does twice here in quick succession, we want to reply, "No, we don't, actually!" But Paul seems to be quite clear. There will one day be a judgment when the secrets of all hearts will be disclosed (Romans 2.1–16; 14.10; 1 Corinthians 4.5; 2 Corinthians 5.10, etc.). Jesus himself will be the supreme judge (Romans 2.16; Acts 17.31). But there will, it seems, be a role within this activity of judgment for "the saints," God's people more largely. That is what, according to this passage, Paul expects the Corinthians to take for granted.

Why? Presumably because Paul, like most early Christians, took Daniel 7 very seriously:

> The holy ones of the Most High shall receive the kingdom and possess the kingdom for ever. . . . [T]hen judgment was given for the holy ones of the Most High, and the time arrived when the holy ones gained possession of the kingdom. . . . [T]he kingship and dominion and the greatness of the kingdoms under the whole heaven shall be given to the people of the holy ones of the Most High; their kingdom shall be an everlasting kingdom, and all dominions shall serve and obey them. (Daniel 7.18, 22, 27)

In its original setting, this prophecy made the striking claim that the Jewish people (or the faithful remnant among them) would be set in authority over the kingdoms of the world, after their terrible suffering at the hands of the "beasts." What has happened to this prophecy within the early Christian understanding?

The primary answer seems to be clear: it has been fulfilled in Jesus Christ himself, in his vindication and exaltation by God after his suffering at the hands of the wicked. This is part at least of what the gospel writers understand when they record Jesus speaking of himself as "son of man" (e.g., Mark 14.62). The phrase is still highly controversial, but I have no doubt that Daniel 7.13, with its vision of "one like a son of man," stands closely behind its main uses.

But already within early Christianity it appears that what was thereby claimed for Jesus was claimed, also, for his people. The plural reference elsewhere in Daniel 7 ("the holy ones of the Most High," who receive royal power) has become plural again after the singular use in the gospels, so that even the muddled and misguided Corinthians were going to share the promised "rule," the judging activity of the Messiah. *So much so that Paul could expect some at least of them to act as wise judges even in the present time.* That which is going to be true in the future, he is saying, must be anticipated in the present. Or at least that is what the church should expect and work toward. Don't hire pagan lawyers, he says. One of your own number will have what it takes. After all, in God's new world you're all going to be judges.

This may perhaps explain the second passage, also from 1 Corinthians, where Paul, speaking with heavy irony, chides his hearers about the way they are giving themselves airs:

> Who is going to concede superiority to you, after all? What have you got that you didn't receive? Well then, if you received it, why boast as if you didn't? Do you really suppose you've already had all the food you need? Do you think you've already become rich? Do you think you've already been crowned as royalty, leaving us behind? I wish you really were already reigning, so that we could reign alongside you! (1 Corinthians 4.7–8)

The sentences I have punctuated here as questions could also be read as ironic statements: "You're already full! You're already rich! You've already become kings—without us!" Paul's response shows that he thinks these boasts are empty, but also that there is a serious theological point underneath: they *are* meant to be kings, in quite a new sense, but their present way of behaving is simply colluding with the

normal, old sense in which people of "importance" puff themselves up
and give themselves airs. But that doesn't undermine the striking claim
made at the end of the previous chapter:

> So don't let anyone boast about mere human beings. For everything
> belongs to you, whether it's Paul or Apollos or Cephas, whether it's
> the world or life or death, whether it's the present or the future—
> everything belongs to you! And you belong to the Messiah; and the
> Messiah belongs to God. (1 Corinthians 3.21–23)

Everything belongs to you! There is the theological principle behind all this, and however much the Corinthians have twisted it so
that it fits into their preexisting cultural expectations, it remains valid
and powerful. Those who are "in the Messiah" already share in his
royal status. However much that royal status has been radically re-
defined around the cross—and the first four chapters of 1 Corinthians are written to make exactly that point—it remains the true royal
status, the status of the true world ruler. That is the status that God's
people in Christ now share.

This mind-boggling sharing of Jesus's royal task in bringing
God's justice to the world emerges in the pastoral epistles as well.
In 2 Timothy 2.8–13 we find the following:

> Remember Jesus the Messiah, raised from the dead, from the seed of
> David, in accordance with my gospel. . . . I suffer everything because
> of God's chosen ones, so that they too may obtain salvation which is
> in the Messiah, Jesus, with eternal glory. The saying is sure:
>
> > If we have died with him, we shall also live with him;
> >
> > if we endure, we shall also reign with him;
> >
> > if we deny him he will also deny us;
> >
> > if we are faithless, he remains faithful,
> >
> > for he cannot deny himself.

"We shall also reign with him." That remains the promise and the hope, the "goal" toward which the New Testament points. In the new heavens and the new earth, those who belong to Jesus will share his sovereign rule over his new world. If it wasn't Paul who wrote 2 Timothy (and most scholars think it wasn't), it was someone closely in tune at this point with what Paul himself says in Romans and 1 Corinthians. And in each case, we note, the point is not argued as a *new* idea, one that the early Christians wouldn't have expected to hear. It is stated as something they were expected to know already, to take for granted.

The same point, finally, is stated explicitly by Jesus himself in Matthew's gospel. The passage in question is one which even skeptics have declared likely to have come from Jesus's own lips. This is partly because the saying appears to be Israel-specific, whereas Jesus's followers, and indeed Matthew himself, quickly concerned themselves with the wider world beyond Israel. Thus it is highly unlikely that such a saying would have been invented later. It is also, even more strikingly, peculiar and "uninventable" because it seems to assign a place in the final judgment even to the traitor Judas! Nobody in the early church would have made *that* up.

The saying comes when Jesus, following the incident with the rich young man, is replying to Peter's question about the coming future:

> Truly I tell you, in the reborn world, when the son of man will sit on the throne of his glory, those of you who have followed me will sit— yes, you!—on twelve thrones, judging the twelve tribes of Israel. And everyone who has left houses or brothers or sisters or father or mother or children or lands for the sake of my name will receive a hundredfold, and inherit the life of the coming age. But many who are first will be last, and the last first. (Matthew 19.28–30)

This, like 1 Corinthians 6, is probably dependent on Daniel 7. Jesus assumes that, since he is the Messiah who is inaugurating God's kingdom, he and his followers will be entrusted with the judgment by which God will sort everything out at last.

Once this passage is in place, we may draw in as well the New Testament's more generalized but still powerful promises about servants who, having been faithful in a little, are then to be entrusted with much (Matthew 25.21, 23; Luke 19.17, 19). So too, we may suppose, we can include the "sheep" who, without realizing it, have already in the present been ministering to the one whom they will subsequently meet as their judge (Matthew 25.34–40). And once we include those passages, we begin to realize that actually a very great deal of what Jesus had to say about the coming kingdom, and the role of his followers within it, is in fact about God's coming rule of the whole world, setting it the right way up at last, and about the way in which those who follow him in the present time are to anticipate, here and now, the role which they are to be given in that ultimate future.

For the full foundation of the Christian reshaping of virtue, in other words, we must look primarily to Jesus himself. As the very early Christians recognized, he had fulfilled the Human roles, the Israel roles, of king and priest. He had brought the great stories of Israel, of Human, and of the world to their climax. He represented in himself the communities that had been called to carry forward the God-given vocation. And he had summoned people to follow him and share that story, that community, and that vocation. It is now time to look, directly and in some detail, at Jesus himself, and at the challenge and invitation he offered to his contemporaries.

4. THE KINGDOM COMING AND THE PEOPLE PREPARED

ONE

When I was first studying theology, some of the scholars whose works I read used to agonize over the Sermon on the Mount. (You'll find it in Matthew 5–7; a different version of some of the same material is found in Luke 6.20–49.) Everybody knew, of course, that in the great and glorious gospel preached by St. Paul people are justified by faith, not by works. So why, the scholars wondered, did Jesus appear to start off his preaching by telling people how to live, what to do and not to do? Surely giving them "rules" for living would simply encourage them into bad spiritual habits, into imagining that they could "make themselves good enough for God" by their own efforts.

One answer that some theologians used to give to this question went like this: "Well, yes, it's true that Paul's gospel was about faith, not about 'how we should live.' But Matthew's gospel wasn't written as 'primary evangelism.' It was written for people who were already Christians. They had already accepted Jesus and the salvation offered through him, by faith alone. Now they needed to be instructed on how to live—not to save themselves by their own efforts, but to respond appropriately to God's grace." I think, for instance, of the careful and thoughtful book on the Sermon on the Mount by the great scholar Joachim Jeremias, who took more or less this line. I think, too, of a lecture in Oxford, many years ago, by the well-known Lutheran

Günther Bornkamm, who managed to demonstrate that, despite appearances, Matthew wasn't actually a "legalist." Why not? Because he was, after all, not only facing Pharisees to the right of him, but also "enthusiasts" to the left of him, people who were casting off all moral restraint and who thought that because they were following Jesus, not the Jewish Law, they could do whatever they liked. Matthew, it thus appeared, was warding off legalism in one direction and antinomianism in the other—just as Martin Luther himself had done. This conclusion was reached, it seemed to me at the time, with something like a sigh of relief.

I remember being suspicious about this approach at the time (it all seemed to fit just a bit too well), but I didn't have anything much to suggest by way of an alternative. Since then I have observed the way in which people who offer the same kind of reading of the text tend to frame everything in terms, not of what Jesus himself meant when he said particular words under discussion, but of what the evangelist (Matthew, or whoever) meant.

This way of reading the gospels is still popular, and at some level it is healthy. Part of human maturity, after all, is learning to read everything with a questioning eye, whether it's this morning's newspaper (in which journalists may have misrepresented things in order to tell the story they wanted to tell rather than what actually happened) or somebody's sacred text (can we trust it? who wrote it and why?). In the same way, many people suppose that learning to read the gospels involves learning to read between the lines and discovering that what's actually going on isn't really "about" Jesus at all, but "about" Matthew's (or Mark's, or Luke's, or John's) theology, about the life of their communities, and so on.

This seems mature, sophisticated, grown-up. And of course at one level it is. Everybody who writes history, everybody who writes a newspaper article on "what happened yesterday," and for that matter everybody who tells somebody else "what I just saw in the street," selects and arranges the material. You can't say *everything,* and if you try you'll be at it all day, and very boring it will be too. So we all select and arrange, and anyone reading what we write can, in principle, try to discover why we've done it the way we have.

But this appearance of sophistication can easily mask a dangerous sophistry. The fact that it's all been selected and arranged *doesn't mean it's all been made up.*

In my part of the world there are three soccer teams that nurse a huge local rivalry. Whenever they play one another, it's fascinating to read the accounts in the different local newspapers. You get a quite different angle on whether the referee was right to give that crucial penalty, whether the left winger was really offside, whether *both* the players who were fighting should have been sent off or only one of them. *But all the newspapers will still tell you who won the game,* what the score was, and so on. If we thought they were making *that* up, we wouldn't buy the newspapers in the first place.

I have gone into this little digression on the question of history and the gospels—a tiny fragment from a much longer discussion we could have had—for one reason only. I have become increasingly convinced that a method of reading the gospels which has been popular among Western scholars for many years is not only flawed in itself, offering an apparently sophisticated reading while denying something quite basic (that Jesus really did and said substantially what the gospels say he did and said), but is flawed *for a particular reason directly related to the subject of this book:* it is flawed because the whole worldview driving the scholarship in question screened out the very possibility that there might be a larger truth that the gospels were trying to express but that didn't fit into the categories the scholars had available. And that larger truth, in which the Sermon on the Mount makes the excellent sense it does, is this: *God's future is arriving in the present, in the person and work of Jesus, and you can practice, right now, the habits of life which will find their goal in that coming future.* This is, if you like, Jesus's answer to Aristotle.

Here is the goal, the *telos:* not "happiness" in the sense of Aristotle's *eudaimonia,* but "blessedness" in the Hebrew sense of *ashre* or *baruch* (Greek *makarios*). That, by the way, is why translations of the

Beatitudes (that familiar series of Sermon sayings announcing blessings) which say "happy" instead of "blessed" are precisely missing the point. And the key point about "bless," "blessing," and "blessed"—one of the things that marks Jesus out over against Aristotle in terms of the source and driving energy of the "virtues"—is that this *includes* "happiness," but it includes it *as the result of something else*—namely, the loving action of the creator God. "Happiness" is simply a state of being for a human, as a self-contained unit. You might, in principle, attain it on your own and develop it for your own sake. "Blessedness," however, is what happens when the creator God is at work both *in* someone's life and *through* that person's life. Likewise, blessedness is what happens when this same God is fulfilling the promises he made to his ancient people, the promises contained in the "covenant" as set out in the closing chapters of Deuteronomy. And both of those—the human blessing and the Israel blessing—are evoked by Jesus's remarkable words in the opening of the Sermon on the Mount in Matthew 5.3–11:

> Blessings on the poor in spirit! The kingdom of heaven is yours.
>
> Blessings on the mourners! You're going to be comforted.
>
> Blessings on the meek! You're going to inherit the earth.
>
> Blessings on people who hunger and thirst for God's justice! You're going to be satisfied.
>
> Blessings on the merciful! You'll receive mercy yourselves.
>
> Blessings on the pure in heart! You will see God.
>
> Blessings on the peacemakers! You'll be called God's children.
>
> Blessings on people who are persecuted because of God's way! The kingdom of heaven belongs to you.
>
> Blessings on you, when people slander you and persecute you, and say all kinds of wicked things about you falsely because of me! Celebrate and rejoice: there's a great reward for you in heaven. That's how they persecuted the prophets who went before you.

These statements, clearly, are not describing "the way things are." They are not suggesting that the mourners are already being comforted, despite appearances. They are not trying to teach hidden, timeless truths about a reality which is normally hidden behind a bleak facade. They are announcing a new state of affairs, a new reality which is in the process of bursting into the world. They are declaring that something that wasn't previously the case is now going to be; that the life of heaven, which had seemed so distant and unreal, is in the process of coming true on earth.

What happens when we put these astonishing declarations into the format we set out at the end of Chapter Two?

1. The goal is God's kingdom: a time of comfort, of heaven coming to earth at last, of the renewal of creation, of plenty, of mercy, of reward, and perhaps above all of seeing God himself.

2. This goal has arrived in the present, now that Jesus is here. How his public career will work out is, from the perspective of those listening to the Sermon on the Mount, not yet clear.

3. Those who follow Jesus can begin to practice, in the present, the habits of heart and life which correspond to the way things are in God's kingdom—the way they will be eventually, yes, but also the way they *already* are because Jesus is here.

How does the ultimate promised future correspond to the present practices and habits Jesus insists upon? In two contrasting ways.

On the one hand, there is a direct correspondence, where the future state is exactly anticipated in the present habits of life: humility, meekness, mercy, purity, peacemaking. When the final kingdom arrives, we won't *stop* being humble, meek, and pure. ("That's enough of that! Now we can be what we've always wanted—namely, proud, arrogant, and impure!") No: these qualities will shine through all the more powerfully.

On the other hand, there is the equal-and-opposite correspondence which demonstrates the tension between that inbreaking future and the way things still are in the present. Consider the mourners, the persecuted, those who are hungry for justice. When the final kingdom arrives, mourners will be comforted, justice-hunger will be satisfied, and persecution will stop. ("Peacemaking" belongs perhaps in both categories, since the attitude of heart that directs peacemaking corresponds directly to the peace of God's new world, but the need for actual peacemaking between warring parties will disappear when God's peace fills heaven and earth, as in the vision of Isaiah 11.) These two types of correspondence obviously go closely together.

But the point of sayings of both types—direct correspondence and equal-and-opposite correspondence—is that Jesus is *not* meaning either "If you can manage to behave in this way, you will be rewarded" (a kind of legalist solution) or "Now that you've believed in me and my kingdom project, this is how you must behave" (the sort of thing some post-Reformation theology might insist on)—though the latter is closer to the truth, albeit not in the sense usually imagined. To shuttle between those two options is to remain impaled on the horns of a philosophical dilemma and its theological ramifications rather than coming round the corner to see things from Jesus's very first-century Jewish point of view.

What Jesus is saying, rather, is, "Now that I'm here, God's new world is coming to birth; and, once you realize that, you'll see that these are the habits of heart which anticipate that new world here and now." These qualities—purity of heart, mercy, and so on—are not, so to speak, "things you have to do" to earn a "reward," a "payment." Nor are they merely the "rules of conduct" laid down for new converts to follow—rules that some today might perceive as somewhat arbitrary. They are, in themselves, the signs of life, the language of life, the life of new creation, the life of new covenant, the life which Jesus came to bring. As we shall see, they are part of that radical Christian modification of the ancient Greek notion of virtue, the modification that quickly settled into the overall pattern of faith, hope, and love.

TWO

At this point we could go straight into the rest of the Sermon on the Mount, beginning with Matthew 5.13, and work carefully all the way through. That isn't necessary for the argument I'm putting forward, but there are various things that need to be said to supplement the basic point already made.

First, as we saw, the Beatitudes could be mistaken for a set of rules. They aren't, however. They are much more like virtues, and that's how they work: grasp the end, the goal, the *telos*, the future, and go to work on anticipating it here and now. That doesn't mean (as I keep stressing) that there are no such things as rules; as we shall see, the Beatitudes are both guidelines for those who are learning virtue and a checklist to which virtuous Christians can refer from time to time. But to read the Beatitudes as rules is to miss the point.

Most of the rest of the Sermon, though, could lead the casual modern reader in a different direction. You must avoid not just murder but hatred, not just adultery but lust, and so on (Matthew 5.21–47); and when you give money, or say your prayers, or fast, you must really mean it, not simply go through the motions (6.1–18). All this could look as though Jesus were commending "authenticity," in line with the romantic movement or existentialism—in other words, the outward forms don't matter; what matters is the attitude of the heart. But again the Sermon can't be drawn down into the categories offered by our contemporary moral discourse, as though Jesus were "really" saying pretty much what some of today's thinkers have urged.

Jesus is in fact inviting his hearers to something much more radical: an anticipation of what we might call *eschatological authenticity*. Yes, there will be a time when God's people will serve and love him, and live out the genuine humanness of which the ancient Law had spoken, "naturally" and from the heart. But this will be a God-given "second nature," a new way of being human. *And you can begin to practice this now,* difficult though it will be, because Jesus is here, inaugurating God's kingdom. It won't happen "automatically," precisely because

God wants you to be, as we might put it, humans rather than puppets. You will have to think about it, to struggle with it, to pray for grace and strength; but it is at least now within reach. You can't collapse the whole question of "how to behave" into the command "It must come naturally; otherwise it isn't authentic." Jesus puts it the other way around: he says, in effect, "Follow me, and authenticity will begin to happen." The authenticity that really matters is living in accordance with the genuine human being God is calling you to become. What the ancient Law really wanted—genuine human life, reflecting God's glory into the world—will start to appear.

The whole of the Sermon is framed within Jesus's announcement that what his fellow Jews had longed for over many generations was now at last coming to pass—but that new kingdom didn't look like they had thought it would. Indeed, in some ways it went in exactly the other direction. No violence, no hatred of enemies, no anxious protection of land and property against the pagan hordes. In short, no frantic intensification of the ancestral codes of life. Rather, a glad and unworried trust in the creator God, whose kingdom is now at last starting to arrive, leading to a glad and generous heart toward other people, even those who are technically "enemies." Faith, hope, and love: here they are again. They are the language of life, the sign in the present of green shoots growing through the concrete of this sad old world, the indication that the creator God is on the move, and that Jesus's hearers and followers can be part of what he's now doing.

That is the context within which Jesus says perhaps the most remarkable thing of all: be perfect, because your heavenly father is perfect (5.48). The Greek is *teleios,* reminding us of Aristotle's *telos,* "goal." You must be people of the goal, people of genuine humanness, people who are "complete." It's the same word which, in Matthew's version of the story of the rich young ruler (19.21), Jesus said to the young man: in effect, "If you want to be 'complete,' *teleios,* then go and sell your possessions, give to the poor, and come and follow me." (The same word, too, is found in a similar context in James 3.2.) And we note that in each case the "perfection" in question consists not of a long list of hard moral commands dutifully obeyed but of *a character formed by overflowing generous love*. When Paul, as we shall see presently, sums up the calling of the Christian in terms of love, he is saying no more than what Jesus said in a variety of ways. And, for that matter, no more than what Jesus *did*....

Which points us to the question which is bound to arise at this stage in the argument. How on earth is Jesus's program for God's kingdom to be put into effect? He sends his followers out into the towns and villages, and they find to their delight and astonishment that the things he has been doing, particularly the healings which were such a striking sign of God's fresh power at work, are happening through them as well. (Notice already, by the way, that the disciples are not given "moral challenges" to be tested on, as though the point of it all were whether their behavior was coming into line, morally and ethically. That will follow—and the early signs are not particularly encouraging, as they squabble among themselves. Rather, they are given things to *do* through which God's new work can go forward. The language of life is the language in which God speaks *through* humans into the world.) But was that all there was going to be to it? Just more followers of Jesus going out and bringing new life and hope to the tiny number of people their lives would touch—while most of the world rumbled on in the same way?

Certainly not. Jesus had something far more radical in mind, something which decisively shaped the emerging movement of his followers. This is what set Jesus and his early followers dramatically apart, in their pursuit of something we can call virtue, from the other theories that go by that name. Basically, Jesus believed that God's future could be fully launched only if the forces ranged against it—the forces of chaos and destruction, of hatred and suspicion, of violence and pride and greed and ambition—were not just outflanked by a cheerful new alternative, but were confronted and defeated. This was at the heart of how he understood his own royal and priestly vocation. Through his own fresh and prayerful reading of Israel's scriptures, Jesus came to believe that this confrontation and defeat would come about through

the twin roles of king and priest: through Israel's Messiah fighting
the battle for the kingdom through his own suffering and death, and
through Israel's true priest offering Israel's God the obedient sacrifice
at the heart of the new Temple. And, as a matter of vocation too deep
for us fully to comprehend, Jesus believed that he himself was Israel's
Messiah and Israel's priest, and that he would therefore suffer that
victory-bringing, obedience-offering fate.

How does this vocation, and its acting out in Jesus's death and resurrection, relate to the challenge he was presenting in the Sermon
on the Mount and elsewhere, the challenge of the coming kingdom,
the challenge to live in the present in the light of God's inbreaking
future?

THREE

Jesus's forthcoming death—and his own deeply scriptural understanding, which led him not only to expect it but to interpret it in advance—
is in fact tightly bound up with his announcement of God's kingdom
and his invitation to his followers to start learning its language right
now. So, at least, all four gospels seem to be saying. For them, there is
no clear demarcation between Jesus's kingdom-announcement and his
approaching death. The two belong closely together. But this brings us
face to face with a problem which runs very deep within the whole of
Western Christianity, and which, unless we deal with it head-on, will
get in the way of any attempt to understand the life of (Christian) virtue to which Jesus calls us, let alone the further question of how that
relates to the other schemes of virtue on offer in the ancient or the
modern world.

Christians, particularly in the Western world, have for a long time
been divided between "epistles people" and "gospels people." The
"epistles people" have thought of Christianity primarily in terms of
Jesus's death and resurrection "saving us from our sins." The "gospels
people" have thought primarily in terms of following Jesus in feeding

the hungry, helping the poor, and so on. The "epistles people" have often found it difficult to give a clear account of what was going on in Jesus's kingdom-announcement and his call to his followers to be "perfect." The "gospels people"—or perhaps we should say the "beginning-of-the-gospels people," since the line of thought they embrace usually screens out the last few chapters—have often found it difficult to explain why the Jesus who was doing these remarkable things had to die, and die so soon. They have often found it difficult, in consequence, to relate to the central themes of Pauline theology.

This either/or split does no justice, in fact, to either the epistles or the gospels. Still less does it do justice to Jesus himself. For him, the kingdom which he inaugurated could be firmly established only through his death and resurrection. Or, to put it the other way around, the main purpose of his death and resurrection was to establish the kingdom he had already begun to inaugurate. The way the gospel writers tell the story of Jesus's death, with prolonged sections of preliminary teaching followed by quite detailed accounts of the "hearings" before the chief priests and the Roman governor, was chosen not for the sake of "local color" or mere historical reminiscence tacked on to the front of an event (the actual crucifixion) whose theological "meaning" must be culled from elsewhere. The "meaning" of the cross, in the gospels, is that it is the execution of the kingdom-bringer, the one who gathers up the "royal" and "priestly" vocations of Israel and of all the human race, the one who at the same time embodies Israel's God coming to establish his kingdom on earth as in heaven. The famous passages which encapsulate what later writers have thought of as "atonement theology" (such as Mark 10.45: "The son of man came not to be served but to serve, and to give his life as a ransom for many") are interpretative clues to understand one key dimension of what the whole story is about, not the superimposition of a supposedly "Pauline" theology (about Jesus "dying for our sins") on a narrative which is basically "about" something else.

Likewise, for Paul the death and resurrection of Jesus did not accomplish merely a "supernatural" salvation having nothing to do with

God's rescue of creation. As we saw in the previous chapter, for Paul the whole point of the achievement of Jesus and his death and resurrection is that, through Jesus, a redeemed people has come to birth, and that through this people the creator will ultimately set the whole world to rights. The point of it all is "new creation" (2 Corinthians 5.17; Galatians 6.15). The gospels, the epistles, and Revelation itself "work" only when you see them as detailed elaborations of the large, complex, but utterly coherent story we sketched earlier: the call of Human to be God's image-bearer into creation, the call of Israel to be the rescuer of Human, and the vocation of Jesus to be the one who, completing Israel's task, rescues Human so that, through redeemed humankind, the whole creation can be liberated from its corruption and death and the project of new creation decisively launched. Shrink this narrative, or leave out one or more key stages within it, and you will never understand the New Testament as a whole, still less its call to learn the habits of heart and mind that anticipate the final goal.

The split of viewpoints we have observed, then, is not so much between the gospels and the epistles as between truncated readings of both, reflecting yet another Great Divide that has come over Western Christianity. (The historical roots of this divide are fascinating, but this is not the moment to trace them back.) Once again, part of the problem is that for many centuries Christians have assumed that virtually the only point in Jesus's death was "to save us from our sins," understood in a variety of more or less helpful ways. But for the gospels themselves, that rescue of individuals (which of course remains a central element) is designed to serve a larger purpose: God's purpose, the purpose of God's kingdom. And in God's kingdom human beings are rescued, are delivered from their sin, in order to take their place (as Jesus already called the disciples to take theirs) not only as *receivers* of God's forgiveness and new life, but also as *agents* of it. In other words: rulers and priests.

How then are Jesus's kingdom-announcement and his "saving" death and resurrection integrated into a single whole? That, of course, is a large and overwhelming question, and it is with considerable temerity that I try a short, and inevitably inadequate, answer. Approach it like this:

Jesus is not going about announcing "God is becoming king!" into neutral territory, like an explorer annexing land that was previously unoccupied. He is announcing God's sovereign and saving rule, and doing things which demonstrate its presence and power, in a world already governed by hostile powers, powers which to our horror include the ruling officials of God's people itself, not least the royal and priestly elites, and also the popular pressure groups and the revolutionary movements within Israel—in addition, of course, to the powers of the pagan world. Saying that God was becoming king, in first-century Palestine, was a way of saying that Israel's God was dethroning pagan overlords and rescuing his people; but the people themselves, it seems, had become part of the problem. But, since the whole point of God's saving rule, as Jesus understood it, is that it is the saving rule *of this God*—the God of gentle, generous, overwhelming love, whose kingdom-way was already articulated in the Sermon on the Mount—it cannot be established by *force majeure,* but only by its proper means: suffering, self-giving love. Hence the deep-level integration of the message of the kingdom and the vocation of the cross. And hence the deep-level resistance, within Western culture, to such an integration, at any level. We have preferred our kingdoms to be of a different sort, and have preferred to see the shameful death of Jesus as bringing about a purely heavenly "salvation."

So, too—this is a major theme in John's gospel, but it's all over the place in the other three as well—Jesus is discovered to be the one in whom God's glory has finally returned to his people. Jesus is, clearly in John and implicitly in the others, the Temple-in-person, the place where Israel's God has come to dwell in fulfillment of his ancient promise. That is why, throughout the gospel narratives but particularly when Jesus goes to Jerusalem for the last time, there is a direct confrontation between the two of them, Jesus and the Temple, with the latter institution represented of course by the chief priests and the high priest himself. This, again, is not a merely accidental bit of "local color," and it is certainly not to be reduced simply to the idea of "the religious establishment" opposing a free-spirited Jesus who is advocating a kind of spontaneous spirituality over against their supposed formalism. Rather, the references to Jesus and Temple convey that just as Jesus is announcing the kingdom and is himself the true though very surprising king, so also he is embodying the true Temple and is himself the true (though shocking) high priest. Jesus thus embodies the two great narratives of Israel, the royal and the priestly strands of the Old Testament, drawing them together and establishing the new way, the royal and priestly way, for Israel and for the human race, for the sake of the world. It is because of this double accomplishment that the human vocation of Genesis 1 and 2 can be reaffirmed, as we saw in the previous chapter in relation to Revelation, Romans, and other texts.

The deepest revolution in virtue that we find at the heart of the gospel—and of the gospels—is found just here. Jesus shouldered the burden, not so much of "sin" in the abstract, in a kind of transaction which took place away from the actual events that led to his death, but rather of the actual weight—the power and results—of human sin and rebellion, the accumulation of the actual human pride, sin, folly, and shame which, at that moment in history, concentrated themselves in the arrogance of Rome, the self-seeking of the Jewish leaders, and the distorted dreams of the Jewish revolutionaries—and, indeed, the failures of Jesus's own followers. I have quoted before, and I quote here again, a matchless sentence from my teacher Professor George Caird: "Thus in literal historic truth, not simply in theological interpretation, the one bore the sins of the many." Some theories of "atonement" detach themselves from the actual events and superimpose on (or even substitute for) the gospel narrative a theological scheme of interpretation culled from elsewhere, in order to "explain" how sinners may ultimately leave this world and go to heaven. Such theories are no better, at the level of a proper theological method, than theories of the kingdom which ignore the cross. Kingdom and cross belong together. The whole story is the whole story. And it is within that whole story, not within some truncated version, that Jesus's call to a new-creation kind of virtue makes the sense which it does.

Jesus's call to follow him, to discover in the present time the habits of life which point forward to the coming kingdom and already, in a measure, share in its life, only makes sense when it is couched in the terms made famous by Dietrich Bonhoeffer: "Come and die." Jesus didn't say, as do some modern evangelists, "God loves you and has a wonderful plan for your life." Nor did he say, "I accept you as you are, so you can now happily do whatever comes naturally." He said, "If you want to become my followers, deny yourself, take up your cross, and follow me" (Mark 8.34). He spoke of losing one's life in order to gain it, as opposed to clinging to it and so losing it. He spoke of this in direct relation to himself and his own forthcoming humiliation and death, followed by resurrection and exaltation. Exactly in line with the Beatitudes, he was describing, and inviting his followers to enter, an upside-down world, an inside-out world, a world where all the things people normally assume about human flourishing, including human virtue, are set aside and a new order is established.

Jesus would have said, of course, that it's the present world that is upside down and inside out. He was coming to put it the right way up, the right way out. That shift of perception is the challenge of the gospel he preached and lived, and for which he died.

What this means is that the normal standards, even the standards of virtue itself, are challenged at their core. No longer is the good life to be a matter of human beings glimpsing the goal of "happiness" in which they will become complete, and then setting about a program of self-improvement by which they might begin to make that goal a reality. They are summoned to follow a leader whose eventual goal is indeed a world of blessing beyond bounds, but whose immediate goal, the only possible route to that eventual one, is a horrible and shameful death. And the reason for this radical difference is not obscure. It is that Jesus's diagnosis of the problem goes far deeper than that of any ancient Greek philosopher.

Jesus believed and taught that humans in general, including God's people Israel, had a sickness of heart which all attempts at self-betterment could not touch. If the project of God's kingdom was to be truly launched, catching up humans into a new life and vocation whose language they would then have to learn, this sickness had to be dealt with. The corruption and decay of the old world and the old human heart, the habits and patterns of thought, imagination, and life, had to be not just reformed, but killed.

Moreover, since one of the primary telltale signs of that corruption and decay was human pride, there could be no place for the kind of "virtue" which saw itself, in effect, as self-made. The greatest of the pagan moralists could only glimpse the reality of a truly human existence in which the goal of human life was realized step by step through training the heart and life into new habits. That reality shimmered like a mirage on the other side of a deep, fast-flowing river that pagan moralism could neither swim nor bridge. Jesus plunged into the river and, being well and truly drowned, was carried to the farther shore. And he told his disciples to follow him. The way to the kingdom is the way of the cross, and vice versa—as long as you remember that "the kingdom," once again, is not "heaven," but the state of affairs in which God's kingdom has come, and his will is being done, *on earth* as in heaven.

All this means that the summary statement we explored in the previous chapter, the idea of God's people as a "royal priesthood," is in fact rooted firmly in the accomplishment of Jesus himself. The royal, priestly destiny of human beings is reborn only because the ultimate Human, the unique son of man, was himself both king and priest. Jesus came to inaugurate and embody the sovereign, saving rule of God within God's creation; he came to embody, also, the long-awaited faithful obedience of the whole creation, of humankind, and particularly of Israel. At the heart of both those vocations—the sovereign movement from God to his creation, and the grateful, obedient movement from creation back to its maker—we find in the gospels the movement, not only of thought, but of action, action that led directly to the cross. The cross is where the true God defeated the false gods and established, with deep and resonating paradox, his kingdom on earth as in heaven. The cross is where the faithful, grateful obedience which God had looked for from his creation, from his image-bearing humans, and from his chosen people, as the appropriate response to his love, was fully and finally offered. There is of course much more to say about the meaning of the cross, but not less.

Jesus was thus both king and priest. That theological judgment brings up in three dimensions, and with heavy irony, the whole story of his messianic entry into Jerusalem and the cleansing of the Temple, his arrest and "trial" before the high priest and, ultimately, before Caesar's representative. In his resurrection, therefore, he *is* now king and priest—and he calls his followers, in an astonishing act of grace and through the power of his Spirit, to join him in working out this double ministry in our lives and in our world. All Christian virtue is located within that vocation, rooted in Jesus's unique accomplishment and looking ahead to the new world in which the task of being "kings and priests," a "royal priesthood," will be undertaken. The goal of human life, the *telos* which the New Testament holds out as the true reality of which Aristotle's *eudaimonia* was a pagan approximation, is given already in Jesus. He is the "end," the goal: as the hymn puts it,

> Jesu, our only joy be thou,
> As thou our prize wilt be;
> In thee be all our glory now,
> And through eternity.[1]

From a Christian point of view, then, virtue cannot be conceived solely in terms of the individual journey from a standing start to a future destination. It belongs within an end that has already begun, an eschatology that has already been inaugurated. Virtue, in the great philosophical tradition, has always said, "Become what you will be." Christian virtue says, "What you will be is what you already are in Christ." This is the whole point of saying, as wise Christian theologians always have, that all is of grace. Once that adjustment has been made, we find that the inner dynamic of virtue, the sense of a character that must be shaped by its future prospect and formed by careful thought, hard choices, and moral effort, is not undermined but rather enhanced. This is the whole point of saying, as wise Christian theologians always have, that the way grace works is by the Holy Spirit enabling us to become, at last, truly human. Hence the overlap with Aristotle—and the radical difference.

Becoming a royal priesthood, becoming genuinely human, always involves a battle, always a struggle, and often an apparent defeat. So it was with Jesus; so it has been, again and again, for his followers. But within those followers virtue has grown up, a quality of character in which the Sermon on the Mount has come true, in which remarkable things come to pass in and through "ordinary" human lives. And at the heart of this phenomenon we find, yes, the human heart.

FOUR

"The heart is deceitful," declared the prophet Jeremiah (17.9), "and desperately wicked." Pessimistic? No: realistic. Jesus would have agreed—and, however much this is a slap in the face for those of us who naturally incline toward a romantic philosophy or ethic, we cannot expect to understand Jesus's moral demands, and how they "work," unless we confront, or rather are confronted by, his analysis of the deep-level human disease and dilemma, and the astonishing way he seemed to assume that he could prescribe a cure for it. Just as Jesus's kingdom-announcement was not made into empty space but into enemy-occupied territory, so his challenge to each human life was not posed to people whose hearts were *tabulae rasae,* wax tablets clean and ready for fresh writing, but rather to people whose hearts were pretty much as Jeremiah had described them. Habits had already been well formed, and, as Shakespeare saw, they were very often the wrong habits. Often—this is what "the deceitfulness of the heart" actually means—they were wrong habits *masquerading as right ones*. Whatever "virtue" might mean in the challenge of Jesus, it means it *within this context*.

The obvious place to begin is Jesus's remarkable saying about clean and unclean foods (Mark 7.14–22 and parallels):

> Jesus summoned the crowd again. "Listen to me, all of you," he said, "and get this straight. What goes into you from outside can't make you unclean. What makes you unclean is what comes out from inside."
>
> When they got back into the house, his disciples asked him about the parable. "You didn't get it either?" he asked. "Don't you see that whatever goes into someone from outside can't make them unclean? It doesn't go into the heart; it only goes into the stomach, and then carries on, out down the drain." (Result: all foods are clean.) "What makes someone unclean," he went on, "is what comes out of them. Evil intentions come from inside, out of people's hearts—sexual immorality, theft, murder, adultery, greed, wickedness, treachery, debauchery, envy, slander, pride, stupidity. These evil things all come from inside. They are what make someone unclean."

I have discussed elsewhere the way in which this little sequence works. Jesus says something so devastating—once you understand it—that it has to remain cryptic while he is out on the street. He only explains it when he is alone with the disciples in the house. (This happens with some other sayings, too, such as Mark 4.1–20.) The point is clear to anyone familiar with first-century Judaism: Jesus was treading hard on some very sensitive toes. Jewish freedom-fighters had died, we're told within the folk traditions of the Maccabees and elsewhere, rather than eat unclean food. The food laws were a vital part of the living tradition which enabled the embattled Israel of Jesus's day to define itself over against the "unclean" pagan nations all around, to retain its God-given identity as Daniel and his friends had done in the court of Babylon. How could Jesus now say that people became unclean, not by eating particular foods, but by things that bubbled up from inside them?

The answer, we may safely assume, was just as unwelcome to many first-century Jews as it is to many contemporary thinkers who hold a "liberal" or "optimistic" view of human nature. (Remember Arthur M. Schlesinger's earlier-quoted comment about those who assume "the unalloyed goodness of spontaneous impulses.") But the answer must be given nonetheless, and it is this: that's just how it is. The diagnosis is accurate. "Unclean" foods are merely a symbol for something else, and that something else lies within, deep in the human heart. The list of horrors in verses 21–22—immorality, theft, murder, and the rest—names and shames characteristics that are not merely "learned" behavior, as though they were accidental add-ons to an otherwise pure human nature. These are things, sadly, that you don't have to work at. You don't have to think through the challenge of how to perform them, and practice hard because they are so difficult and demanding. No: they bubble up, unbidden and unhindered, from within, even from within those of us nursed and schooled in traditions of piety, devotion, worship, study, and self-denial. They can of course be encouraged and solidified by particular circumstances or choices; like any other pattern of behavior they can reshape the "wiring" of the brain so as to become "automatic"; but they do not have to be consciously thought about and practiced in order to be present. They are the real "uncleanness."

But what is the point of Jesus drawing attention to all this? Has he come simply to tell people that they all have an incurable sickness? Of course not. He speaks of himself as the doctor coming to visit the sick (Mark 2.17), but—as we gradually come to see—he believes that his kingdom-project contains, at its core, a cure for this deadly disease, this unclean heart. He forgives on his own authority; he heals the sick (including those whose illnesses have rendered them technically "unclean"—e.g., Mark 5.24b–34); he casts out "unclean" spirits (e.g., Mark 5.1–20). Furthermore, he warns against a superficial "cleansing" that leaves the heart untouched (Mark 7.1–8; Matthew 12.43–45). But he does not issue these warnings about "uncleanness" in order to say, "That's how you are, and that's how you'll stay"—though if his hearers do not repent that would indeed be true. His intention is that, somehow, those who hear and accept his kingdom-announcement are to have their hearts cleansed. He is doing the work of the royal priest, sovereignly providing the "cleansing" of heart for which the regular and God-ordained Temple practices were an advance (but ultimately ineffective) signpost.

This was taken for granted in the early church, as we see, for example, in Acts 15.9, where Peter speaks of God "cleansing the hearts [of Gentile converts] by faith." We see the same thing in 1 John 1.7, which declares that "the blood of Jesus cleanses us from all sin." Jesus himself, in the so-called farewell discourses in John's gospel, comments, almost in an aside, that his disciples "have already been made clean by the word which I have spoken to you" (John 15.3). Three different agencies—faith, the blood of Jesus, and the word of Jesus—but a single result: cleansed.

We can approach the same point from a slightly different angle if we look again at Jesus's comment about divorce in Mark 10.2–12. As we saw, there was a political angle: everyone in Jesus's world knew perfectly well what Herod Antipas had done in taking his brother's wife, and a pointed inquiry about divorce was no more a "neutral" question about an abstract ethical issue than it would have been at the court of Henry VIII. Jesus therefore gives an oblique but no less powerful answer, getting his interlocutors to tell him what *they* think scripture says. They come up with Deuteronomy, where Moses allows divorce under certain circumstances. Yes, says Jesus, but from the beginning it wasn't so. God made them male and female and declared that the two would become one flesh, meaning that God had joined them and they should not therefore be separated. Why then Deuteronomy's permission? "Because," replies Jesus, "your hearts were hard" (Mark 10.5). This is extraordinary. What sense does it make to say that permission was given because people's hearts were hard, but permission is now being withdrawn? Here, as often, the scale of Jesus's understanding of his own kingdom-bringing work emerges, breathtakingly, on the back of an apparently incidental discussion. Jesus believes that he, and the kingdom of God which he is launching, *will contain a cure for hardness of heart*. He believes that he has come to undo the effects of human hard-heartedness and to restore the original purpose of creation. He has come to put all things right, and, as part of that, to put humans back together again.

The source of this astonishing claim, that through his kingdom-bringing work human hearts are to be both cleansed and softened, ought not to be difficult to find. Jesus, as we know from multiple sources, was steeped in the Hebrew scriptures, not least in those passages which spoke of God renewing the covenant, restoring his people, enabling Israel to be Israel at last and humans to be humans. And Jesus believed, as again we know from several sources, that these very prophecies were finally coming true in and through his own work. When it comes to unclean and hard hearts, the likely passages jump out at us:

> The days are surely coming, says YHWH, when I will make a new covenant with the house of Israel and the house of Judah. It will not be like the covenant that I made with their ancestors when I took them by the hand to bring them out of the land of Egypt—a covenant that they broke, though I was their husband, says YHWH. But this is the covenant that I will make with the house of Israel after those days, declares YHWH: I will put my law within them, and I will write it on their hearts; and I will be their God, and they shall be my people. No longer shall they teach one another, or say to each other, "Know YHWH," because they shall all know me, from the least of them to the greatest, declares YHWH; for I will forgive their wickedness, and remember their sin no more. (Jeremiah 31.31–34)

> I will sprinkle clean water upon you, and you shall be clean from all your uncleannesses, and from all your idols I will cleanse you. A new heart I will give you, and a new spirit I will put within you; and I will remove from your body the heart of stone and give you a heart of flesh. I will put my spirit within you, and make you follow my statutes and be careful to observe my ordinances. (Ezekiel 36.25–27)

We have good reason to suppose that Jesus had the Jeremiah passage in mind, because he spoke at the Last Supper of establishing a "new covenant" in which sins would be forgiven (Matthew 26.28; Luke 22.20; the manuscripts have several variations at these points, but the overall drift is clear). And his ministry had begun with John's baptism, a washing with water to represent a completely new start for Israel as part of the launching pad for God's kingdom. Behind both Jeremiah and Ezekiel stands Deuteronomy, which speaks of loving God with all one's heart (6.5) and then, when all has apparently failed and the covenant has been broken (28.15–68), of God "circumcising your heart" so that you will, after all, love him with heart and soul (30.6), with the result that the covenant is renewed and Israel restored.

There can be little doubt that Jesus saw himself as the heir to these traditions, and as being charged with a vocation to make them come true. Everything that he says to his followers about their hearts and lives flows from this point; everything his first followers believed about themselves and their calling in the years immediately following his resurrection indicates that they shared Jesus's vision. The kingdom which Jesus came to bring on earth as in heaven must take root in, and be implemented through, the cleansed and softened hearts of his followers.

Nor does this happen simply by Jesus's hearers signing on as "disciples." The story told in the gospels makes it quite clear: when the crunch comes, they all abandon him and run away. No doubt we cannot psychoanalyze them at this distance, or undertake a careful examination of their spiritual state. They were in a unique position, privileged beyond measure to be with Jesus himself, having "faith" enough to go on following, and yet, again and again, unable to comprehend what was happening before their eyes or to respond to it appropriately. Within the story line, they too needed the events of Jesus's death and resurrection before the kingdom-work could take hold of them with its full transforming power. (That's the point of John's cryptic line in 7.39: the Spirit was not yet available, because Jesus was not yet glorified.) But when that kingdom-work does indeed catch them up fully, as happens at Pentecost, they are radically changed people: not yet perfect, as Acts reveals all too painfully, but transformed from the inside out in a way for which the only available explanation was a combination of scriptural prophecy, the events concerning Jesus, and a new power breathing within them. And with that they discovered that Jesus's stated aim of launching God's kingdom on earth as in heaven had come true—but, once more, not at all in the ways they, as first-century Jews, had imagined.

Rather, it had come true through Jesus's defeat of the powers of corruption, sin, and death and his becoming, in himself, the kingdom-in-person and the Temple-in-person. Jesus's own resurrected body was the one bit of "earth" to be already fully and completely colonized by the powerful, life-giving energy and glory of "heaven." The disciples, as Jesus's followers, were then commissioned to put the kingdom into effect, neither by military conquest nor by otherworldly retreat, but by announcing Jesus as the world's true Lord and calling people to believe in him and know his healing, rescuing power in their own lives and communities. In other words, the evidence for the changed hearts of the disciples is that they became, in turn, heart-changers; or rather, as they would have put it, they became the instruments of God's work of heart-changing (notice how Paul calls God "the heart-searcher" in Romans 8.27). And part of their work, all through, was that they suffered persecution and danger in order to become kingdom-bringers, glory-bearers. The way of the kingdom and the way of the cross were one and the same for them, as they were for Jesus.

What does all this tell us about Christian virtue? Simply this: that the life to which Jesus called his followers was the kingdom-life—more specifically, the kingdom-*in-advance* life—the life which summoned people to be kingdom-agents through the kingdom-means. We could sum it up the way Peter and Revelation do, echoing the ancient call of Israel: they were to be kings and priests. The habits and practices of heart and life to which they were called were the habits and practices which demonstrated in advance that God's kingdom was indeed turning the world the right way up, cleansing the world so that it would become the dwelling place of God's glory. And that work would begin with, so that it could work through, their own hearts, minds, and lives.

Central among these practices were, of course, the baptism which spoke of God's washing and renewal (renewal of heart, renewal of covenant), and the shared bread-and-wine meal which spoke of Passover, of Jesus and his death and resurrection, and again of covenant renewal. But flowing from these practices, these corporate habits which formed the heart habits of individual disciples, was the acquiring of the habits of heart, mind, body, and fellowship which spoke of the *telos* of the kingdom itself and gave evidence of that quest to be *teleios*, "complete": the meekness, the peacemaking, the purity of heart (there it is again), and so on which Jesus had urged from the beginning in the Sermon on the Mount.

Jesus called his people to share in the task of bringing his kingdom—and to share in the cost of that work. That double challenge speaks volumes about the revolutionary nature of virtue within a Christian perspective, and about the fact that, though the Christian believes that virtue is itself a work of grace, it is not a work which happens automatically, easily, or without the Christian equivalent of the hard moral effort of which the pagan theorists had spoken. Jesus's challenge extends and transforms that of Aristotle, but the main lines of the ancient pagan wisdom, however much they are changed by being placed within such a different framework, are nevertheless enhanced. That, as we shall see, is the basis on which the wider challenge of the kingdom can go forward.

FIVE

Before we can continue, we must face one particular question. Many people, reading a chapter about Jesus and virtue, would expect a discussion of Jesus himself as the great *example*. Surely, many will think, part of the point of his life was to show us how it's done?

A counter-question: To what extent would this be a helpful, or even possible, line to pursue?

At one level, it certainly wouldn't be helpful and might well not even be possible. Holding up Jesus as an example of how to live a moral life seems rather like holding up Tiger Woods as an example of how to hit a golf ball. Even if I started now and practiced for eight hours a day, it is highly unlikely that I would ever be able to do what Woods can do; and there are many people out there, younger and fitter than I, who are trying their hardest to do it and still find they can't. Similarly, watching Jesus—with his astonishing blend of wisdom, gentleness, shrewdness, dry humor, patience with blundering followers, courage in confronting evil, self-control in innumerable situations of temptation (managing, says Hebrews 4.15, to remain without sin though he was tempted in all respects as we are)—makes most of us, all but the most proud or ambitious, feel like we do when watching Tiger Woods hit a golf ball. Only more so.

What's more, the suggestion that we treat Jesus as a moral example can be, and in some people's thinking has been, a way of holding at arm's length the message of God's kingdom on the one hand and the meaning of his death and resurrection on the other. Making Jesus the supreme example of someone who lived a good life may be quite bracing to contemplate, but it is basically *safe:* it removes the far more dangerous challenge of supposing that God might actually be coming to transform this earth, and us within it, with the power and justice of heaven, and it neatly helps us avoid the fact, as all four gospels see it, that this could be achieved only through the shocking and horrible events of Jesus's death. Jesus as "moral example" is a *domesticated Jesus,* a kind of religious mascot. We look at him approvingly and decide we'll copy him (up to a point at least, and no doubt he'll forgive us the rest because he's a decent sort of chap). As if! If all we need is a good example, we can't be in quite such a bad state as some people (including Jesus himself) have suggested.

Over against all such notions stands the entire tradition from Jeremiah with his warnings about the deceitful heart, through John the Baptist, with his warnings about the ax being laid to the roots of the tree, through Paul, with his warnings that if righteousness had come by the Law the Messiah wouldn't have needed to die, through to Ambrose, Augustine, Luther, Kierkegaard . . . and a host of others. And of course Jesus himself. He doesn't go about saying, "This is how it's done; copy me." He says, "God's kingdom is coming; take up your cross and follow me." Only when we learn the difference between those two challenges will we have grasped the heart of the gospel and, with that, the taproot of a reborn virtue.

And yet, in one respect at least, the New Testament does hold Jesus up as an example to be followed. It is striking that this occurs in one of the areas where Jesus was *not* modeling a "standard" virtue, but was doing something that nobody had ever imagined before—namely, forgiving those who were torturing and killing him (Luke 23.34). Up to this point, the Jewish tradition, like the pagan one, had assumed that the right thing to do, under such circumstances, was to call down the wrath of God upon the torturers and executioners: so, at least, we see in the grisly stories in the books of the Maccabees and elsewhere. Here, however, exactly in line with what we saw in the Sermon on the Mount, we find Jesus portrayed, not as an example of how to face a standard temptation, but of how to do something completely different:

> If, when you do what is good and suffer for it, you bear it with patience, this is pleasing to God. That, you see, is what you were called to, because the Messiah, too, suffered for us, leaving you a pattern so that you could follow in his footsteps. He did no sin; no deceit was found in his mouth; when he was abused, he did not return the abuse, and when he suffered, he did not threaten, but gave himself up to the one who judges justly. (1 Peter 2.20b–23)

The passage goes on to speak of the atoning value of Jesus's death, but the message at this point is different: here is a new way of behaving that nobody has attempted before, let alone taught. Look carefully at Jesus, and copy him. There is some evidence in the early church that Jesus's followers did exactly that, starting with the first martyr, Stephen (Acts 7.60). You only have to read the stories of the great Maccabean martyrs, who call down lurid curses on their persecutors, and even some of the Psalms (e.g., 58.6–9; 69.22–28), to see what a startling innovation this was.

This may be the meaning, too, of those passages where Paul speaks of "imitating the Messiah," or at least of imitating him, Paul, as he in turn imitates Jesus. Thus in 1 Corinthians 11.1 Paul says, "Imitate me, as I imitate the Messiah," summing up a particular point—namely, that one ought to give no offense, but rather determine not to please oneself but to seek the good of others (1 Corinthians 10.32–33). This, interestingly, fits closely with Romans 15.2–6:

> Each one of us should please our neighbor for his or her good, and to build them up. The Messiah, you see, did not please himself. Instead, as the Bible says, "The reproaches of those who reproached you are fallen on me." Whatever was written ahead of time, you see, was written for us to learn from, so that through patience, and through the encouragement of the Bible, we might have hope. May the God of patience and encouragement grant you to come to a common mind among yourselves, in accordance with the Messiah, Jesus, so that, with one mind and one mouth, you may glorify the God and father of our Lord Jesus the Messiah.

In other words, the pattern of Jesus's messianic life—not pleasing himself, but acting in obedience to God's vocation and thus giving himself for the rescuing of the world—was to be held up as an extraordinary example, not so much of *how* to do it as of *what* to do, in an area where, without this example, one might simply not have known that such an unprecedented attitude was expected. Here too, we may suppose, belongs another, better-known passage:

> This is how you should think amongst yourselves: with the mind that you have because you are in the Messiah, Jesus. (Philippians 2.5)

Paul goes on, in this passage, to speak of the voluntary self-emptying of the Messiah, and his subsequent glorification. This both undergirds the striking appeal for a unity of heart and mind in 2.1–5, and forms the basis for the subsequent appeal to "work out your salvation in fear and trembling" (2.12), which I take to mean, in effect, "Think through very carefully the new patterns of life to which you are committed by the 'salvation' which is yours in the Messiah." Once again, we remind ourselves that the death and resurrection of Jesus did indeed inaugurate a new pattern of life. Nobody in the ancient world, pagan or Jewish, had ever imagined living like this. Jesus had actually done it, and the Sermon on the Mount showed that he expected his followers to do it too. These Pauline exhortations show that at least some of Jesus's followers took this very seriously.

Jesus's "moral example," then, is hardly what it is often taken to be, a suggestion that an ordinary human being can actually resist sin if he or she tries hard enough, and that observing how Jesus did it will enable us to do so. Nobody ever says anything like that in the New Testament. In fact, the New Testament's references to Jesus's own sinlessness, a remarkable enough determination for people to have reached so soon after his lifetime, make no attempt to conclude with ". . . therefore you too can be sinless." Their meaning is different: ". . . therefore his death was God's rescue operation" (2 Corinthians 5.21); "therefore he knows what temptation is like and is there to help when you need him" (Hebrews 4.15, already referred to); "therefore he is the unique high priest" (Hebrews 7.26); "he is the one who takes away sins" (1 John 3.5). Insofar as Jesus's life constitutes a "moral example," it is that he has modeled an entirely new aspect of "morality"—namely, humility, a willingness to suffer without recrimination, and a determination to forgive even those who were not asking for it. But these are not "examples of how to do it." They are indications that a new way of being human has been launched upon the world. And it is the habits of heart that generate and sustain this new way of being human that the specifically Christian "virtue" is designed to produce.

To this extent, then, can Jesus be seen as an example of virtue? At first sight we are inclined to answer no; or, at least, not in the ordinary sense. The earliest Christians were convinced that Jesus was in a category of one: he was, to be sure, a fully human being, and tempted as we all are, but he was also identical with the one "through whom all things were made." Does it make sense to think of this Jesus going through the same laborious learning process, in terms of moral struggle, that the rest of us have to face?

Surprisingly, perhaps, it may. Three of the gospels begin, after all, with an account of Jesus's temptations in the wilderness (Matthew 4.1–11 and parallels), and though these abbreviated and stylized accounts can be misread as an apparently rather easy victory, we are no doubt meant to understand that these were severe and prolonged attacks on the very heart of Jesus's understanding of his own vocation and identity and the character of the kingdom he was called to inaugurate. Successful resistance to temptation may result in an increase in moral muscle, but that's because one is going to need it: a temptation resisted may become more, not less, fierce, since to give in is to decrease the tension, at least for the moment. That may be the meaning, at least in part, of the following interesting statement in Hebrews 5.7–9:

> During the time of Jesus's earthly life, he offered up prayers and supplications, with loud shouts and tears, to the one who was able to save him from death. He was heard because of his devotion; although he was a son, he learned the nature of obedience through what he suffered. When he had been made complete and perfect, he became the source of eternal salvation for all who obey him.

This refers primarily, of course, to Jesus's experience in Gethsemane (Mark 14.32–42 and parallels), but it seems to have a wider application as well. Jesus, son of God though he was, *learned the nature of obedience*. What the passage says literally is simply that "he learned obedience," though clearly the writer does not think this meant that he was sometimes disobedient and only gradually discovered how to be obedient instead. Rather, he found out, through practicing it, what it felt like to obey at all points even when tempted to disobey.

This sounds, after all, very much like what we have been talking about in terms of virtue. Even Jesus had to learn what it meant to obey when he didn't want to do so. As his suffering increased, so he discovered more and more what obedience meant in practice. The result was that he became *teleios,* "perfect," "complete" (Hebrews 5.9); not that he had been "imperfect" in the sense of "sinful" prior to that, but that he had not at that stage grown into the fully developed human being he became through his completed work. And that, as the wider context in Hebrews indicates, is what Christians need to do. Because they are starting from a different point—that of forgiven sinners who are still themselves prone to sin—they need to learn not only obedience but also courage, so that they can "hold fast their confession" (Hebrews 4.14). The goal, the *telos,* is up ahead. The habits of heart we need to learn in the present are those which will take hold of Jesus's accomplishment and make it our own.

What we do not find, in the New Testament or the writings that immediately followed, is any attempt to categorize Jesus's life in terms of the normal "moral values" or virtues. His life was full to the brim, if we are to believe the gospels, of faith, hope, and above all love, but nobody ever actually makes that point. If it comes to that, his life was a wonderful model, too, of courage, prudence, temperance, and justice, but again nobody actually comes out and says that. What the earliest Christians were struck by, and what they returned to again and again, was that in Jesus they had seen (and the stories testified of this to those who had not seen) a way of being human which nobody had ever imagined before. This was a way of generosity and forgiveness, a way of self-emptying and a determination to put everyone else's needs first, which was both original in itself and the source of those other virtues that are commonly recognized as Christian innovations—namely, humility, charity, patience, and chastity—all four of which, as contemporary secular philosopher Simon Blackburn notes drily, would have been "unintelligible as ethical virtues to ancient Greeks."[2] And, as noted above, the stories of Jesus's temptation, and the (albeit brief) reflection on it offered by the letter to the Hebrews, suggest that in pursuing this goal Jesus himself did indeed have to go by the route we have described as "virtue": that is, by finding out through painful practice what it actually meant to obey—in particular, to obey the Father's commission to live and to die by the rule of self-giving love.

What we do not find, then, is Jesus held up, or holding himself up, as an example of someone who "kept the rules," reinforcing or reinterpreting them. The way of life he was modeling was precisely not something that could be reduced to rules, or undertaken simply by the effort to conform to certain laid-down norms. Nor could it be arrived at (as the utilitarian would wish to do) by the calculating and weighing of likely effects of certain behaviors, with those calculations leading to decisions and actions. Nor, certainly, was Jesus saying that people should "do what comes naturally": indeed, what comes "naturally," from the heart, was precisely the problem, as far as he was concerned. The only way we can get to the heart of understanding the moral challenge Jesus offered, and offers still today, is by thinking in terms not of rules or of the calculation of effects or of romantic or existentialist "authenticity," but of virtue. A virtue that has been transformed by the kingdom and the cross.

Of course Jesus took for granted, as his contemporaries did, that the behaviors he enumerated in Mark 7.21–22 (immorality, murder, theft, and so on) are wrong. He wouldn't have had any time for someone who said that, since what mattered was character (what a person *was*) rather than rules (what a person *did*), one could cheerfully break the rules (say, steal or kill) so long as one's character was developing in the right way. Wickedness, treachery, debauchery, envy, slander, pride, wanton stupidity, and all the rest are still evil. The rules still matter; one cannot play off virtue against rules and hope still to be talking sense. But what matters, since all of the above can be forgiven, is that the heart be renewed. And when the heart is renewed, it has a fresh set of tasks: to learn the habits that will make the avoidance of all manner of wickedness a matter of "second nature." Learning that obedience will be a hard and painful road. But it will teach us the language of life.

What this discussion has done is to displace "ethics" from the position it is often assumed to hold within discussion of Jesus and his achievement, and to relocate it at a different point within a different framework. Jesus did not come to "teach a new ethic." Nor did he come to teach people that everything they'd ever thought about human behavior was wrong and that they should begin again from the beginning. Nor did he come to show us how to keep God's Law, or, for that matter, to warn us that we couldn't do so even if we tried, so we'd better come to him for forgiveness. Jesus didn't come, in other words, to reinforce any of the normal ways in which Western Christians— and Western non-Christians, too—have thought about "behavior." He came to inaugurate God's kingdom, in his life and public ministry, and through the climax of both in his death and resurrection. He came to rescue Israel, to rescue humankind, and thereby to rescue creation. And, with that, everything is different.

Jesus came, in fact, to launch God's new creation, and with it a new way of being human, a way which picked up the glimpses of "right behavior" afforded by ancient Judaism and paganism and, transcending both, set the truest insights of both on quite a new foundation. And, with that, he launched also a project for rehumanizing human beings, a project in which they would find their hearts cleansed and softened, find themselves turned upside down and inside out, and discover a new language to learn and every incentive to learn it. God's kingdom was bursting in to the present world, offering a "goal" the like of which Aristotle had never imagined. Human beings were called at last to rediscover what they had been made for, what Israel had been created for. They were, after all, to be rulers and priests, following Jesus's ultimate royal and priestly achievement, and they would have to learn from scratch what that meant. They were to practice virtue—virtue of a kind never before imagined. And in this, as in so much besides, the first great theoretician among Jesus's followers was that tireless, restless, lovable, and often puzzling man named Paul.

5. TRANSFORMED BY THE RENEWAL OF THE MIND

ONE

I often think St. Paul must have been what we call a morning person. Mind you, he was quite capable of staying up late at night as well. In fact, one of the best-known stories in Acts is of him talking on and on in an upstairs room until eventually one young man, overcome with sleep, fell out of a window. Paul, undaunted, picked him up, checked that he was all right, and carried on till morning (Acts 20.7–12).

But there are telltale passages in his letters which give a hint, I think, that Paul was one of those people who sensed, and relished, the excitement of being up before sunrise, and of being able, like a surfer picking up the energy of a wave, to let the power and promise of the breaking dawn stimulate fresh thought, prayer, and action. "Don't you know what time it is?" he asks. "Night is nearly over; day is about to break! It's time to stop sleeping and wake up!" (Romans 13.11–12). "Wake up, sleepyhead!" he insists. "Rise up from the dead, and the Messiah will give you light!" (Ephesians 5.14). And, perhaps most telling,

Now when it comes to specific times and dates, my dear family, you don't need to have anyone write to you. You yourselves know very well that the day of the Lord will come like a midnight robber. When people say "Peace and security!" then swift ruin will arrive at their doorstep, like the pains that come over a woman in labor, and they won't have a chance of escape. But as for you, my dear family—you are not in darkness. That day won't surprise you like a robber. You are all children of light, children of the day! We don't belong to the night, or to darkness. So, then, let's not go to sleep, like the others, but let's stay awake and remain in control of ourselves. People who sleep, you see, sleep at night. People who get drunk get drunk at night. But we daytime people should be self-controlled, clothing ourselves with the breastplate of faith and love, and with the helmet of the hope of salvation; because God has not placed us on the road to fury, but to gaining salvation, through our Lord Jesus the Messiah. He died for us, so that whether we stay awake or go to sleep we should live together with him. So strengthen one another, and build each other up, just as you are doing. (1 Thessalonians 5.1–11)

Yes, all right. Paul has well and truly mixed his metaphors here. You should stay awake in case a thief tries to burgle your house. You need to wake up because it's nearly morning. And, for good measure, the woman is going into labor, so you mustn't get drunk, but should put on your armor . . .

But behind the breathless early-morning rhetoric there's a fundamental point which shows just how similar, *and just how different,* the early Christian approach to virtue was to that of the pagan world all around. "We daytime people should be self-controlled, clothing ourselves with the breastplate of faith and love, and with the helmet of the hope of salvation." There is the goal, the *telos,* the full day which is already dawning; here are the steps toward that goal, the habits of heart, mind, and body which will prepare you to be a daytime person, a complete, renewed human being. First Thessalonians is almost certainly one of Paul's earliest letters, but already we can glimpse the mature position which he sketches more fully elsewhere, a proposal about virtue which will turn, over the centuries, into a massive structure of Christian exploration, renewing the ancient classical tradition of virtue and radically transforming it in the process. Faith, hope, and love form, for Paul, the fundamental character of the person who is anticipating in the present, by patient and careful moral discipline, the goal of genuine humanity which is set before us. (Note especially the phrase "self-controlled." These things don't happen by accident. We will come back to that in due course.)

The goal, he insists, is already given in Christ. That's why, from one point of view, the day has already dawned, while from another it's still on the way. Paul, innocent of the modern phenomenon of jet lag, nevertheless expresses something similar here. He is like someone taking off just as dawn is breaking and flying rapidly westward, catching up with the end of the night and arriving in the new country in time to experience dawn all over again. His body and mind know it's already daytime, while the world around him is still waiting for the dawn to break. That is the picture of the Christian, living in the new day of God's kingdom—a kingdom launched by Jesus—while the rest of the world is still turning over in bed. Paul's vision of Christian virtue, centered here as elsewhere on faith, hope, and love, is all about developing the habits of the daytime heart in a world still full of darkness.

To begin here is to note again, as we saw in the previous chapter, that everything we now say about the moral life as seen from Paul's perspective is held firmly and unbreakably in the context of the overarching grace of God. Never for one moment does Paul imagine, as one might from reading Aristotle, that morality is simply a matter of a human being deciding to adopt a particular set of characteristics and discovering in herself or himself the capability and energy to get on and reform one's life in that way.

Paul would not have doubted that such reformations are in principle possible. Plenty of people, perhaps after some years of dissolute and disorganized living, notice that there seem to be better, more effective, and happier ways to live, and decide to take themselves in hand and sort their lives out. Better that than nothing. But with that moral effort, Paul would have insisted, come the further temptations to pride, arrogance, greed, and a host of other things. And even in the most serious pagan moralists—Aristotle, Seneca, and so on—there remains the puzzle that one can tell people how to live but not be able quite to do it oneself. For Paul, faith, hope, and love are already given in Christ and by the Spirit, and it is possible to live by them. But you have to work at it. And to work at it you have to *want* to live in the daytime. You have to understand how your own moral life functions. You have to think through what it all means and how it all works. You have to develop, consciously and deliberately, the habits of heart, mind, soul, and strength that will sustain this life of faith, hope, and love. In other words, you have to practice the specifically Christian form of virtue.

Knowing that the day has already dawned, and that you are caught up within its new life and new possibilities, is the framework which enables proper Pauline reflection on the virtues to take place. It is the framework, too, which guarantees that as we go forward we will not, in any way, endanger Paul's well-known theological position that we are justified, and ultimately saved, by grace through faith.

Paul's vision of the dawning day, and of justification, faith, and the Christian life, is itself held within a larger theological framework. For him, all Christian life, faith, thought, and action takes place within the creative and redemptive (or new-creative) action of the one true God, who had made himself known in and as Jesus the Messiah, and was now active in and through the Spirit of Jesus, the Holy Spirit. The implicitly and sometimes explicitly trinitarian framework of Paul's thought has been explored many times, and we do not need to develop it here, except to note that if we were to ask Paul for his definition of the ultimate goal, the *telos,* of all our faith and life, he might reply "the resurrection," or he might reply "the new creation," but equally, and perhaps more profoundly, he might reply "God himself."

"For us," he writes to the Corinthians, "there is one God, the Father, *from whom are all things and we to him*" (1 Corinthians 8.6). That little phrase, "we to him," echoes what he says at the end of one of his greatest arguments: "from him and through him *and to him* are all things" (Romans 11.36). This is tied closely to the repeated similar phrase in Colossians 1, though in the latter it is Jesus Christ "to whom" all things tend: all things were created "through him and for him" (1.16), and all things were reconciled "through him and to him" (1.20). For Paul, God remains in the center of the picture, and if we focus on the renewed humanity, the new creation, the world restored by God's love and saving justice and filled with his glory at last, we must not forget that the point of the whole thing is "so that God may be all in all" (1 Corinthians 15.28).

But if we were to replace the *telos* of "happiness" or "human flourishing" or, in Christian mode, "resurrection" and "new heavens and new earth" with the answer "God himself," and were to inquire how this affected the framework of thought which generates the discourse of virtue, we would quickly find, in Paul, what we might expect from a Jew soaked in the ancient scriptures of Israel. If the creator God is the goal, then what that means for human beings is not that they will be absorbed into God, losing their identity and individuality, but that they will come once more *to reflect the divine image* fully and completely—from God into the world, and from the world back to God. In other words: rulers and priests.

This idea of being restored as genuine image-bearers is exactly what we find Paul exploring. Daytime people, in Paul's perspective, are people who are making the choices in the present, developing the character in the present, which will tend toward the goal which is God himself, by being "renewed in knowledge according to the image of the creator" (3.10). And with that we find ourselves in one of Paul's main expositions of Christian virtue: the letter to the Christian community in Colossae.

TWO

> When the Messiah is revealed, the one who is your life, then you also
> will be revealed with him in glory. So put to death the earthly parts . . .
> since you have put off the Old Human with its deeds, and have put on
> the New Human, which is being renewed in knowledge according to
> the image of the one who created it. (Colossians 3.4–5, 9–10).

There is Paul's understanding of virtue. Interestingly, it is also John's:

> Now, children, abide in him, so that when he is revealed we may have
> boldness and not be ashamed before him at his royal appearing. . . .
> Beloved, we are now God's children, and it has not yet been revealed
> what we shall be. But we know that when he is revealed, we shall be
> like him, because we shall see him as he is. And everyone who pos-
> sesses this hope in him purifies themselves, just as he is pure. (1 John
> 2.28, 3.2–3)

The future event will demonstrate our true, ultimate existence: we must therefore do the hard work in the present of becoming the people we are destined to be. In each case, in both Paul and John, this future destiny (to stress the point once more) is already given in Jesus Christ and in our membership in him. We are not starting with raw human material and working it up from scratch. We are starting with a human character already in Christ, "risen with him" (Colossians 3.1) and "abiding in him" (1 John 2.28); we are greatly beloved and marked out as "children of God" (1 John 3.1; Galatians 4.1–7). But what interests us now is both the logic of the Pauline and Johannine virtue and, just as much, the practical steps that are to be taken to attain that virtue.

First, as to the logic. Paul's commands clearly belong within the discourse of virtue, albeit in Christian mode. They cannot be reduced either to a Christian deontology (that is, the quest for a new or revised set of "rules" or "duties") or to a Christian utilitarianism (seeking, and perhaps calculating, the likely resultant happiness of the majority), still less a Christian romanticism or existentialism.

Let's take these one by one. The commands of Colossians 3.1–17, one of the fullest and most theologically ordered of Paul's ethical passages, are not to be seen as "Christian rules" in the sense people so often suppose today. (I'm not talking about serious philosophers, who know of course that virtue is not to be played off against proper rules, but about the popular mind in which anyone who tells anybody else how to behave is perceived to be projecting his or her own prejudices or psychology upon other people in an arbitrary and unwelcome fashion.) Nor are Paul's commands here to be explained on the grounds that behavior of this kind will produce the greatest happiness of the greatest number. Paul is far too much a realist for that, far too aware of the suffering which comes when people set themselves to follow the crucified Jesus. Yes, "the sufferings of this present time are not worth comparing with the glory that is to be revealed" (Romans 8.18), but this is hardly a prudent argument to be advanced by a would-be Christian utilitarian. Finally, nor, in particular, is Paul saying, as the romanticist or existentialist might hope, that the moral positions he is commending will "come naturally," so that once one is a Christian one should simply expect to be able to do what he says without reflection, without thought, without moral effort.

No: what counts is the formation, in the present time, of a character that properly *anticipates* the promised future state, in the sense we explored earlier. As we saw, that future state is, for the Christian, the resurrection to a body like that of the risen Jesus Christ, a resurrection to share in the new world, the new creation that has already begun with him, and in which God's people are to be a royal priesthood, the genuine human beings through whom God's world is brought into glorious flourishing and order. The Messiah is already "seated at God's right hand"—that is, in the position of executive authority over the world; very well, says Paul, you are in Christ, so you are there as well. So, just as the "cardinal virtues" within the pagan scheme of virtue pointed toward, and actually anticipated aspects of, the eventual *eudaimonia* or "human flourishing," so the styles of life Paul is commending point toward, and actually anticipate aspects of, the eventual renewal of humanity.

Within this logic, it is important to note what Paul is *not* saying. "Think about the things that are above," he says, "not the things that are on the earth" (Colossians 3.2). Centuries of dualist misunderstanding have encouraged today's readers to imagine that when he talks about "things above" as opposed to "things on the earth," he is adopting a straightforward antithesis between the world of space, time, and matter ("things on the earth") and an "upper" world, a pure spiritual existence, where these messy and unfortunate inessentials are abandoned with a sigh of relief.

Not so. If that were his meaning, he would have reinforced the prohibitions against certain kinds of food and drink, instead of declaring such prohibitions unnecessary (2.16–23). He would not have recommended all the practical aspects of character to which we shall presently turn (3.12–17). No: when he says "on the earth," he is referring, as becomes clear in 3.5–9, to those styles of behavior which are turned away from God the creator, which are reflecting the present corruption of creation rather than reflecting God's love and stewardship. We might note the parallel with Philippians 3.14–21. There, Paul makes the same contrast of "above" and "on the earth," making it clear that "on the earth" doesn't mean "part of the world of space, time, and matter" but "behavior which carries on as though earthly appetites were all that mattered." That passage ends, not with Jesus snatching people away from the present physical world, but with his return from heaven in order to bring heaven and earth together and, ruling both, to transform our present corruptible bodies to be like the one he already has. And, as has often been remarked about the list of "works of the flesh" in Galatians 5.19–21, most of what we see here in Colossians 3.5–9 could in fact be practiced by a disembodied spirit (anger, slander, blasphemy, and above all lying). In other words, Paul adopts the language of "upper" and "lower" to make the moral point, but he is not thereby importing ontological dualism (matter = bad, non-matter = good) into his argument. Rejecting the good created world is, at best, a gross parody and severe distortion of Christian virtue.

What then is Paul saying in Colossians that Christians must *do*? Answer: he is telling them to develop, in the present, the *character* which will truly anticipate the life of the coming age. We shall consider below the detailed practical things he sets out, which overlap very largely with similar lists elsewhere. What we need to grasp, as being of the essence of his summons to Christian virtue, is the *moral ef-*

fort involved. "Put to death . . ." (3.5), "put away . . ." (3.8), "put on . . ." (3.14)—these are the points of particular interest.

The main thing to notice is that none of these things "comes naturally." Even for the Christian this is not going to be so, certainly to begin with. The point of virtue, as we have seen, is that eventually, as a person's character becomes more fully formed, such things may indeed begin to "come naturally." But the steps it takes to get to that point involve hard decisions and hard actions, choices that run counter to the expectations, aspirations, desires, and instincts with which every human being comes equipped.

Paul does not mince his words at this point. He does not say, "You might like to try giving up a bit of this" or "If it feels all right to you, think about doing without some of these things." He says, "Put them to death." If you don't kill them, they will kill you (3.6). This is not, we must stress, because God will suddenly invoke some arbitrary and tyrannical divine prohibition to cramp our style, stop us having a good time, or punish us if we step out of line. Rather, it is because these styles of behavior lead directly, as a matter of necessity, into corruption, decay, and death and hence away from the new creation where heaven and earth come together and resurrection results.

An obvious example. As I mentioned earlier, I was writing this book during the financial turmoil of the so-called credit crunch of 2008–2009. Those with old and wise financial heads said, "Well, banks and investors were lending people money they couldn't afford to borrow to buy houses that weren't worth as much as they were selling for, and thus this crash was inevitable, sooner or later." The result wasn't an arbitrary punishment, like a court locking someone up for five years as a punishment for fraud. It was a foregone conclusion, a necessary consequence *within the behavior itself.* Do that sort of thing, and these consequences *will unfold* from within it. So it is with the behaviors Paul lists here. They are the habits of life which already share in the death they court.

Some things, then, are to be "put to death." Others are to be "put away," placed out of reach, pushed away with a sense of revulsion.

Indeed, the development of that sensitivity—the recognition and sustained awareness that these negative aspects of character (anger, wrath, malice, blasphemy, evil speaking of every sort) really are dehumanizing—is a vital part of the development of character. If these things, or the list in verse 5, have become habits, as Paul indicates that they have for the people to whom he is writing (verse 7), then the first new habit to acquire is that of breaking the old ones. Consider the self-taught tennis player who has been doing everything wrong for years. Such a person may need to unlearn all sorts of things which, if continued, will prevent her from playing the game properly. Only after that unlearning can she acquire the new habits which will enable her to play tennis not only properly but also with success. In the same way, converts need to learn that there are some habits of body, mind, imagination, speech, and so on which have to be unlearned in order to make way for the new habits which have to be learned.

That illustration, however, is limited, because tennis is a game you can play one on one. In other words, it's normally an individual pursuit. But Christian behavior isn't like that. It's a team sport, like soccer, football, rugby, or hockey. There's no room on this team for "passengers"—that is, players who allow the others to do the hard work and coast along hoping all will be well. But equally there's no room for the lonely individual who supposes that he or she can play simultaneously in attack, support, and defense. That's why the virtues which Paul encourages the Colossians to develop are the virtues of *community:* mutual kindness, truth-telling, forgiveness, acceptance across traditional barriers of race, culture, and class. It isn't just that building up and fostering such community is itself one of the virtues. Since "love" is the primary virtue (3.14), community is the primary context. And—to anticipate a much later point—it is of the very essence of this kind of community that we are not clones of one another. All Christians are to exhibit the Christian virtues, but each one is called to a different set of tasks.

Paul then turns to the positive side. "Put on, then, as God's chosen ones . . ." The point, once again, is that *this doesn't happen automati-*

cally. Community is vital, but all members must make it their own. It's no good hoping that because you've been converted, because you attend church, because you say your prayers, because you have Christian friends, you are going to discover that the qualities of kindness, gentleness, humility, and the rest just happen, without any effort on your part. That context is indeed essential. Being in a supportive and like-minded company (or having a healthy genetic makeup and a happy upbringing) can, but need not necessarily, create a context within which an individual can find the courage and energy to make moral progress. But sooner or later, preferably sooner, each individual Christian must make the key choices to "put on" the things which genuinely anticipate, in the present, the life we are promised in the future, the life we have already been given in Christ. And, having made those key choices, each Christian must acquire the habit of making them over and over again.

As with the "putting off," so the "putting on" is a matter of consciously deciding, again and again, to do certain things in certain ways, to create patterns of memory and imagination deep within the psyche and, as we saw from contemporary neuroscience, deep within the actual physical structure of our mysterious brain. Gradually, bit by bit, the "putting on" of these qualities—qualities that seem for the moment so artificial, so unnatural, so "unlike me"—will in fact transform the character at its deepest level. Colossians 3 is indeed a primer in Christian virtue.

We often use the phrase "putting on," of course, in terms of people pretending to be something they are not. The phrase "putting it on" is a bit of a sneer. "You're just putting it on," we say to someone apparently feigning deep emotion; "you don't really feel like that." Our culture, soaked in romanticism and existentialism, is quick to spot and laugh at hypocrisy. This reaction is really the modern secular counterpart of the older theological anxiety about people trying to "make themselves good enough for God" instead of relying on God's grace. As we saw earlier, Martin Luther, writing nearly five centuries ago, reckoned that all "virtue" was really "hypocrisy."

But part of Paul's point, which is utterly characteristic of "virtue ethics," is that you have to go through that stage if you're going to get anywhere. To risk another individualistic sporting illustration, when a golf coach finally showed me what I was doing wrong in the way I was gripping the club, for days afterward my whole game felt "unnatural." I badly wanted to go back to doing it the way I'd always done it, because it felt fine to me that way. That was what my hands and wrists were used to. The trouble was that the ball didn't usually go where I wanted it to . . . whereas, at least sometimes, the new grip—unnatural though it felt—was beginning to improve my aim. Likewise, I remember a piano teacher pointing out to me that the reason I was having trouble with a piece I'd taught myself to play was that I'd paid no attention to the fingering which the composer himself had suggested. When I first tried the "proper" fingering, after months of stumbling through the piece in my own sweet way, it felt very strange. I could hardly concentrate on the feeling in the music because I was so bothered by the odd feeling in my fingers. But, again gradually, not only did I get used to the new fingering, but the piece began to sing in a way it hadn't before. That's what it's like when someone seriously begins to "put on" the things Paul is talking about.

Then we have to transpose these individualistic illustrations into the key of a whole community. It's not uncommon to hear football coaches (and supporters) complain that their team consists of a bunch of expensive individuals who haven't learned to play together. Such a team—a team in name only—will be at the mercy of a team with less talented individuals who know each other's strengths and how to play to them, know how to bring out the best in one another, and rely on one another to be in the right place at the right time. Likewise, put the piano player into a chamber group, or make her instead a viola player in a large orchestra. The good musician is not simply playing the music on the stand in front of her. She is playing, consciously and delightedly, as part of a much larger whole, making her own contribution but aware of the music's whole sweep and flow, and of the other contributions which are so different to her own, but so thoroughly complementary.

"Put on, then, compassion, kindness . . ." "Putting on" is of course also a metaphor referring to what happens when you get up in the morning and decide which clothes to wear. Imagine a man who has just changed jobs and has gone from being a chartered accountant to looking after a garden center. For years he has been getting up in the morning and automatically putting on his suit to go to the office. Hasn't had to think about it. Now, however, he has to put on the tough clothes he will wear for outdoor work. You can imagine how it might go. On some of the early days, eagerly thinking about the new work, it wouldn't be difficult to get the right clothes out of the closet. But before that new habit has really stuck fast, it wouldn't be surprising if, getting up one morning with something else on his mind, he discovered he'd put a suit on, tie and all, before he stopped to think. A silly illustration, perhaps. But it makes the point: clothes don't just fall out of the wardrobe and put themselves on you; you have to think about what you're going to wear, making conscious and repeated decisions to put on the clothes appropriate for the new life you're going to follow.

That's exactly what Paul is saying. The new life is the life "in Christ." The new clothes—which, to be sure, will feel unnatural and uncomfortable to begin with—are the list we find in verses 12–17: compassion, kindness, humility, meekness, patience, forbearance, forgiveness, and above all love. Sounds a bit like the Beatitudes, doesn't it? And, as with Jesus's own list of characteristics, you have to *decide* that you *intend* to put them on. You have to get them out of the closet. You have to learn how to put them on the right way, like someone learning how to do up a bow tie.

Paul extends the metaphor: there is one garment which goes over all the others and holds them all in place, like a belt. That is *agapē,* or love (verse 14). We shall come back to the meaning of *agapē* in Paul later on, but notice here what he says about it: love is "the bond of perfection," the *syndesmos tēs teleiotētos,* the thing which ties it all together and makes it "complete." There is the root which connects this whole theme to Aristotle on the one hand, with his *telos,* the "goal," the final end of all our endeavors, and to Jesus on the other hand, with his

command to be "perfect" or "complete," *teleios*. Here is the goal; these
are the steps toward it. There are some things that abide, that last, that
form (as it were) a bridge between this world and the next one; and,
of these things that last, the greatest is love (1 Corinthians 13.13, which
we shall look at in the next chapter).

This is how virtue works. Keep your eye on the goal of a "complete" character—in the Christian case, the full humanity promised
in the resurrection, through which we are called to be a royal priesthood. Practice the skills in the present which will gradually enable you
to do and be what will go to make up that complete character. This
will seem "unnatural" at first, but eventually it may, if we stick at it,
become "second nature." When you do this, he says, you will be turning into a genuine, God-reflecting human being. The world will see in
you a reflection of who God truly is. God will see in you a reflection
of the world as it has been and will be renewed in the resurrection of
Jesus Christ.

For any of this to make sense, there is one key element which Paul
insists on again and again. There are two interlocking reasons why we
can't do without this element. First, it is a vital ingredient within a genuinely human existence, so that to leave it out—as many, sadly, seem
to want to do—is to collude with what is at best a semi-human state.
Second, it is the ingredient without which this whole scheme simply
won't function. I refer to the mind. "Be transformed," urges Paul, "by
the renewing of your mind" (Romans 12.2).

THREE

Paul's summons to let the mind be renewed, and so to be transformed
all through, comes at the start of the "so what" section of Romans, his
greatest letter. The brief passage is worth quoting in full:

> So, my dear family, this is my appeal to you by the mercies of God:
> offer your bodies as a living sacrifice, holy and pleasing to God. This is

your true and appropriate worship. What's more, don't let yourselves
be squeezed into the shape dictated by the present age. Instead, be
transformed by the renewing of your minds, so that you can work out
and approve what God's will is, what is good, acceptable and complete. (12.1–2)

Note, first, that Paul frames the command to be transformed
within the call to *priestly worship*. We are to offer sacrifices; we are to
worship the living God in the true and living way. And the sacrifices in
question, exactly as in Romans 8, are our whole selves. Those who have
been assured of their "access" into God's presence, as in the Temple
(Romans 5.2), and who are promised that they will "reign" with Jesus
Christ (5.17), are now told, as it were, to come into the Temple not
just as worshippers but as sacrifices. They are to present themselves on
the altar—in other words, to give their whole lives to the God whose
mercy has rescued them. By so doing they will, like the humans in Revelation 4 and 5, be gathering up the inarticulate praises of all creation
and presenting them before the creator. They will share, in this sense,
in the obedient and grateful worship offered in Jesus Christ.

The word Paul uses for "true and appropriate" is actually a term
which pagan moralists would have recognized (though they might not
have understood Paul's particular point). This word, *logikos,* is hard to
translate, because in addition to "true and appropriate" or "logical," it
can also carry the meanings of "rational" on the one hand and "spiritual" on the other. Paul seems to be saying three interlocking things.
First, offering your body (by which he here means your whole self)
to God is the utterly fitting thing to do, since God has redeemed you
and will transform that body to be like the risen body of Jesus Christ, a
transformation which you must anticipate in appropriate behavior here
and now. Second, this self-offering is not merely of your body, but of
your body *as directed by your reasoning mind*. Third, when you worship
God in this way, with your whole self, you are not (of course) actually
lying down on an altar and cutting your own throat, but you are doing
so "spiritually"—not just metaphorically, but in the realm of spiritual

reality. This is, as it were, the true "priestly" work toward which the earlier sacrifices in the Jerusalem Temple had been pointing all along.

Paul develops this "priestly" theme in a variety of ways elsewhere. In Romans 15.16, he sees himself going to Jerusalem as a priest, taking an offering to the Temple—but the offering is the Gentile converts, in the form of the money they have donated, which has been made holy (in case anyone should question it) by the Holy Spirit. In Philippians 2.17 he sees the Philippians and their faith as a sacrificial offering to God, with his own life like the drink-offering which is poured out on top of it. These images of sacrificial worship came naturally to Paul. Since he had thought through carefully the fact that the significance of the Jerusalem Temple had been transferred to Jesus Christ, and to those in whom the Spirit now dwelt, he was quite easy about drawing on such imagery to highlight the nature of Christian worship, of the "priestly" aspect of the "royal priesthood" vocation.

This same theme is highlighted at the end of the "epistle of priest-hood," the letter to the Hebrews:

> We have an altar from which those who minister in the tabernacle are not allowed to eat. For the bodies of the animals whose blood is taken into the sanctuary by the high priest as a sin-offering are burned outside the camp. That's why Jesus too suffered outside the gate, so that he might make the people holy with his own blood. So, then, let's go out to him, outside the camp, bearing his shame. Here, you see, we have no city that lasts; we are looking for the one that is still to come. Our part, then, is to bring, through him, a continual sacrifice of praise to God—that is, mouths that confess his name, and do so fruitfully. Don't neglect to do good, and to let "fellowship" mean what it says. God really enjoys sacrifices of that kind! (13.10–16)

Once more: the royal priesthood, transcending the world of ancient Judaism but picking up its essential vocation.

To return to Romans 12.1: Paul has hereby created the context for the key command which sets all of his ethics apart from any suggestion of "spontaneity," as though once you were in Christ, indwelt by the Spirit, all you had to do was let the new life "come naturally." No: *the mind must be transformed,* so that you can think out for yourself, weigh up and consider, what God's will actually is. Unless the mind is fully involved, not only are you not growing up as a fully (and fully integrated) human being; you are not engaging in virtue at all.

When Paul talks about the "mind," he is not ranking Christians in terms of what we would call their intellectual or "academic" ability. Some Christians have that sort of mind. Plenty of others don't. But Paul wants all Christians to have their minds renewed, so that they can think *in a different way.* We all face many challenges, not only in the sphere of morality as such, but in a thousand different contexts. It won't do simply to go into autopilot and hope to get through somehow. That will work, as with our initial examples of virtue, only when we have already trained ourselves in the necessary habits. But to do that requires careful and disciplined thought in this new mode, probably over some time. We have to be able to think about what to do—what to do with our whole lives, and what to do in the sudden crisis that faces us this very minute. Being trained to think "Christianly" is the necessary antidote to what will otherwise happen: being, as Paul says, "squeezed into the shape dictated by the present age."

Once again, the substructure of what Paul is saying should be clear. In the first eleven chapters of Romans he has set out at considerable length the way in which the creator God has, in Jesus Christ and his death and resurrection, been faithful to his covenant promises to Abraham and his family, and has provided the way by which human beings, despite their idolatry and sin, can be rescued and set on the path to the promised land, to the renewal of the whole creation. In particular, he has shown that even the apparent failure of most Jews to believe in their own Messiah is somehow contained within the larger overall purpose of the one God. His whole exposition is dominated by his core belief that in the Messiah, Jesus, the "age to come" has already burst into the "present age." Many Jews of the time expected the present age to come to an end and then the age to come to begin, whole and entire. Paul sees that in Jesus Christ the long-awaited age to come has already begun. And that is where Christians must consciously choose to live.

Yes, the present age continues on its weary way as well, so that the two overlap. Like waves on the ocean shore, God's new age has come thundering in through the resurrection of Jesus Christ, but the present age acts as a powerful undertow, preventing the incoming waves from having their full force. The undertow of the continuing present age does its best to persuade those who through faith and baptism are already part of the age to come that in fact nothing much has changed, and that they should simply continue as they were, living the same life that everyone else is living. "The way the world is" is a powerful, insidious force, and it takes all the energy of new creation, not least of faith and hope, to remind oneself that the age to come really is already here, with all its new possibilities and prospects.

The antidote to the power of the present age, then, is to have the mind renewed so that one can think clearly about the way of life which is pleasing to God, which is in accordance with God's will, good and acceptable and (here it is again) "perfect," *teleios,* complete. This renewal of the mind is at the center of the renewal of the whole human being, since the "darkening" of the mind was identified as central to the problem of idolatry, dehumanization, and sin in an earlier chapter of Romans:

> Though they knew God, they did not glorify him as God or give him thanks, but became foolish in their reasonings, and their senseless heart was darkened. Giving themselves out to be wise, they became fools, and they exchanged the glory of the immortal God for the likeness of the image of mortal humans, and birds, animals and reptiles. . . . And, just as they did not "see fit" to hold God in their mind, God gave them up to an "unfit" mind, to do things that are inappropriate. (1.21–23, 28)

The words for "see fit" and "unfit" here are from the same root as "work out and approve" (*dokimos, dokimazein*) in 12.2. Once again this is hard to bring out in translation, but essential to grasp if we are to understand Paul's overall flow of thought. The mind that is in rebellion against God, that refuses to worship him, becomes "unfit"—that is, incapable of thinking straight about what constitutes appropriate human behavior—whereas the mind that is renewed will learn the habit of clear, wise thinking and approval. The "unfit" mind is, in Romans 1, the root from which a whole host of evil things grow, all of which in Paul's understanding reflect the fracturing of the "image," alluded to here in a passage which clearly has the first few chapters of Genesis in mind. It isn't the case that the body leads the mind or heart astray. Rather, the failure to *worship* the one true God leads to a failure to *think,* and thence to a failure to *act* as a fully human being ought. It is worth noting (for the avoidance of doubt) that Paul is here describing the human race as a whole, not specific individuals within it. He is diagnosing a disease from which we have all suffered, even if the symptoms vary from person to person.

Perhaps the most telling point is the one with which Romans 1 concludes: "They know God's decree that those who do such things deserve to die, but *they not only do those things but approve of those who do them*" (1.32). It is one thing to insist on walking south when the compass is pointing north. But to "fix" the compass so that it tells you that the wrong way is the right way is far, far worse. You can correct a mistake. But once you tell yourself it wasn't a mistake there's no way back.

The redemption of the whole human being, anticipated in the case of Abraham in Romans 4, is then remarkably characterized by the reversal of this whole process:

[Abraham] did not weaken in faith when he considered his own body, which was already dead because he was a hundred years old, and the deadness of Sarah's womb. He did not waver in unbelief when faced with God's promises, but gave glory to God, and was fully convinced that he had the power to perform what he had promised. (4.19–21)

That is part of the significance of Abraham in Paul's thought, particularly in Romans. Because of God's call and promise, Abraham is the beginning of the truly human people. He is the one who, in a faith which Paul sees as the true antecedent of Christian faith, allows his thinking and believing to be determined, not by the way the world is, and not by the way his own body is, but by the promises and actions of God. This then sets the tone for the "truly human" exposition in chapter 5, which we looked at earlier, where the same root word (*dokimos*) is used when Paul is talking about the "tried and tested character" in 5.4.

Again, it isn't easy to bring this wordplay out exactly in English, but because an understanding of Paul's phrasing might help us to track his sequence of thought, let's take a closer look. Humans had not "seen fit" to hold God in their minds, and so were "unfit" in their thinking and consequently in their acting (1.28). Being justified by faith, they have peace with God and access to grace, and they are launched on a pattern of character development where suffering produces patience, and patience makes them "fit," and their "fitness" gives them hope (5.4). Then, being transformed by the renewal of their minds, they are to assess the "fitness" of God's will, determining what is good, acceptable, and "perfect" (12.2). For Paul, the mind is central to Christian character: virtue is the result of thought and choice.

All this helps us, too, to understand the exhortation in chapter 6 to "reckon yourselves dead to sin and alive to God in Christ Jesus our Lord" (6.11). This is calling for an act, not of guesswork, nor of fantasy or speculative imagination, but of *mental deduction:* you are in the Messiah; the Messiah has died and been raised; therefore, you have died and been raised; therefore, sin has no right to hold any sway over you. That mental homework, and that alone, is the basis for the appeal which follows instantly: "So don't let sin reign in your mortal body, to make you obey its desires" (6.12). All of this—and much more, actually, but at least all of this—stands now behind Paul's deceptively brief instruction at the start of chapter 12: don't let yourselves be squeezed into the shape dictated by the present age, but be transformed by the renewing of your minds.

What does this mean in terms of Paul's vision of virtue? Virtue, as we have seen, is hard work. It requires the building up of muscles. It is the learning of a new and complex language which, to begin with, people find it hard to get their minds and tongues around. But it isn't a language you can learn parrot-fashion. Yes, it may help if you spend quality time with others who are also learning it. Yes, it will be good if you go to classes and listen to radio programs in the new language. But ultimately you have to get your *mind* around it: you have to think through its verb formations and sentence structure, learn how the vocabulary has arisen and why certain words now carry complex metaphorical associations you'd never have imagined at first sight. Only when you have *thought it through* will you become anything like fluent.

How does that apply to our present topic? Part of our difficulty in the Christian world of late Western modernity has been that the mind, the faculty of thought and reasoning, has become detached. As happens if you have a detached retina in your eye, when your thinking becomes detached you stop seeing things clearly. "Thought" and "reason" seem to have been placed to one side, in a private world reserved for "intellectuals" and "academics." (Note, for example, the way in which sports commentators use the word "academic" to mean "irrelevant," as in "from now on the result of the race is academic.") Furthermore, we often speak of our thoughts as if they were feelings: in a meeting, to be polite, we might say, "I *feel* that's wrong," because it sounds less confrontational than saying, "I *think* that's wrong." Similarly, perhaps without always realizing it (which itself is a sign of the same problem!), we sometimes allow feelings to override thoughts: "I feel very strongly that we should do this" can carry more rhetorical weight than "I think we should do that," since nobody wants to hurt our *feelings*. As a natural next step, we allow feelings to replace thought processes altogether, so that what looks outwardly like a reasoned discussion is actually an exchange of unreasoned emotions, in which all participants claim the high moral ground because when they say, "I feel strongly we should do this," they are telling the truth: they *do* feel strongly, so they *will* feel hurt and "rejected" if people don't agree with them. Thus reasoned discourse is abandoned in favor of the politics of the playground.

On the day I was drafting this chapter someone wrote to the newspaper I read to express a view about "assisted suicide"—that is, euthanasia. "That is how I feel about it," he said after stating his opinion, "and I know a lot of other people feel strongly the same way." I don't doubt it was true. But his feelings were irrelevant to the question of whether the proposal was right or wrong. Lots of people feel very strongly that we should bomb our enemies, that we should execute serious criminals and castrate rapists, that we should abolish income taxes and let the fittest survive. Lots of other people feel very strongly that we should do none of those things. An exchange of feelings may tell us where the pressure points are likely to come, but it won't tell us what is the right thing to do.

Unless a person can give *reasons*, there is, literally, no reason why anyone else should take that person seriously. But without reasons, all we are left with is emotional blackmail. We sometimes call it "moral blackmail," but it has nothing to do with morals, only with the implied juvenile threat of having a tantrum unless everyone else gives in. As a result, the making of moral *decisions* has been downgraded to the weighing of quasi-moral *feelings* and thence into a squadgy morass where, yes, the present age has quietly but firmly squeezed us back into its own shape. It is as though the resurrection had never happened; as though the new age had not dawned. That is precisely the point.

Or rather, it is half of the point. From that angle, Paul's moral teaching begins with the command, as in Romans 6.11, to "think through who you really are in the crucified and risen Messiah," looking *back* to the messianic events of Jesus's death and resurrection. But here, launching in on a characteristic "virtue" exhortation, he is equally looking *forward:* the point of "being transformed by the renewing of the mind" is so that you can work out, test out, think through, and come to a settled judgment about (all of this contained in the rather dense Greek expression *eis to dokimazein hymas*) what God's will is, what will make you a *complete* renewed human, what will get you to the *telos,* the goal. You don't get there by "going with the flow," or even by taking an intuitive leap. Yes, your intuition *may* get you to the right place, but until you've done the mind-renewing work, you will have no guarantee that the intuition is accurate, that you aren't simply being deceived once more by the present age.

Another passage which sits tightly alongside Romans 12 is found near the start of the letter to the Philippians:

> This is my prayer: that your love may abound more and more, with *knowledge* and *all discernment,* so that you can *figure out properly things that differ from one another,* so that you may be blameless and innocent *for the day of the Messiah,* filled with the fruits of righteousness which come through Jesus the Messiah to the glory and praise of God. (1.9–11)

The parts I have put in italics show how the same theme works out. Thinking of and praying for his beloved people in Philippi, Paul wants them, of course, to grow in love; but this love is not a matter of "undisciplined squads of emotion," but a thought-out habit of the heart—the heart knowing why it approves what it approves and why it disapproves what it disapproves.

All this has the forward look that is common to classic virtue-teaching. "The day of the Messiah" is coming, when you will be "complete," as he has said earlier in verse 6: "The one who began a good work in you *will bring it to completion* [*epitelesei,* the *telos* root again] at the day of the Messiah, Jesus." There once more is the *telos,* the goal, and there too is the grace, the sovereign work of God, that will get you to the goal; but don't suppose for a minute that this grace will work without your mind being fully engaged. Here we find it yet again: God wants us to be people, not puppets; real human beings who think things out and make actual decisions, not straws in the wind to be blown this way and that. You need to "figure out properly things that differ," says Paul—and the word he uses for "figure out properly" is our old friend *dokimazein,* as in the *dokimos* root in Romans 1, 5, and 12. Part of the problem in contemporary Christianity, I believe, is that talk about the freedom of the Spirit, about the grace which sweeps us off our feet and heals and transforms our lives, has been taken over surreptitiously by a kind of low-grade romanticism, colluding with an anti-intellectual streak in our culture, generating the assumption that the more spiritual you are, the less you need to think.

I cannot stress too strongly that this is a mistake. The more genuinely spiritual you are, according to Romans 12 and Philippians 1, the more clearly and accurately and carefully you will think, particularly about *what the completed goal of your Christian journey will be* and hence *what steps you should be taking, what habits you should be acquiring, as part of the journey toward that goal, right now.* Thinking clearly and Christianly is thus both a key element within the total rehumanizing process (you won't be fully human if you leave your thinking and reasoning behind) and a vital part of the motor which drives the rest of that process.

Once again, none of this can be seen in an individualistic sense. Of course, those who have particular gifts of mind and intellect must use them in God's service. But, as Romans 12 goes on at once to say, we should not think of ourselves more highly than we ought, but should think with sober judgment, since God made us members one of another in Christ, within the one body (Romans 12.3–5). But even here, stressing the corporate nature of Christian discipleship and hence the absolute requirement of appropriate humility, Paul also stresses that each person must think this out individually: "I am saying this," he writes, "to every single one of you." And again what matters is *thinking:* he's saying, in effect, "Don't *overthink* what you ought to *think,* but *think* with *reasonable thinking.*" Paul's wordplay here (*hyperphronein, phronein,* and *sōphronein*) climaxes in a word which readers might well recognize as cognate with *sōphrosynē,* "reasonableness" or "moderation," well-known in classical discussions of virtue. All Christians are called to think things through—indeed, to think through the way in which thinking through things makes a radical difference to the life of the body of Christ.

This note, in my judgment, is urgently needed today. One of the ironies in the story of Western theology during my lifetime has been the way in which the "liberal" tradition, which used to pride itself above all on clear, rational thinking, has quietly been taken over by emotivism, not least in the area of ethics. Meanwhile, the "conservative" tradition, which used to pride itself on carefully articulated ethical as well as doctrinal stances, has often been so worried about the danger of "works-righteousness" that it has turned a blind eye to the nature of moral understanding and effort upon which Paul is doing his best to insist, and has effectively ruled out virtue before it begins, lest people should suppose themselves to be contributing to their own salvation. No wonder that, when we try to debate key issues, we find ourselves in a dialogue of the deaf.

This discussion of the mind, and its renewal, leads us to the tricky and delicate subject of the conscience. What, for Paul at least, is its role in the formation and practice of virtue?

FOUR

We sometimes speak of a "troubled conscience," but conscience itself is a somewhat troubling concept in early Christian writing. But if the mind, and its renewal by the power of God, is so important for Paul and other early Christians as part of Christian training in the habits of genuinely human behavior, then this faculty, whose original word (*syneidēsis*) literally means "knowing-together-with," can hardly be omitted from our consideration.

First, some clear key passages. Paul, on trial for sedition before the Jewish council in Jerusalem, declares that he has maintained his conscience in a good state all his life long, and still does so now as a Christian:

"My brothers," he said. "I have conducted myself before God in a completely good conscience all my life up to this day." (Acts 23.1; compare 2 Timothy 1.3)

Paul gets into trouble for this: the high priest commands that he be struck on the mouth for daring to say such a thing. But he repeats the point five days later before Felix, the governor:

> This much I will confess to you: that it is true that I do worship the God of my ancestors according to the Way which they call a "sect." I believe everything which is written in the Law and the prophets, and I hold to the hope in God, for which they also long, that there will be a resurrection of the righteous and the unrighteous. For that reason I make it my settled aim always to have a clear conscience before God and all people. (24.14–16)

The word for "clear" here is *aproskopos,* the same word Paul uses in a similar context in 1 Corinthians 10.32:

> So, then, whether you eat or drink or whatever you do, do everything to God's glory. Be blameless [*aproskopos*] before Jews and Greeks and the church of God, just as I try to please everybody in everything, not pursuing my own advantage, but that of the great majority, so that they may be saved. Copy me, just as I'm copying the Messiah. (10.31–11.1)

Paul, in other words, has always kept a close eye on his own state of mind and heart, watching out for points at which there might be something he could be accused of, something where blame might be levied against him. He has, as we say, kept short accounts with himself and with God. Indeed, in Acts 23 we can see him at it, as his angry response to the high priest's order to strike him on the mouth earns a further rebuke for insulting the high priest, which in turn wins an instant apology from Paul himself, who had not realized that the person in question was indeed the high priest. He should have respected the office, he says, and apologizes for not doing so.

The same perspective emerges when we go back further in 1 Corinthians:

> I regard it as a matter of minimal concern to think that I should be interrogated by you, or indeed by any human court. I don't even interrogate myself. I don't actually know of anything [*ouden synoida*] that stands against me, but that isn't what vindicates me; it's the Lord who interrogates me. So don't pass judgment on anything before the time when the Lord comes! He will bring to light the secrets of darkness, and will lay bare the intentions of the heart. Then everyone will receive praise—from God. (4.3–5)[1]

There are two points to notice here. First, *synoida* in verse 4 is cognate with *syneidēsis,* the regular Greek word for "conscience." Paul "knows nothing with himself against himself"—in other words, he has nothing on his conscience in relation to his ministry in Corinth. However, second, what matters is the final judgment, when dark secrets will be uncovered and the intentions of the heart will be revealed. Conscience, he implies, might or might not shine a bright enough light all the way down to illuminate what will emerge on the final day.

Paul's ministry is again assessed by his own conscience and found to be in the clear—despite all the agony he has been through!—at the start of 2 Corinthians:

> This is what we boast of, you see; this is what our conscience is telling us: that our conduct in the world, and in particular in relation to you, has been marked by holiness and godly sincerity, not in merely human wisdom but in God's grace. (1.12; compare the similar reflection in Hebrews 13.18)

Once again, Paul has looked into his own heart as far as he can see, and declares that he finds there nothing to be ashamed of. Indeed, on this occasion his conscience is not merely acquitting him of potential accusations, but congratulating him on holiness (another reading is "single-mindedness") and godly sincerity, and telling him that what he has done has displayed not merely his own human wisdom but God's grace.

Paul thus appears to have a clear idea of what conscience is, or can be: an inner witness, a voice within one's self, assessing the moral worth of what has been done and, perhaps, what might yet be done (though none of the passages yet examined has a forward look). That, however, is all very well for him. Other people do not seem to have such an easy time:

> Some have been accustomed up to now to eating idol-food with the assumption that it really does belong to the idol. This has given them a weak conscience, and now that conscience will be polluted. But the food we eat won't recommend us to God. We won't be any worse off if we don't eat, and we won't be any better off if we do. But you must take care in case this official right of yours becomes a danger to the weak. Look at it like this: if someone with a weak conscience sees you, a person with "knowledge," sitting down to eat in an idol-house, that conscience of theirs is likely to make up its mind actually to eat idol-food, isn't it? And so, you see, the weak person—a brother or sister for whom the Messiah died!—is then destroyed by your "knowledge." That means you'll be sinning against your brother or sister, and attacking their weak conscience; and in doing this you'll be sinning against the Messiah. So, for this reason, if food causes my brother or sister to stumble, I will never ever eat meat, so that I won't make my brother or sister trip up. (1 Corinthians 8.7b–13)

The details of the particular discussion here need not concern us. What matters is the phenomenon of the "weak conscience" that can now be "polluted" (verses 7, 10, 12). Paul implies that all humans possess a conscience to which appeal can be made (as also in 2 Corinthians 4.2 and 5.11). However, when people distort their God-given humanness through idolatry, the conscience is pulled this way and that. Initially, it approves of the actions in question; then, following conversion to Jesus Christ, it is horrified by the very thought of them.

Paul wants to argue that, once conscience is properly informed by a strong monotheism, it will come to see that all meat is created by God and therefore fit to eat (1 Corinthians 8.1–6; 10.25–30). However, in the passage quoted above and in 10.27–29, he bends over backward to insist that if a fellow Christian has a weak conscience about such things, due to a background in the world of idolatry, such a person is to be respected. Paul will not ride roughshod over another's scruples, presumably because once you do so, you crush the moral compass altogether. The fact that he is unwilling to do this—though he will continue with the task of trying to educate Christians to think through the issues and come to a different mind—indicates that, for him, paying attention to one's conscience is more important, in some matters at least, than arriving instantly at the "right" solution. This is a tricky place for Paul to be, but it shows not only pastoral wisdom but a clear sense that when we are considering the interior makeup of a Christian whose character is being formed by the Holy Spirit and the practice of Christian habituation, there is something to be set alongside the transformed and renewed mind: a conscience that may, to be sure, need educating, but also needs listening to.

This is presumably what is meant in 1 Timothy:

> What we aim at in our teaching is the love that comes from a pure heart, a good conscience, and sincere faith. (1.5; compare 3.9)

Indeed, the same chapter goes on to emphasize that one cannot simply reject conscience:

> . . . so that, as they said, you may fight the glorious battle, holding on to faith and a good conscience. Some have rejected conscience, and their faith has been shipwrecked. (1.18–19)

Thus one must still attend to conscience, even though it needs to be trained, and may quite possibly either not get fully to the bottom of things or actually give misleading signals. Indeed, Paul believes that when he himself is preaching, or explaining himself to one of his own churches, he is appealing, not just to the minds of listening pagans, but to their consciences. There is something inside them which should give moral as well as intellectual approval to what is being said.

None of this takes us very far in terms of the much later debates about what exactly "conscience" might be, how it operates, what it can know and not know, whether it is always to be trusted, and, not least, what weight to give to it when it appears to conflict with other authority, whether that of scripture, the pope, or anything else! Fortunately, for our purposes we simply need to draw the threads together as follows. Paul is aware, as he looks ahead to the final day when God will judge all secrets of all hearts, that part of the appropriate preparation for that day is to keep a clear conscience. Indeed, he wants to enable people to maintain this clear conscience even when he thinks the conscience in question needs further educating or even realigning.

Whether he would have said all this in all circumstances we may properly doubt. Supposing, for instance, the man guilty of incest in 1 Corinthians 5 had declared that his conscience had told him to do it? (This is, sadly, not uncommon. I recently heard of a clergyman who excused his affair with a married parishioner by explaining that he felt Jesus very close to him when he was engaging in the illicit relationship.) But Paul clearly regards moral self-knowledge as a vital element in the formation of overall moral character. It is, in other words, part of the equipment which sustains the Christian in anticipating in the present time the moral character that will be completed in the future. And, tellingly, conscience is something shared in principle by all people—Jew, Gentile, and Christian alike. It is part of the universal human makeup, subject to the same problems that we find in other aspects of human life but nevertheless to be respected, appealed to, and ultimately brought in line with the gospel.

It would be good if we could ask Paul to explain himself further on all this; but granted that we can't, we return to a cognate subject on which he does have more to say. We come back to Colossians, and to a theme which has been hovering in the air for some time and must now come in to land. Colossians is all about Christian maturity; it is all about learning to give thanks to God; it is all, supremely, about Jesus; and it is therefore, because of and contributing to all of the above, about wisdom.

FIVE

As with Philippians, so in Colossians, Paul describes in lavish detail the prayer he has been praying for the new young church. He has been asking God, he says,

> . . . to fill you with the knowledge of what he wants for you, in all wisdom and spiritual understanding. This will mean that you'll be able to conduct yourselves in a manner worthy of the Lord, and so give him real delight, as you bear fruit in every good work and grow up in the knowledge of God. I pray that you'll be given all possible strength, according to the power of his glory, so that you'll have complete patience and become truly steadfast and joyful. And I pray that you will learn to give thanks to the Father, who has made you fit to share the inheritance of God's holy ones in the light. He has delivered us from the power of darkness, and transferred us into the kingdom of his beloved son. (1.9–13)

This is one of those summary prayers where we find many of the themes of the subsequent letter already set out. Paul first prays that his hearers will come to a particular *understanding,* and then proceeds to spell it out for them in more detail, hoping that the rest of his letter will be part of the means by which God answers his prayer.

Knowing God! That is the heart of it. Knowing God, knowing his will, knowing what he wants for you, and arriving at that knowledge through "all wisdom and spiritual understanding." For this, young Christians will need the strength that likewise comes from God, and they will need to develop patience, steadfastness, joy, and gratitude. And all this is because of the hope that is set before them, as Paul has already said in verse 5: they are to share the inheritance of God's holy ones, and to live within the sovereign rule of God's son, Jesus the Messiah. They are, in short, called to develop those virtues which will fit them for the goal that has been placed before them as a free gift. And central among these virtues is the wisdom which then becomes a main theme of the letter.

Not everyone will notice this, because not everyone will realize that the great poem which then bursts forth in verses 15–20 is in fact based on the ancient Jewish notion of the divine "Wisdom," God's second self, the one through whom all things were planned and created. This theme goes back at least as far as Proverbs 8, which we cannot explore in detail here but in which the figure of Lady Wisdom is calling people to come to her to learn how to be genuinely human. In doing so, she describes her role as YHWH's handmaid in creation itself (verses 22–31). This theme was then developed through various later Jewish writings, and provided a rich context within which the earliest Christian reflection on Jesus's identity came to birth, not only in Paul but also in John and elsewhere.

From within this context Paul (or whoever wrote the poem which he quotes here) places Jesus where Wisdom had been:

> He is the image of God, the invisible one,
>   the firstborn of all creation.
> For in him all things were created,
>   in the heavens and here on the earth.
> Things we can see and things we cannot,
>   —thrones and lordships and rulers and powers—
> All were created both through him and for him.

And he is ahead, prior to all else
    and in him all things hold together;
and he himself is supreme, the head
    over the body, the church.

He is the start of it all,
    firstborn from realms of the dead;
    so in all things he might be the chief.
For in him all the Fullness was glad to dwell
    and through him to reconcile all to himself,
    making peace through the blood of his cross,
through him—yes, things on the earth,
    and also the things in the heavens.

Jesus is the one through whom the creator made all things, and he is now the one through whom the same God has reconciled all things to himself. The second half of the poem, starting with "he is the start" halfway through verse 18, provides the groundwork upon which much of the rest of the letter can then build. Paul's aim is to assure the Colossians that, possessing Jesus Christ, they already have the key to the wisdom they need to develop if they are to attain the goal (here it is yet again) of "completeness," "maturity," "perfection." Such a person is to become *teleios*. It is Christ we proclaim, declares Paul, "warning everyone, and teaching everyone in all wisdom, so that we may present everyone mature [*teleion*] in Christ" (1.28).

And, as we have seen at every stage of our argument, this same setting of the goal—the goal of a complete and finished product of humanness—drives and shapes the habits of mind, heart, and body which will lead to that finished product and, in addition, drives and shapes the way in which those habits must be clearly understood, chosen, and learned.

This is the direction the whole letter takes from this point forward. Paul's basic aim is to draw young Christians toward the full knowledge of God's mystery, Christ himself, "in whom are hidden all the treasures of wisdom and knowledge" (2.3), in contrast to the deceitful human schemes which abound in the present age (2.4, 2.8–23). Once they realize that they are complete in Christ, having been baptized into him and so having died to the present world and come alive in Christ, they do not need the fake varieties of a so-called wisdom, or the schemes of a pseudo-holiness which they will find here and there (perhaps in varieties of Judaism, perhaps in certain types of paganism). This is where one of the passages we examined earlier, Colossians 3.1–17, comes into its own: Christian virtue says to these other schemes, in effect, "Anything you can do, I can do better."

Throughout the second and third centuries, indeed, the early Christians were at pains to make that point, even as their pagan opponents mocked them and killed them. They were modeling a different way of life, a different kind of virtue, outflanking those on offer elsewhere but still with the recognizable classical shape: a clear perception of a goal (*telos*) up ahead, giving rise to fresh, chosen, and worked-at habits of heart, mind, and life. (By the way, I think this helps to explain why Paul doesn't use the normal pagan word for virtue, *aretē:* he is upstaging the entire pagan tradition at this point. In addition, the word itself had by his day developed several related meanings which would have taken him in a different direction.)

Central to this vision of human renewal is part of a verse we deliberately held back in our earlier discussion: Colossians 3.9–10. Do not lie to one another, urges Paul, since you have put off the Old Human with its deeds, and have put on the New Human, *which is being renewed in knowledge according to the image of the one who created it*. Clearly this goes closely with the great poem of chapter 1, where Christ himself is "the image of God, the invisible one, the firstborn of all creation." But equally, too, we have here arrived at a central and vital clue to Paul's whole vision of what Christian virtue is all about. It is about being remade in God's image.

It is, in other words, about becoming genuinely human. Where Aristotle had *eudaimonia,* Paul has "the image of God." This has brought us back at last to where we began—namely, Genesis 1. The call to reflect God's image is the touchstone by which we may judge the "renewal in knowledge" of which Paul speaks. Just as in Romans 12, here the way to the goal is to have the mind renewed.

All this raises a further question: How then is the mind to be renewed? Have we not chased the logic of virtue back to its starting point and discovered that here, after all, there is still something required which the individual Christian must, as it were, summon up from his or her own resources? Not at all. The virtues, as many classical moralists insisted, need one another for completeness. Each depends on the others to stay in place. The other virtues will not work properly unless the mind is fully engaged; but for the mind to be fully engaged, thinking through what Christian behavior involves and aware of the process of developing the necessary moral muscles, there must be fellowship, there must be love, there must be prayer and mutual Christian support. And, above all, there must be a constant fresh word from the Lord himself: "Let the word of Christ dwell in you richly, as you teach one another and warn one another in all wisdom, singing psalms and hymns and spiritual songs, making music with grace in your hearts toward God" (3.16).

A rich mutual ministry of the word, then, is what Paul has in mind: the word both taught and sung, telling and retelling the story of God, the world, Israel, Jesus Christ, and (not least) the future hope. The aim is that individual Christians might have their minds and hearts awakened and alerted to fresh visions of God's reality, of the final hope set before them, and be able to discern in a fresh way what habits of mind and heart and body are necessary if they are to grow into the people God intends.

Colossians is a wonderful resource for reflection on Paul's vision of Christian virtue. But there remains one other source which is arguably greater still.

SIX

The foundation of the letter to the Ephesians, like that of Colossians and Philippians, is prayer. The letter opens with a great paean of praise for God's grace, holding before us the vision of hope which sees God gathering up "all things in Christ, things in heaven and things on earth" (1.10). This is the ultimate promise of the recreated world, which sets the context for the ultimate promise of renewed human beings. Paul then turns at once to describe his prayer for his readers in terms of the *goal* to which they are aiming and the *power* by which they will get there:

> I pray that the God of King Jesus our Lord, the Father of glory, would give you, in your spirit, the gift of being wise, of seeing things people can't normally see, because you are coming to know him and to have the eyes of your inmost self opened to God's light. Then you will know exactly what the hope is that goes with God's call; you will know the wealth of the glory of his inheritance in his holy people; and you will know the outstanding greatness of his power toward us who are loyal to him in faith, according to the working of his strength and power. (Ephesians 1.17–19)

This is once more the classic structure of virtue: glimpse the goal, work out the path toward it, and develop the habits which you will need to practice if you are going to tread that path. This passage does not yet mention the specific moral muscles needed to accomplish all this. It simply assures the faithful of God's power, which will enable those muscles to be developed, those choices made. It prepares the way for the dramatic and decisive opening statements of God's free rescue of sinners (2.1–10) and his resultant incorporation of Gentiles into his ancient people, forming one body in the Messiah and, in consequence, a new Temple where God himself will come to dwell through his Spirit (2.11–22). This picture in the first two chapters— more or less a summary of Paul's entire message—leads to a further explanation of Paul's apostolic agenda (3.1–13) and a further summary prayer (3.14–21).

The first three chapters of Ephesians, breathtaking in their scope and sweep, set the scene for what is often described as the "ethical" section of the letter, chapters 4–6. What is striking about this section is the way in which, again, Paul is operating with what we may call a Christianized virtue ethic, holding before his readers the promise of full human maturity in Christ and urging them to embrace the habits of heart, mind, and life which will lead toward it.

The center of the long opening exhortation may be discerned in 4.13–16. Working toward that central point, Paul notes that Christians are to strive after unity, working hard at loving one another and developing humility, gentleness, and patience (4.1–3), since they are called together to belong to the one God (4.4–6). This is the reason God gives diverse ministries to the church (4.7–12): to build up the body of Christ,

> in order that we should all reach unity in our belief and loyalty, and in knowing God's son. Then we shall have a mature and genuine human life, measured by the standards of Christ's fullness.
>
> As a result, we won't be babies any longer! We won't be thrown this way and that on a stormy sea, blown about by every gust of teaching, by human tricksters, by their cunning and deceitful scheming. Instead, we must speak the truth in love, and so grow up in everything into him—that is, into Christ, who is the head. He supplies the growth that the whole body needs, linked as it is and held together by every joint which supports it, with each member doing its own proper work. Then the body builds itself up in love. (4.13–16)

"A mature and genuine human life": that brings out the full flavor of *eis andra teleion* in verse 13. There it is yet again: the Christian embracing of the goal of being *teleios,* mature, complete, "perfect." The perfection is of course that of Christ himself (which is why, I think, Paul uses the word *andra,* which is specifically masculine, rather than *anthrōpos,* "human"), and the virtues of truth and love are the ways in which we are to "grow up into him," even as the growth is supplied by him in the first place. And, with this initial statement in place, Paul can launch into the quite detailed instructions of 4.17—5.20, which find several parallels in Colossians 3 but, in most cases, with fuller development in Ephesians.

Thus, again, we find Paul emphasizing the renewal of the *mind*. Put away, he says, the Old Human, which is corrupt in accordance with its deceitful desires (deceitful, presumably, because they promise a full and genuine human existence but give exactly the opposite), and "be renewed in the spirit of your minds" (4.23, which we might equally well translate, "Be renewed, in your minds, by the Spirit"), and put on the New Human, who is "created in accordance with God in righteousness and in the holiness which belongs to the truth" (4.24). This is close to Colossians 3.10, and also to Romans 12.2, and with the same import: the goal is the renewed humanity which at last truly reflects God's image, and the pathway to that goal is the renewal and full activity of the mind. There then follows a catalogue of the new habits that must be acquired, and of the old habits and practices that must now be shunned (4.25–5.2; 5.3–20). As always, the eschatological note is never far away: these are not (as the heading in one translation puts it) "Rules for the New Life," but *habits* of heart and mind, ways of learning how to think Christianly about the ultimate future and about the pathway toward it—the pathway which is, as it were, a daily resurrection (5.14). (Again, for the avoidance of misunderstanding: I am not saying that rules are irrelevant or unnecessary within the life of virtue, merely that they are neither the starting point nor the destination.)

SEVEN

All this, from Romans, Philippians, Colossians, and Ephesians, ought to leave us in no doubt that Paul is thinking substantially in terms of an eschatologically driven virtue ethic which outdoes anything the pagan world can offer. He has glimpsed a fresh vision of the ultimate future, which has given him in turn a fresh vision of the habits of life by which humans can already live in the present as people shaped by that future. The goal is God's new creation, and the full human maturity and dignity which will ultimately be celebrated in the resurrection. The pathway to that goal is the complete set of learned habits of life—of heart and body and especially *mind*. Straight, clear, sharp thinking not only grasps the goal and the pathway but is itself part of that maturity of which Paul speaks. To put it the other way around, if the mind is downgraded, one will be less than fully and truly human, partly because one will not grasp the goal or the path and thus will wander off course, but even more so because one part of the fully human makeup will not be in operation, and will not therefore be integrated with everything else.

Thus, as we have seen earlier, *thinking* about what one ought to be doing is one of the key elements in virtue ethics, as opposed to schemes of ethics based either upon mere rules obeyed unthinkingly or upon "spontaneity" or "authenticity." In the former case, you don't need to think anymore once you've got the rules—but, like certain rugby players who have learned dozens of formal "moves" but have never really acquired a second-nature instinct for the game, you will be lost when a new situation arises for which the rules (the formal moves within the rugby game) provide no clear answer. In the latter case—spontaneity or authenticity—you shouldn't think too hard (in fact, you shouldn't really think at all), because what matters is what "comes naturally." Paul does of course want the young Christians to develop to the point where, as mature followers of Jesus Christ, they will gradually find that the Christian habits of heart and life "come naturally." But to get to that point they must learn to *think,* must be "transformed by the renewal of their minds," and must then allow that transformation to inform and redirect their habits of life.

Here, in fact, is one of the major differences between virtue ethics and other schemes of thought: the thinking is front-loaded. A person relying on a duty- or rule-based ethic, faced with a challenge or dilemma, needs to think on the spot: Is there a rule? Is there a duty? Someone using a utilitarian-based ethic needs to do quite a bit of thinking: How will doing this (or not doing it) affect the sum total of human happiness? A person following a spontaneity ethic, of course, won't want to think at all. For someone developing a virtue ethic, on the other hand, the hard thinking has already been done some time before a particular crisis or challenge presents itself. The character has been formed by conscious choice and habit. Whether or not there is time for thought, the emergency will be met and dealt with.

Paul is very much aware that the entire mode of Christian living, more than the sum of its individual "ethical" parts, is a new thing, to be thought through, studied, reflected upon, and practiced, and that without this effort churches will simply slide back into the ways of the old world. And, fully aware of the risks he is taking by going this route, he draws attention to himself (and his close associates) as examples of what this new way of life will look like. His converts will never have seen anyone living this way before, and they must hold before their minds and memories the examples they have:

> So let me appeal to you: copy me! That's why I have sent Timothy to you; he's my child in the Lord, and I love him and trust him. He will remind you how I conduct myself in the Messiah Jesus, just as I teach everywhere, in each assembly. (1 Corinthians 4.16–17)

> Be blameless before Jews and Greeks and the church of God, just as I try to please everybody in everything, not pursuing my own advantage, but that of the great majority, so that they may be saved. Copy me, just as I'm copying the Messiah. (1 Corinthians 10.32–11.1)

> I hope in the Lord Jesus to send Timothy to you soon, so that I may be encouraged in my turn by getting news about you. I have nobody else of his quality: he will genuinely care about how things are with you. All the rest, you see, are looking after their own interests, not those of Jesus the Messiah. But you know how he has proved himself; like a child with a father he has slaved with me for the sake of the gospel. (Philippians 2.19–22)

> Join together in imitating me, my dear family, and pay careful attention to people who behave according to the pattern you have in us. (Philippians 3.17)

This is what you should do: what you learned, received, heard, and saw in and through me. And the God of peace will be with you. (Philippians 4.9)

You know what sort of people we turned out to be, for your sake, when we were amongst you. And you learned how to copy us—and the Lord! (1 Thessalonians 1.5b–6)

You yourselves know, after all, how you should copy us. We didn't step out of line, nor did we eat anyone's food without paying for it. We worked night and day, with labor and struggle, so as not to place a burden on any of you. It wasn't that we don't have the right; it was so that we could give you an example, for you to copy us. (2 Thessalonians 3.7–9)

Throughout these passages, Paul is indicating that there is a new way of living to which Jesus's followers are now committed, and that one of the ways to sustain the commitment to live that way is to hold before the mind such examples as there may be. To this we shall return.

In and through all of this, Paul is explicitly developing an ethic of "character." At the key transition between Romans 4 and Romans 5, in a passage at which we have already glanced in another connection, he sketches out a theory of how character is formed, pointing forward to and deriving its meaning from the ultimate hope, hope for "the glory of God":

The result is this: since we have been declared "in the right" on the basis of faith, we have peace with God through our Lord Jesus the Messiah. Through him we have been allowed to approach, by faith, into this grace in which we stand; and we celebrate the hope of the glory of God.

That's not all. We also celebrate in our sufferings, because we know that suffering produces patience, patience produces a well-formed character [*dokimē*], and a character like that produces hope.

> Hope, in its turn, does not make us ashamed, because the love of God
> has been poured out in our hearts through the Holy Spirit who has
> been given to us. (Romans 5.1–5)

There are two key things here for our present purposes: hope and character construction.

The hope is, as Paul states clearly, "the glory of God." We have spoken of this already in terms of two interlocking themes: the sovereign stewardship over creation entrusted by God to humankind, and the return of the divine glory to dwell amidst God's people after the long years of the Exile. This latter theme seems to be in the back of Paul's mind in several of his writings, but not least here in Romans 5 and in the continuation of the same theme in chapter 8, where the Spirit "dwells within" believers, evoking the theme of God "dwelling in the Temple" in the Old Testament (8.4–11). Frustratingly, the word "glory" is so often used in Christian circles as a vague word for "going to heaven" that these important overtones to the concept of "the glory of God"—overtones that would have been audible to Paul and his first hearers—are often ignored altogether.

What Paul is saying—and it is of central importance for this whole book—is that the hope to which we press, the *telos* or goal of all our pilgrimage, is "the glory of God." When this is explained, it means on the one hand the "royal priesthood" we studied earlier, the vocation of genuine humanness, and on the other hand the place where the living God himself comes to dwell in fulfillment of his ancient promise.

Both parts of this were realized by Jesus himself, as we saw. Paul's point, throughout Romans 5–8 but particularly in chapter 8, is that both are also realized, through the presence and power of the Holy Spirit, in and through God's people. Some people say that the early Christians had no trinitarian theology, but that position can be sustained only by carefully putting the telescope to the blind eye.

But if God's glory is the goal, what is the route toward it? What are the character-forming habits that put together the genuine humans, the God-bearing, Spirit-filled humans, who will one day rule

God's new creation and sum up its praises? In answer we are brought up short with a theme which, as Paul well knew (not least when writing 2 Corinthians), would have been anathema to the whole classical tradition, Aristotle included, and also to anyone, including any Christian, who had not fully thought through the way in which the gospel of Jesus Christ transformed the ideal of human living. The theme is stark and challenging: in order to develop Christian character, the first step is suffering.

Two impulses pushed Paul to this shocking and unwelcome conclusion. There was, first, the suffering of the Messiah himself. Second, there was the suffering which he, Paul, had formerly inflicted upon the church, and had then undergone himself at the hands both of zealous Jews and of pagan authorities and mobs. Acts gives a small window on all this; from 2 Corinthians 11 we may deduce that there was much more besides. But what provided Paul with the theological framework for coming to terms with all this, and indeed making it central in his understanding?

The tradition of ancient Israel within which Paul stood had come, slowly but surely, to understand suffering as somehow falling within the saving purposes of God. This finds expression particularly in books such as Isaiah, Jeremiah, and Daniel, and of course in the Psalms. We know, in addition, that Paul made Jesus's crucifixion thematic for his own life and teaching, as we see in many places, perhaps particularly 2 Corinthians. We do not know, though I think it likely, whether he knew any of the specific traditions stemming from Jesus, such as the Beatitude on those who were persecuted and the challenge to take up the cross. He certainly reflected on suffering in terms of Christians being out of step with the world around them, and at odds with the "powers" that exercise authority within that world. People whose lives cut across the expectations of the world and its rulers can expect to suffer suspicion, hostility, and various forms of attack. People who find themselves in that sort of situation as a result of following a crucified Messiah, and who see his own suffering within the context of the Jewish expectation of God's saving purposes, will have a grid of understanding within which to interpret what is happening to them, and to give it theological and moral meaning.

What we find here in Romans 5 is that Paul incorporates suffering, not only into a general statement about suffering with Christ in order to be glorified with him (see also 8.17; compare 2 Corinthians 4.10 and similar passages such as Philippians 3.10–11), but into a remarkable, almost unique statement about character formation. Suffering produces endurance or patience, endurance produces character (not just any sort of character, but one that has been tried and tested and has proved its worth), and character gives birth to hope, a hope which does not disappoint. This sequence, coming at a crucial turning point in the letter, shows beyond any doubt that Paul did indeed envisage the whole question of Christian living on the model of the classical virtue tradition, but that he had radically rethought this tradition around Jesus and the Spirit, changing both its content and its shape but retaining the key elements, the sense of an ultimate *telos* and the insistence on working toward that goal by character-building, habit-forming steps.

I said that Romans 5.1–5 was almost unique; but there are two other New Testament passages which offer similar sequences of thought, looking for all the world like carefully thought out agendas for the development of virtue:

> Reckon it all joy, my dear family, when you fall into the middle of different kinds of testing. You know that the trying and testing [*dokimion*] of your faith produces patience. And let patience produce its perfect work [*ergon teleion*], so that you may be complete [*teleioi*] and fully kitted out, lacking in nothing. (James 1.2–4)

> That is why you must bring every bit of energy you have to bear on the task of supplementing your faith with virtue [*aretē*, one of only three uses of the word in the New Testament], and virtue with knowledge, and knowledge with self-control, and self-control with patience, and patience with godliness, and godliness with family affection, and family affection with love [*agapē*]. If you have these things in plenty,

you see, they will ensure that you are not wasting your time or bearing no fruit in the knowledge of our Lord Jesus Christ. (2 Peter 1.5–8)

Here we are clearly in the same world of thought. All these characteristics lead to one another, of course. The point is not to spend some years acquiring the first, and then move on to the second, and so on; they work together. And the point is their *forward* look: the aim of it all is to be fruitful in working for Jesus (2 Peter); to be "complete," *teleioi,* ready for whatever contingency may arise, since your character has been formed to be prepared for anything and everything (James). We could no doubt spend much longer on these passages, but the general point is clear.

All this leads to a number of major and interlocking questions which will take us into the next chapter. If this was Paul's theory about Christian living, how did the practice work out? More particularly, where do things such as the "fruit of the Spirit" and the "gifts of the Spirit" fit in? Why does Paul highlight the character traits he does, and what is he able to take for granted when he refers simply to "good" and "evil" in the apparent assumption that his readers will know what he's talking about? When he spells out other instructions, is he simply supplementing his virtue ethic with a few "rules" to carry on with; and if so, is there a reason for this? In particular, and growing out of all of these, why does he again and again highlight faith, hope, and love? What role do those traits play within his overall thinking about Christian character? Are they virtues in any classical sense; and if so, how does putting them in this privileged position alter the very character of virtue itself? And, over and around it all, how does Paul's sense of the church as a single body, a united community, form part of the necessary context for the practice of Christian virtue?

6. THREE VIRTUES, NINE VARIETIES OF FRUIT, AND ONE BODY

ONE

"When 'the perfect' comes, then 'the partial' will be abolished." Some of Paul's hearers might have detected echoes of Aristotle, for whom "perfection," *to teleion,* was the goal. Paul is undoubtedly aware of the tradition of pagan moral thought, but he has translated it into a different register. The line comes, of course, from the heart of Paul's greatest chapter on the greatest virtue, which tells us an enormous amount not only about how he saw that virtue in particular, but about how he understood virtue in general. "We know in part," he says, "and we prophesy in part," contrasting the temporary gifts with the permanent virtue of love, "but when 'the perfect' comes, then 'the partial' will be abolished" (1 Corinthians 13.9–10).

First Corinthians 13 is one of the best-known passages in all of Paul—partly, I suspect, because many couples still choose to have it read in public at their wedding, though if they reflected on it line by line they might find it quite a daunting challenge:

Love is great-hearted; love is kind,
knows no jealousy, makes no fuss,
not puffed up, no shameless ways,
doesn't force its rightful claim;
doesn't rage, or bear a grudge,

doesn't cheer at others' harm,
rejoices, rather, in the truth.
Love bears all things, believes all things;
love hopes all things, endures all things.
Love never fails. . . .

Fair enough to hold before yourselves that astonishing portrait. But don't imagine that you can just step into it on a cheerful sunny morning and stay there effortlessly forever. The last lines tell their own story: bearing, believing, hoping, enduring, never failing—all these speak of moments, hours, days, and perhaps years when there will be things to bear, things to believe against apparent evidence, things to hope for which are not seen at present, things to endure, things which threaten to make love fail. The phrase "tough love" now sounds hackneyed, a relic of social debates from the day before yesterday. But the love of which Paul speaks *is* tough. In fact, it's the toughest thing there is.

The love of which Paul speaks is clearly a *virtue*.

It is not a "rule" of the sort that is so out of fashion nowadays, imposed in an arbitrary fashion and to be obeyed out of a sense of duty. (We shall discuss the more serious question of proper rules and their relation to virtue later on.)

It is not a "principle," a generalized rule which a person either obeys or disobeys.

It is not a "prudential maxim based on calculated effects"; though it has to be said that if even a few more people lived in the way Paul describes, a lot more people would be a lot more happy.

Nor, especially, is it the result of people "doing what comes naturally." At every single point in Paul's catalogue of what love does, and what love doesn't do, we want to say, "Yes, I see what you mean. However, left to my own inclinations, I would be small-minded, unkind, jealous, fussy, puffed up, shameless, and so on. In particular, left to myself, there are some things I wouldn't bear, many things I wouldn't believe, several things I wouldn't be able to hope for, and a whole mul-

titude that I wouldn't endure. Left to myself, doing what comes naturally, I would fail." But the point of love is that it *doesn't*.

That is why love is a virtue. It is a language to be learned, a musical
instrument to be practiced, a mountain to be climbed via some steep
and tricky cliff paths but with the most amazing view from the top. It
is one of the things that will last; one of the traits of character which
provides a genuine anticipation of that complete humanness we are
promised at the end. And it is one of the things, therefore, which can
be *anticipated* in the present on the basis of the future goal, the *telos*,
which is already given in Jesus Christ. It is part of the future which can
be drawn down into the present.

Here—as most people are vaguely aware but few really reflect
on—we have a problem of language. A problem about this particular
blessed word, "love." The English word "love" is trying to do so many
different jobs at the same time that someone really ought to sit down
with it and teach it how to delegate.

It isn't simply a matter, as some people used to think, of getting
back to the "true" meaning of the Greek word *agapē*. That word, actually, had almost as much of a checkered career in the centuries before
and after Paul as our word "love" (and, for that matter, "charity") has
had in the last three hundred years. A glance at the Greek lexicon indicates that *agapē* and its cognates were used across several spectrums
of meaning, covering affection, erotic passion, contentment with
something or someone, prizing something highly, and so on. Sometimes *agapē* was distinguished from *philia* (which we often translate
as "friendship"), and sometimes the two appear to have been interchangeable. The specific meaning of *agapē* which we find in the New
Testament isn't the result of the early Christians discovering a word
which already said exactly what they wanted to say and latching on
to it. Rather, they seem to have settled quickly on this word as the
best available one, and they then gave it the fresh privilege of carrying a new depth of meaning in which some aspects of its previous career were highlighted and others were set aside. The early Christians,
in fact, did with the word *agapē* pretty much what they did with the

ancient notion of virtue. They picked it up, soaked it in the message and achievement of Jesus, and gave it a new life, a new *sort* of life.

It isn't surprising that in the ancient world, just as today, words for "love" would carry a wide variety of meaning and would slide to and fro between those variations. After all, the question of how we humans relate to one another, and of how we mark the fact that we delight in and approve of (or are appalled by and disapprove of) certain styles of that relating, and how these perceptions and moral beliefs change across time and culture, is enormously complex. Novels, poems, plays, and movies—not to mention ordinary experience in families and among friends—scatter so much information on the subject that it's a bit like looking up at the sky on a clear and cloudless night and see- ing not only millions of stars and planets but also meteors, shooting stars, and satellites. There are not just four things called "love," as in the title of C. S. Lewis's important book on the subject. As Lewis him- self would readily have agreed, there are four thousand and four, or perhaps four million and four. We need a huge range of words (as, at least in urban mythology, the Inuit peoples have for different kinds of snow) to map the complex and shifting nature of what, in English, we still just call "love."

Fortunately, in terms of our present argument we don't need to get into that mapwork. We just need to note that Paul, like the other early Christians, settled on the word *agapē* to do a job which nobody had realized needed doing until then. Nobody until then had really glimpsed, in quite the way those early Christians did, the challenge to embody a virtue so profound, so life-changing, so community- defining, so revolutionary—both in its nature and its effects, and in the moral character needed to aspire to it—that people in Paul's own day thought he was mad. Indeed, people ever since, even within the church, have balked at the challenge and settled for second best. Or twenty-second best. *Agapē* sets the bar as high as it can go. The first thing to do before we can discuss it is to acknowledge that we have all failed quite drastically to clear that height. Then, with that on the table, we can set ourselves the task of thinking through, in the first place, what Paul is saying about "the perfect" and "the partial." This is the key to understanding how he supposes virtue works, and what it consists of.

TWO

"When 'the perfect' comes, 'the partial' will be abolished." The word Paul uses for "the perfect" is our old friend *teleios*—the adjective, treated here as a noun, "the perfect [thing]," *to teleion*. This word carries two adjacent meanings which, as with "love" itself, are difficult to bring out in English. On the one hand, it indicates a sense of something having reached its goal at last, of a cup slowly filled but at last brim-full, or a long and winding pilgrimage which has finally arrived at its goal. On the other hand, it gives the slightly different sense of "maturity" or "completeness," contrasting the former in particular with "youthfulness" or "immaturity." That's the sense which Paul then develops in the next verse: having said "when 'the perfect' comes, 'the partial' will be abolished," he goes on at once, "When I was a child, I spoke, thought, and reasoned like a child, but when I became a man, I got rid of [literally, "abolished," as in the previous verse] childish ways."

Paul thus stresses the permanence of *agapē* as the main reason for urging the muddled Christians of Corinth to work at it. This is the language of virtue, albeit obviously in a Christian accent. Aristotle, and the tradition stemming from him, would have seen human maturity simply in terms of "human flourishing," the complete human character in the present life, rather than looking into a coming age in which the partial vision of the present time would give way to face-to-face knowing (verse 12). For Paul, it is the permanence which counts.

The chapter is carefully and beautifully structured in three "movements." In the opening paragraph (13.1–3) Paul stresses that all other Christian experience without *agapē* is worthless. Tongues, prophecy, mystery, knowledge, mountain-moving faith, self-sacrificial living— unless there is *agapē*, you might as well not bother. Then comes the lyrical middle paragraph, quoted at the start of this chapter. Then the final section, balancing the first, and gently but firmly pushing home the point: it is the *permanence* of faith, hope, and love, but especially love, which makes it worthwhile to work at it. First Corinthians 13 advances its point almost as much by its aesthetic appeal as by its logic, though that too is profound.

The final section of the chapter is all about things that won't last and things that will:

> Love never fails. But prophecies will be
> Abolished; tongues will stop, and knowledge, too
> be done away. We know, you see, in part;
> we prophesy in part; but, with perfection,
> the partial is abolished. As a child
> I spoke, and thought, and reasoned like a child;
> when I grew up, I threw off childish ways.
> For at the moment all that we can see
> is puzzling reflections in a mirror;
> then, face to face. I know in part, for now;
> but then I'll know completely, through and through,
> even as I'm completely known. So, now,
> faith, hope, and love remain, these three; and of
> them all, love is the greatest.

This notion of some things that won't last and others that will is based on the assumption, which underlies the argument of Paul's whole letter and will finally be unveiled in chapter 15, that the present life is the first phase in a much longer existence, and that between the present and the ultimate future there will be strong continuity as well as some radical discontinuity. The promise and hope of resurrection, in other words, is the thing that has both reshaped how virtue works and also given it fresh moral content. "If for this life only we have hoped in the Messiah, we are of all people most pitiable" (15.19), and "you know that in the Lord your labor is not in vain" (15.58b).

All this brings into clear focus what was said in scattered fashion earlier in the letter: "Don't judge anything until the time when the Lord comes, who will bring to light things now hidden in darkness and disclose the intentions of the hearts" (4.5); "God raised the Lord and will raise us by his power . . . ; therefore glorify God in your body" (6.14, 20). The continuity between the present life and the future one undergirds much of Paul's teaching about how to behave in the present.

Yes, there are indeed some elements of present Christian life which will no longer be needed: ironically, they include some of the things which the Corinthians, like some people today, are tempted to regard as very "spiritual" and hence superior to the humdrum disciplines of "ordinary" Christian living. Impermanent things include those strange phenomena which can carry the life of heaven into parts of the earth in the present time: tongues, prophecy, and special gifts of "knowledge." All three will be made redundant when the reality comes, as candles are made redundant by the sunrise. A great transition, a great transformation, is on the way, which for us will be like the transformation from childhood to mature adult life, the transition from peering into a smoky mirror to seeing someone face to face (13.12), the shift from glimpsing parts of a jigsaw puzzle but having no idea how they fit together to seeing the whole thing, complete, at a single glance (13.12b)—or, to match more exactly what Paul says, from glimpsing parts of the puzzle to realizing that the Puzzle is not only complete but is looking back at us. "Now I know in part; then I shall know, even as also I am known."

Paul is writing here with a careful subtlety. The contrast of immature childhood and mature adulthood is a metaphor for the coming transition from the present life to the resurrection life, yet it seems more than just a metaphor. There is also a sense, similar to that in Galatians 4.1–7 (though making a slightly different point), that we are indeed God's immature children now, and will one day be grown up. The contrast between looking in a cloudy mirror and seeing face to face is a metaphor for the coming transition, yet for Paul there is a sense that we do indeed at the moment peer into the mist of the present world and dimly discern God and his ways, and that one day we will see clearly. And when he comes to "knowing in part" and knowing fully, as we are fully known (picking up a theme from earlier in the letter, at 8.1–3), we are passing beyond figures of speech into as direct a statement as is possible in such matters. It is as though Paul, though at one level inevitably employing picture language, is constantly working back as best he can toward the reality itself. With that we may perhaps grasp, as well, the explanation for why *agapē* is one of the three things that will last from the present world into the future, and is indeed the principal one of those three things. To know as we are known is to pass beyond virtue into worship; or perhaps we should say it is the point where virtue becomes worship, or where worship becomes the summit of the heart habits we call virtue. It is the point at which we are formed by God's Spirit into a royal priesthood. First Corinthians 13 comes, after all, in between the two chapters in which Paul discusses the church's worshipping life. This is the center of it all.

Thus the *agapē* we are called to practice in the present, to learn like a difficult but powerful language and to practice like a beautiful but complex musical instrument, will last into the future world—indeed, will be gloriously fulfilled in the future world—because it is the very essence of the God we know in Jesus Christ. The God whom Paul had come to recognize in the face of the crucified and risen Jesus is the God of utter self-giving love, and if we humans are called to reflect this God, to be "renewed in knowledge according to his image," then it is not surprising that love of this sort is the key element in that future life and in its anticipation here and now. It will "abide" (13.13); it will remain. It is the supreme example of the principle Paul articulates two chapters later (15.58): what we do in the present, in the Lord, is not wasted. Love is the language they speak in God's world, and we are summoned to learn it against the day when God's world and ours will be brought together forever. It is the music they make in God's courts, and we are invited to learn it and practice it in advance. Love is not a "duty," even our highest duty. It is our destiny.

Welcome, then, to Paul's greatest exposition of the greatest virtue. Here is the goal, the *telos,* the state where we are to share in *to teleion,* "the perfect," "the complete," "the mature." One day the whole cosmos will attain "perfection," "completeness," "maturity." Within that renewed cosmos, human beings will attain the "perfection" proper to them, the "maturity" which will enable them at last to be the royal priesthood, mediating God's wise stewardship to the world and the world's glad worship back to its maker. And if that is the goal, here are the "virtues," the "strengths," the habits of heart, mind, and life which will form you into the person you need to be for that day, and will anticipate, even within the present partial and incomplete world, something of the life of the new and complete one. Virtue, for Paul, is part of inaugurated eschatology, part of the life of the future breaking in to the present. That is why it is both hard and glorious work.

THREE

Before we look any further at the three great virtues, however—not least at the quite natural question, "That's all very well, Paul, but how can we even begin to reach toward such a high ideal?"—we must look at the second great Pauline theme which stands beside it. In Galatians 5 Paul speaks of "the fruit of the Spirit." And here, as in the three great virtues, the top of the list is *agapē.* Clearly these belong together. But how?

When Paul lists nine varieties of the "fruit of the Spirit" (Galatians 5.22–23), he does so having just announced a crucial introductory point: "If you are led by the Spirit, you are not under the Law" (verse 18). In today's climate of thought, with a certain set of questions directing our ethical search, that great statement is almost bound to be misheard and seriously misunderstood.

To show you what I mean about mishearing something because you're thinking of a different set of questions, imagine sitting in a coffee shop and overhearing a snatch of conversation from the next table.

You have no idea who the people are, or what they're talking about. All you hear is a single sentence: "We shall end it at C."

What does it mean?

Perhaps the people are part of an educational board, trying to produce a new structure for recording and tabulating exam results. Do we want a structure with five "passing" grades, A, B, C, D, and E, with F meaning "Fail"? Or is that too drastic? Do we really need *five* grades? No, declares, the chairman; the list will be long enough with just three categories: "We shall end it at C." That's as far as we need to go.

Or supposing they're from a publisher's office, trying to decide where to divide a multivolume encyclopedia. Clearly the book is going to spread way beyond a single volume, or even two or three. But all the early material is now in hand, and the question is, at what point in the alphabet are we going to call a halt to volume 1? Answer: "We shall end it at C." The next volume will, perhaps, run from D to F.

Or supposing they're discussing a possible Mediterranean cruise. The ship will be stopping at various ports, but one of the participants is hoping to meet up with a friend who will be on shore near one of the scheduled port calls. She is asking the organizers whether it would be possible for her friend to come to the party on board ship that night, and then disembark again before the ship sails. Sorry, no, comes the reply. The ship will need to catch the evening tide. As for the party, "We shall end it at sea," the ship having already sailed.

We might imagine other examples, too—think, for instance, of the composer Jean Sibelius, planning to end his matchless Seventh Symphony at the point where the music finally resolves into a great chord of C major—but the point is no doubt clear already. A single sentence can carry quite different meanings, depending on the implicit question or set of questions the hearer has in mind to which the sentence is perceived as the answer.

So with Paul. "If you are led by the Spirit, you are not under the Law." Someone today catching just that snatch of conversation is very likely to hear it in terms of the strong implicit debate between those who think you should order your life by "rules" and those who think that what matters is "doing what comes naturally," living "spontaneously" or "authentically." And it isn't just our *cultural* climate that makes us assume that's the sort of conversation we're overhearing. For four hundred years the *religious and theological* climate has conditioned us to hear a religious version of the same point. Ever since the Reformation at least, a large number of Christians have assumed that the foundation of Paul's thinking goes like this: He spent the first part of his life trying to keep the rules of his religion, and then discovered not only that he couldn't but that rules weren't the point. God didn't want rule-keeping; he wanted "spontaneity." God had forgiven him all his rule-breaking, in and through Jesus Christ, and was now giving him his Spirit, who would produce the "fruit" without all that horrible moral striving.

But is that what the conversation at the next table was really all about?

In this way of interpreting, the listener assumes that when Paul says "law" or "the Law," he isn't meaning the Jewish Law, the Law of Moses, or at least not particularly. If there is a reference to it, it's just because that was the particular type of "law" Paul knew. From this point of view, we are all "under the law" in some sense or other, since all human beings are aware of some kind of moral code hanging over them, telling them what to do and making them feel guilty when they don't. And Paul's message, within this way of thinking, is, "You're free from all that! The Spirit will guide you from within, and you don't need to bother about all those rules that come at you from somewhere else, from tradition or philosophy or the Old Testament! Stop worrying about all that moralism; lighten up and be spontaneous. You don't have to *try*! Moral effort is a sign that you're still on the wrong track. All you have to do is to go with the flow of the Spirit!"

All of which is no more relevant to what Paul is actually talking about than the "encyclopedia" meaning is when someone overhears the travel agent saying, "We shall end it at sea." Paul is *not* discussing the question of rules versus spontaneity. He is talking about the great change that has come over the people of God with the death and resurrection of the Messiah and the gift of the Spirit.

"The Law"—that is, the Mosaic Law—was God's gift for the period of time that came to an end with the Messiah. Paul argued that point in Galatians 3.15–29. This, however, has come as news to some in the Galatian church, who had been taught that the Mosaic Law—at least those stipulations (such as circumcision and the food laws) which marked out Jews from their pagan neighbors—was to be required of all converts from paganism, to make sure they were genuinely members of God's people, were truly Abraham's children. Paul disagrees: Abraham's children consist of all those who believe in Jesus the Messiah and are baptized into him, no matter what their ethnic origin, and no matter what their relation to the Jewish Law.

Paul then turns the tables on his opponents with considerable irony, and this is the context in which he expounds the various "fruit of the Spirit," with *agapē* at the head. All this concentration on the Mosaic Law, the Torah, has resulted in huge fights within the Galatian church. Isn't that a sign that something has gone wrong? After all, the best available summary of the whole law is "Love your neighbor as yourself" (Galatians 5.14). As in Romans 13.8–10, which we shall consider later on, Paul here in Galatians is quoting from Leviticus 19.18. Yes, he says, "the whole Law is summed up in this one saying: Love your neighbor as yourself." So how can you be law-abiding if you are breaking the most fundamental principle of the Law itself? On the contrary: you are going in the opposite direction, and asking for mutual destruction (5.15).

What is the alternative? Summarizing in a dense couple of sentences what he will later spell out in much more detail in Romans, Paul indicates that there is a way to fulfill what the Law was really trying to accomplish—but it isn't the way of "the flesh." Here the argument turns on the ambiguity of this key term. For Paul, "flesh" is not simply "physicality." It always carries the connotation of "corruptibility" or actual "rebellion," of the turning away of humankind in general, or Israel in particular, from God. Paul has been specially concerned to emphasize that circumcision is merely a matter of "flesh": not that he has suddenly become a dualist, rejecting the physical world of space, time, and matter, but that for him the word "flesh" is a way of denoting "that which will decay and die." "Flesh" is not something that will *last*. There it is again, as in 1 Corinthians 13: "When 'the perfect' comes, then 'the partial' will be abolished."

So now he says, You need to escape from "the flesh," not go courting it! If you emphasize "flesh," see what company you will be keeping! You will be putting yourselves alongside those very pagans whose lifestyle you so despise! So you need to order your life in line with the Spirit; that is the way—the only way—to avoid "the works of the flesh" that you see all around you within paganism. You can't do it through circumcision and outward or ethnic adherence to the Mosaic Law.

Now at last we can understand the significance of the throwaway line we have overheard from the next table. "If you are led by the Spirit, you are not under the *Mosaic* Law." This has nothing whatever to do with preferring spontaneity to rules. It has everything to do with the new covenant in which God is pouring out his Spirit upon those who are "in Christ" so that in them the life which the Law wanted to produce, but could not, will at last be fulfilled (see Romans 8.1–11). And when that happens—this is the point of being "not under the Law"—the Mosaic Law has no role in producing this behavior, even though, as it were, it might now look on and applaud from the sidelines. In other words, *you do not have to become a Jew, by taking on the Mosaic Law, in order to be a flourishing and fruitful member of God's people*. In fact, paradoxically, if you *do* go that route you will find yourself stuck at the same level as the pagans from whom you want to distance yourself!

Thus Paul launches into the list of those behaviors he associates with "the flesh"—many of which, as we noted before, could be practiced by a malevolent disembodied spirit, so there's no question of his disapproving of these styles of action because they have anything to do with "physicality." Rather, he disapproves because they're what happens when humankind turns in on itself and away from God:

> Now the works of the flesh are obvious. They are such things as fornication, uncleanness, licentiousness, idolatry, sorcery, hostilities, strife, jealousy, bursts of rage, selfish ambition, factiousness, divisions, moods of envy, drunkenness, wild partying, and similar things. I told you before, and I tell you again: people who do such things will not inherit God's kingdom. (5.19–21)

Notice the last line: the kingdom is coming, on earth as in heaven, and these are the roads which do *not* lead in that direction. They are the ways in which people on earth keep the life of heaven at bay, and so make a covenant with death, declaring by their behavior that they want to keep earth just the way it is, in its present corrupt and decaying form. As with virtue, so with vice: the point is not that these styles of behavior are prohibited by some arbitrary legalistic divinity, determined to stop humans "being themselves" or "having a good time." These are things which exhibit the signs of dehumanization, of that corrupt version of humankind which, left to itself, is keeping God's promised future at bay. What's more, as Shakespeare saw only too well, they are customs of the heart—habits—which will solidify and prove next to impossible to shift. That's the point of the word "vice": once the habits settle down, they will have you in a grip which you won't be able to loosen.

By contrast, "the fruit of the Spirit is love, joy, peace, greatheartedness, kindness, generosity, faithfulness, gentleness, self-control. There is no law that opposes things like that!" (5.22–23). The last line is heavily ironic: "I think you'll find that none of those things is against the Law!"—in other words, "If this is what God's redeemed people look like, don't you think the Law would be extremely pleased?" It indicates the main thing Paul is saying. He is *not* saying, "Once the Spirit has taken up residence in a person or community, these are the things which will happen automatically," as though thereby to reinforce the romantic or existentialist approach to behavior against some kind of legalism. Nor is he saying, "Now that you've got the Spirit, isn't it great that you can get rid of that silly old Law with all its moral restrictions?" Rather, he is saying, "This, after all, is the behavior which the Spirit produces; can't you see that you don't need to impose the Mosaic Law on converts in order to generate people like that?"

We should note carefully that Paul writes here of the fruit, singular, not the fruits, plural, of the Spirit. Just as Plato and others insisted that if you want truly to possess one of the cardinal virtues you must possess them all—because each is, as it were, kept in place by the others—so Paul does not envisage that someone might cultivate one or two of these characteristics and reckon that she had enough of an orchard to be going on with. No: when the Spirit is at work, you will see all nine varieties of this fruit. Paul does not envisage specialization.

And, just to be clear what is *not* meant, he rounds off the discussion with a sentence which functions as a warning to his readers not to imagine that they can stay with "the flesh" and expect still to be part of the Christ-people, the messianic community. "Those who belong to the Messiah Jesus," he says, "crucified the flesh with its passions and desires" (5.24). They *crucified* the flesh: this corresponds to what Paul said near the start of the theological argument of the letter: "I have been crucified with the Messiah" (2.19). And this sentence, though designed for another purpose, serves to alert us, with our own questions, to a key point which could otherwise be overlooked.

The key is this: the "fruit of the Spirit" *does not grow automatically*. The nine varieties of fruit do not suddenly appear just because someone has believed in Jesus, has prayed for God's Spirit, and has then sat back and waited for "fruit" to arrive. Oh, there may well be strong and sudden initial signs that fruit is on the way. Many new Christians, particularly when a sudden conversion has meant a dramatic turning away from a lifestyle full of the "works of the flesh," report their own astonishment at the desire that springs up within them to love, to forgive, to be gentle, to be pure. Where, they ask, has all this come from?

I didn't used to be like this. That is a wonderful thing, a sure sign of the Spirit's working.

But this doesn't mean it's all downhill from there. These are the blossoms; to get the fruit you have to learn to be a gardener. You have to discover how to tend and prune, how to irrigate the field, how to keep birds and squirrels away. You have to watch for blight and mold, cut away ivy and other parasites that suck the life out of the tree, and make sure the young trunk can stand firm in strong winds. Only then will the fruit appear.

And, in case anyone should think I am imposing an alien note on Paul's cheerful list of these wonderful characteristics (surely, thinks the easygoing romantic Christian, all these things will just happen by themselves now that the Spirit is within me!), we note the final characteristic in the list: self-control. If the "fruit" were automatic, why would self-control be needed? Answer: it isn't, so it is: it isn't automatic, so it is needed. All the varieties of fruit Paul mentions here are comparatively easy to counterfeit, especially in young, healthy, happy people—except for self-control. If that isn't there, it's always worth asking whether the appearance of the other sorts of fruit is just that, an appearance, rather than a real sign of the Spirit's work.

That, we may guess, is why Paul immediately adds the note of crucifixion. "Those who belong to the Messiah Jesus crucified the flesh with its passions and desires" (verse 24). There are many parasites, many alien shrubs that will threaten to choke the fruit-bearing tree, many predators ready to nibble the roots or snatch the fruit before it ripens. There must be a conscious choice of mind, heart, and will to deal with all such enemies without mercy. Suddenly we realize that we are in exactly the same place Colossians 3.5 took us: "Put to death therefore all that is earthly." For "earthly" in Colossians read "flesh" in Galatians: Paul's point is substantially the same in both places, as we see in the overlap between the things that need to be killed off in Colossians and the "works of the flesh" in Galatians. Only when this putting to death is done can Paul's closing command be obeyed: "If we live by the Spirit, let's line up with the Spirit" (5.25). The second clause could be translated "let's walk by the Spirit," but the root for "walk" can also refer to things lined up in a row, and in either case the point is clear: just because you "live in the Spirit," that doesn't make following the Spirit's direction automatic. You have to *choose* to do it. And you can.

This is the very point on which, many centuries later, Paul could have been invoked to settle a long-running argument in discussions of morality. Some theologians have distinguished carefully between the sort of virtue you can acquire by unaided hard work and the sort you can have only if God gives it to you. The question is then raised, Is there no work involved in the latter kind? Paul's answer is emphatic, here and throughout his writings. Christian virtue, including the nine-fold fruit of the Spirit, is *both* the gift of God *and* the result of the person of faith making conscious decisions to cultivate this way of life and these habits of heart and mind. In technical language, these things are both "infused" and "acquired," though the way we "acquire" them is itself, in that same language, "infused." We are here, as so often in theology, at the borders of language, because we are trying to talk at the same time about "something God does" and "something humans do" as if God were simply another character like ourselves, as though (in other words) the interplay of God's work and our work could be imagined on the model of two people collaborating on a project. There are mysteries here that we do not need to explore further at this point. It is sufficient to note that the varieties of spiritual fruit Paul names, like the Christian virtues, remain both the work of the Spirit and the result of conscious choice and work on the part of the person concerned.

We could make the same point by a different route, joining up with some of our earlier discussions. The basic command to human beings (and to the whole animal kingdom; as I wrote this sentence, two sparrows outside my window were delightfully obeying the Creator's command) was to "be fruitful and multiply." Paul can draw on exactly that language to refer to the early growth in faith and life of the young Christian churches (e.g., Colossians 1.6, 10). But the point about spiritual fruit is that, however healthy the tree, it has to be looked after.

Leave it for too long untended and unpruned, and it will go wild. Once again, the conduct which Paul expects the Spirit to produce will not come by the Spirit's bypassing the mind, the will, the conscious choice of young Christians. They have to crucify the flesh. They have to be transformed by the renewal of their minds. Then, when they are "led by the Spirit," they will not be "under the Law"; but they will not be living in the romantic ideal of spontaneous, unreflective behavior either, any more than they will be blindly following a list of arbitrary rules. They will be discovering the true meaning of human "freedom" (5.1, 13), the meaning for which humans were made in the first place, the meaning to which the Jewish Law pointed, but which they can attain only through dying and rising with the Messiah. They will be truly "free," walking on the high road that leads to that full authenticity which is the goal of Christian living. And the road consists of the Spirit-led practice, like the practice of a language or a musical instrument, of the Christian virtues.

FOUR

So where do the three virtues and the ninefold types of fruit join up? How do they work together, as Paul clearly thinks they do? The serious reader of Paul naturally approaches this question from one angle, trying to see Paul's ethical thought as a clear and coherent structure, but of course Paul himself approaches it from a variety of different angles, depending on which question he is addressing to which church. We can, however, begin to draw some threads together before moving on to the third main theme of this chapter, the appeal for unity—and the habits of heart, mind, and practice which contribute toward it.

First, does it not look as though—despite our insistence that virtue is the deep center of what Paul is exploring—that he is bringing in "rules" again, but by the back door? When he describes in detail how *agapē* behaves—not jealous or boastful, not arrogant or rude, and so on—and when he insists that "the whole Law is summed up in this commandment," is he not saying, "Well, you must cultivate these habits, but this is because that's the best way to keep the rules"?

The answer to this question is no, but explaining that leads us to an interesting point. There is an old saying: Give someone a fish and you feed them for a day; teach someone to fish and you feed them for life. Paul's normal practice, in teaching his converts, is the latter. His version of the saying seems to be: Give people a command for a particular situation, and you help them to live appropriately for a day; teach them to think Christianly about behavior, and they will be able to navigate by themselves into areas where you hadn't given any specific instructions. But what Paul does, again and again, is to give *initial guidelines,* especially in areas where the outworking of Christian virtue will lead people into behavior patterns that will look surprising to them, and perhaps shocking to their neighbors. They will need to be reassured that this is indeed the way to go. Instructions that could look like simple old "rules" are, for the most part, guidelines to keep them on track while they are learning the habits of the heart. Just as he is certainly not lapsing back into a legalism which would undermine his teaching on grace and faith—that was always a strange suggestion, which could only have grown out of a misreading of him in the first place—so he is not lapsing back toward a rules-based ethic while purporting to advocate a virtue-based one.

Another illustration may help—and may show that this is not a matter of playing rules and virtue off against each other, but of seeing the former within the larger framework of the latter. When the local authorities build roads for cars to travel long distances—highways, motorways, call them what you will—they naturally intend that people should drive along these roads in full control of their cars. Ideally, nobody will ever stray from their side of the road into the path of traffic coming in the other direction. But because from time to time people have been known to lose concentration, to fall asleep at the wheel, to be distracted by a pet dog in the back seat, or whatever—and because sometimes a puncture or other mechanical failure may cause a car to behave erratically, no matter what the driver is doing—

the wise highway builders construct a central barrier so that any car drifting toward the oncoming traffic will be stopped in its tracks. Better to bounce back among cars going in the same direction than lurch into a head-on collision. Likewise, they build a "rumble strip" at the outer edge of the highway, short of any fence or ditch, which makes a loud noise if your wheels touch it, to keep drivers from running off the road. Those responsible for building roads are not saying, "There you are; there's a nice crash-barrier. Bounce off that and you'll be all right." They're saying, "You are supposed to drive down the road without touching the barriers. But if something goes wrong, you may need to know that the barrier is there."

Applying this to Paul's ethics, we may want to add that, amid the multiple moral muddles of ancient paganism, and with his wide and diverse pastoral experience, Paul is no doubt well aware that however much he may want the virtues and the fruit to be chosen, developed, and put into practice by every single Christian and by the church as a whole, there are going to be many cases where one cannot simply wait for that to happen. One cannot, in the meantime, leave people with no guidelines as to where the virtues ought to be leading, any more than you can leave new converts without clear indications of which styles of behavior will in fact cohere with "being in Christ" and which won't. (Think, for example, of 1 Thessalonians 4.) This could appear to be circular reasoning (seeing right actions as the things which stem from the virtues, and then seeing the virtues as the things which produce right actions—which is producing which?), but that would be to flatten out what Paul is doing. He is engaged in active pastoral ministry, not simply in moral theorizing. And if he sees a car careening out of control, well off the track that faith, hope, and love should have been directing, he won't wait for the crash to happen, and lessons to be learned, if he can possibly help it. Stepping in with some firm "rules," as (for instance) in 1 Corinthians 5 and 6, does not mean that he has given up inculcating virtue and is going back to rules, let alone to "the Law" itself. Rather, he is displaying the skill of the pastor: knowing when to let the young pupil learn from mistakes made, and when to push the theory toward the back burner and go to the rescue.

We could develop the driver/car/highway image in a different direction as well. I was driving the other day in a part of the country I know vaguely but, as it turned out, insufficiently. The main highway was blocked by an accident, so I turned off onto a side road. Following my nose, I zigzagged across country lanes in roughly the right direction, but frequently came to turnings and junctions where there was no signpost. Obviously the locals who use those roads know which way to go; but I, a comparative stranger, did not. I could have benefited from "rules"—signposts that said, in effect, "This is the way"—until the day when I had "learned the road" and didn't need them any more. Experienced local drivers would only glance at such a sign, because of course they know already which way to go. Rules and virtue go together; but, in a society where rules have often been perceived as arbitrary and restrictive, we need to remind ourselves how they should actually work, not so that we can rehabilitate an unthinking keeping-the-rules mentality but so that we can see, on a broad canvas, the truth which Paul highlights in Romans 8.3: what the Law could not do . . . God has done.

All this leads us to two other questions which are often asked about virtue, and to which Paul's virtue ethic offers clear answers. First, isn't it self-centered to shine the spotlight of moral discourse on the virtues that the individual is supposed to be cultivating? Isn't morality supposed to be about directing attention toward others? And, second, doesn't a focus on virtue mean that the moral value of the individual is going to be determined to a large extent by accidents of birth, personality, nature, and nurture?

No; and no. Answering these two questions will draw us to the heart of what Paul says about the virtues and the ninefold fruit. These characteristics are precisely generated by, and constitutive of, the life and work of an entire community, not of isolated individuals, and they are designed to contribute to that life and work, not to draw attention to the individual who is exercising them. And, however much they are deliberately thought out, chosen, and practiced, they remain, for the Christian, the gift of God's grace.

To explain this, we need first to broaden out the picture to include the two characteristics which Paul declares will "last" into God's new world alongside love: faith and hope. It's worth noting that this trio, found at the climax to 1 Corinthians 13, regularly occur together in Paul, in letters normally regarded as both early and late:

> We remember before God our father your work of faith, your labor of love, and your patient hope in our Lord Jesus Christ. (1 Thessalonians 1.3)

> We who are of the day should stay awake, and put on the breastplate of faith and love, and for a helmet the hope of salvation. (1 Thessalonians 5.8)

> We have heard of your faith in Christ Jesus and the love which you have for all the saints, through the hope which is stored up for you in the heavenly places. (Colossians 1.4–5)

Two of these sentences are found in opening greetings, indicating that these are the categories for which Paul reaches when he wants to say, "You are showing all the signs of being a healthy Christian community." It's interesting, too, that the passage from 1 Thessalonians 5 is the passage we noted earlier, which says, We are daytime people, even though the world sleeps on! As in 1 Corinthians, then, the three virtues are to be found in an eschatological context. These are the things which belong to the new day that is dawning, and which you must make every effort to put on in the present time.

But now a further puzzle appears. It may be clear that love is a virtue, in the sense of being an aspect of present hard-won discipleship which genuinely anticipates the central feature of the life of the coming age; but how does this apply to faith and hope? Surely they are temporary, along with tongues, prophecy, and the other features of

present Christian living which we will do without in the age to come?
One hymn puts it like this:

> Faith will vanish into sight;
> Hope be emptied in delight;
> Love in heaven will shine more bright;
> Therefore give us love.[1]

This stanza comes from the nineteenth-century hymn "Gracious
Spirit, Holy Ghost," by Bishop Christopher Wordsworth; this is the
more surprising, in that Wordsworth was an expositor of the New
Testament, and much of the hymn in question is directly drawn from
1 Corinthians 13. But that chapter insists, as we have seen, that these
three *abide*. They will last into the future world. Faith and hope will
not vanish or be emptied. Why not?

It is true that faith and hope do at present seem to us to be looking
forward to the new age, so that we might assume that when that new
age comes they will be redundant. But Paul is seeing much deeper than
that. Faith is the settled, unwavering trust in the one true God whom
we have come to know in Jesus Christ. When we see him face to face
we shall not abandon that trust, but deepen it. Hope is the settled, unwavering confidence that this God will not leave us or forsake us, but
will always have more in store for us than we could ask or think. I do
not imagine for a minute that in the coming age we shall arrive at a
point where we shall have experienced everything the new world has
to offer, and will become bored (as is imagined by some scornful contemporary visions of "heaven"). That is a gross caricature, born of the
bland talk about "heaven" which has characterized "afterlife" specula-
tion in the Western world over the last century or two. In contrast,
because I believe that the God we know in Jesus is the God of utterly
generous, outflowing love, I believe that there will be no end to the
new creation of this God, and that within the new age itself there
will always be more to hope for, more to work for, more to celebrate.
Learning to hope in the present time is learning not just to hope for a

better place than we currently find ourselves in, but learning to trust the God who is and will remain the God of the future.

So, back to the two objections: Is this virtue ethic actually self-centered, and does it lean too much on accidents of character given at birth? This brief analysis of faith and hope, and the more obvious analysis we could give of love (where love in the present is the anticipation of the mutual delight and affirmation that passes between God and his creatures, and between the creatures themselves), ought to be sufficient to answer the first of these. To speak of "virtue" is indeed to say that we are concerned with the moral growth, the habits of the heart, of every single individual. But to insist that the three primary virtues are faith, hope, and above all love is to insist that to grow in these virtues is precisely to grow in *looking away from oneself* and toward God on the one hand and one's neighbor on the other. The more you cultivate these virtues, the less you will be thinking about yourself at all.

We have here stumbled upon one of the most obvious differences between Christian virtue and that of the ancient pagans. Pagan virtue aimed at cultivating hero-figures, brave, resourceful leaders, especially in war. Aristotle's ideal of virtue was, granted, developed within the context of the *polis,* the city-state, since (as he rightly saw) humans are social animals. But the virtues remain those of the individuals who stand out from the crowd. Christian virtue is, by definition, not like that. As we said earlier, it is a team sport, and it can be effective only when each member of the large and diverse team is playing his or her unique and distinctive part, in careful relation to every other member and for the good of the team as a whole.

Is it paradoxical to say that cultivating virtue is a matter of looking away from yourself? If so, the paradox is only apparent, not real. Of course morality must take root deep within the individual. To insist on that, as virtue does, is to insist that it is neither an externally imposed rule, nor a calculation of consequences that could in principle have been done by a computer, nor a matter of discovering what is in the depth of one's heart and being true to it. But if "morality" ends up coming to its focal point in faith, hope, and love, then—though it will spring from deep within—its actual focal point is outside the self and in the God and the neighbor who are being loved, in the God who is the object of faith and hope and the neighbor who is to be seen, and loved, in the light of that faith and that hope. Or, to put it another way: at this point, even the words "faith," "hope," and "love" can let us down. The point of all three is not "Look, here are three qualities I'm developing in myself." To say that of faith, hope, and love is to perform a self-contradiction. All three, themselves gifts from God, point away from ourselves and outward: faith, toward God and his action in Jesus Christ; hope, toward God's future; love, toward both God and our neighbor.

The second objection was that a focus on virtue might appear arbitrary, in that some people seem to have the right sort of character as an accident of birth or as the product of a particular upbringing. And of course there is apparent substance to this claim. Bill may appear to have a head start in some of the relevant areas, and that is not to be scorned; he grew up in a loving, supportive family, and so was much more likely to be outward-looking and generous than Ben, who grew up surrounded by selfishness, abuse, and violence. But Paul's answer would be, without a doubt, that this is beside the point when it comes to the Christian character of virtue. "Those who belong to the Messiah Jesus crucified the flesh": there are no exceptions, no categories of people who can, as it were, slide sideways into the holiness which the gospel generates without going the painful route of crucifixion with the Messiah and then the hard moral effort needed to cultivate the virtues in all their fullness. (Think, for a start, of the number of areas of life covered by Paul's brief analysis of *agapē*!) Bill may well imagine that his background makes him a superior kind of being. Much is expected of those to whom much is given, and the deadliest snake of all, pride, is always lurking in the long grass, ready to bite those who fancy themselves effortlessly superior to their disadvantaged neighbors. Ben, glimpsing the difference between his background and the life of genuine Christianity, may take a flying and grateful leap into the new world. We come back to the question of being "renewed in knowledge according to the image of the creator." This is not a matter of preformed character, but of choices thought through, reasoned out, and implemented, of the new language learned, practiced, and spoken, at first stumblingly and then, gradually, with increasing fluency.

As with the virtues, so with the fruit of the Spirit. In fact, the closer we get to understanding the two categories, the more we realize that they are two ways of saying the same thing. We shall study the lists of virtues and spiritual fruit more fully in a moment, in search of their inner dynamic and practical outworkings, and we shall discover that Paul is simply coming at the same deep-level reality from different angles, in obedience to the rhetorical needs of the different contexts he is addressing. The point of using the term "fruit," after all, is that these are things which grow from within rather than being imposed from without. Once we get over the common misperception that, if it is fruit, it ought to happen without our making any effort or thinking it through—actually, any Christian with any self-awareness ought to realize the flaw in that quite quickly!—then we are free to recognize that the different varieties of fruit are, like the virtues, characteristics that need to be thought through, chosen with an act of mind and will, and implemented with determination even when the emotions may be suggesting something quite different. That is how you acquire a taste, or a skill. That is how you learn a language. That is how you are recreated as a fully human being, reflecting God's image. That is how you become, in advance, part of the "royal priesthood."

That, after all, is where all this is going. Ultimately, God does not want, and Paul does not suppose that God wants, human beings as perfected individuals, all clean and scrubbed but with nothing to do. Morality, surprisingly to some, is part of *mission*. Cleansed vessels are to be put to fresh use; conversely, fresh use requires cleansing. But before we can explore this further, we must look at the *corporate* virtue in which the virtues and the sorts of fruit come together. Paul insists that the church must be, must think of itself as, and must make every effort to remain, one body.

FIVE

It isn't difficult, when you read Paul's lists of virtues and vices, to see one of the principal effects of following the one list or the other. Imagine living in a community where, day by day, the normal habit of life for most people includes immorality, bad temper, jealousy, factions, envy, and so on. Then imagine living in a community where, day by day, the normal habit of life is patience, kindness, gentleness, and self-control—not to mention love, joy, and peace. In one of C. S. Lewis's most memorable images, sketched in *The Great Divorce,* hell is a place where people live further and further apart from one another, since they are always quarreling and moving off somewhere else, muttering about how badly everyone else has behaved and how it's all someone else's fault. Of course, anyone with a bit of experience of the church knows that "getting on with one another" may sometimes be only skin-deep. There are, sadly, plenty of communities which are outwardly very pleasant but which, deep down inside, are pits of snakes. But the fact that many of us find the ideal hard to attain doesn't mean it isn't what we should aim at. In fact, our frustration when we meet that kind of split-level community, shiny on the surface and rotten underneath, ought simply to increase our sense that the corporate virtue of unity is well worth working for.

But work we shall have to do. Commands such as the following seem quite extraordinary and unreal to us today, and we have no reason to suppose that they were any easier in the first century:

So if there is any comfort in the Messiah; if there is any consolation from love; if there is any partnership in the Spirit; if your hearts are at all moved with affection and mercy—then make my joy complete! Bring your thinking into line with one another, in this way: hold on to the same love; bring your innermost lives into harmony with each other; set your minds on the same object; do nothing from selfish ambition or vanity, but in humility reckon each other as superior to yourselves; don't look after your own interests, but each other's. (Philippians 2.1–4)

It's breathtaking, but it looks as though Paul really meant it. And it's not an optional extra, a further moral mountaintop for the intrepid few who have already climbed all the other peaks in the district and are looking for new challenges. This, you might say, is what Paul means by declaring that love is the virtue that binds all the others together (Colossians 3.14). This *is* love-in-action; or, rather, it is the starting point for love-in-action. Unity of heart and mind among believers is only the beginning. From here, the gospel of active, generous love can go out into the rest of the world.

There were, of course, particular pressures in the first century which made it vital that the Christians should cherish their unity. Persecutions came and went; but when the early Christians and their bizarre message met blank incomprehension, and when their gatherings aroused multiple suspicions of unpleasant, illicit rituals (were they really talking about *eating* someone?) and worries about political subversion (were they really talking about "another king"?), the followers of Jesus needed to stick closely together. Any divisions in the tiny little fellowships would be potentially disastrous, both for their internal health and for their external witness. One of the regular tragedies to this day among small groups of Christians who are faced with hostility from outside is how easily, addressing that threat, they turn their frustrations on one another in factional fighting within the community itself.

And even where that doesn't happen, we who have lived for many generations with the phenomenon of "denominations" may well sigh and throw up our hands. Our denominations, with all their ambiguities and puzzles, are often rooted in the very kind of ethnic distinctions or personality-based divisions which Paul went out of his way to combat. Perhaps that is one reason why moral discussions in the church tend to go round and round in small circles on a few favored issues, especially sex: discussing how, why, and when two human beings come together in a loving or quasi-loving act may be, after all, a displacement activity when we can't cope with the question of how, why, and when a whole family of Christians should (but can't) come together in mutual love and support. That doesn't mean that sexual ethics are unimportant. On the contrary, they are symptomatic of the health or unhealth of the wider community. But we shouldn't focus all our worries on the fact that the church secretary has run off with the organist's spouse when the promised unity of Jesus Christ with all his people is flouted by structures and customs—and sometimes, yes, theology!—which destroy the fabric of the church just as surely as adultery destroys the fabric of the community. And we shouldn't concentrate all our attention on the fact that the church treasurer has embezzled a thousand dollars, reprehensible though that is, when the entire banking system has crashed into chaos through the mind-blowing greed of those at the top. Personal morality is enormously important, but overconcentration on it can function as a displacement activity when we don't want to address the larger, equally important issues.

(Having said that, the two examples, of adultery and embezzlement, demonstrate the danger of allowing morality to be thought of solely in terms of "rules" which are either obeyed or disobeyed. All right, the treasurer has taken money belonging to the church. But now that he has confessed, shouldn't we be gracious, not inform the police, remind ourselves that Jesus welcomed sinners, and reinstate him? It's not that simple. What this fails to take into account is the extent to which the breaking of the "rule" against embezzling funds is far more than just cutting across an arbitrary injunction. It destroys trust. Will people give money to the church if they don't trust the treasurer? So too with adultery: how often one hears it said, when a couple has abandoned previous spouses and "gotten together," that Jesus welcomed sinners, that one should be "supportive," that we shouldn't be self-righteous or "judgmental." This fails to take into account the way in which entire communities—villages, churches, colleges, businesses, you name it—suffer a kind of moral electric shock when two people who have publicly committed themselves elsewhere suddenly turn out to be "an item." It isn't just that they have "broken a rule." They have undermined part of the moral fabric of their world.)

The command to be united, then, is worked out by Paul in sharp focus and detail. The passage from Philippians with which we began comes at it from one angle after another: learning to think the same way as each other, learning to love one another in the same way, practicing a harmony of thought and feeling, uniting in the object of thought . . . how many more ways, we wonder, can Paul say the same thing?

And he places these extraordinary commands within a framework which itself speaks volumes. Comfort, consolation, partnership, affection, mercy, and joy! If there is any sign of any of these, that is the place to start. Any Christian fellowship that lacks these is hardly a Christian fellowship: and when you see the spark of any of them, like the small glow at the back of the fireplace, blow gently and bring it into a small flame, then feed the flame with more fuel until the whole fire comes to life. That's how it's done. And then, at the other side of the picture: whenever you find selfish ambition or vanity, you know that's the wrong way to go. Whenever you find yourself thinking you're superior, learn the habit of pushing the thought away. (Remember Mark Baxter, the father who, by acting quickly, saved his young daughter from drowning: "Every time I thought a bad thought, I forced myself to think of something else.") Whenever you find yourself looking after number one, stop and think, and find a way of reversing that priority. Philippians 2 is all about looking away from yourself and concentrating on everybody else.

Yes, I know: someone is already saying to herself, "Okay, so Paul thinks we should be doormats for Jesus. I used to be like that, and everyone just walked over me. Now I've learned that if you don't stand up for yourself, you'll be used and abused." That is the normal critique of what is taken to be a Christian ethic; you will find it in plenty of places, both inside and outside the church.

But it's a critique of a parody, not of the reality. Many modern Christians have become so used to taking Paul's commands with a large pinch of salt that these instructions have lingered on, like the grin of the Cheshire Cat, in debased forms: the simpering pseudo-humility of Anthony Trollope's character Mr. Slope, and the self-hatred of those who, for whatever reason, are always putting themselves down and pretending to themselves that by so doing they are following Jesus and Paul. We are less accustomed, perhaps, to recognizing the robust, cheerful community where genuine mutual submission goes hand in hand with, and indeed creates a supportive context for, energetic exercising and celebrating of individual gifts, including strong and wise leadership. Happily, such communities do exist, and where they do, they are a joy.

Actually, as with all virtues, once you begin to learn the language, and especially once you begin to speak it in groups where other people are learning it too, it doesn't seem so impossible, but actually begins to acquire its own sense of "second nature," of a second-order spontaneity, as with skilled actors, footballers, or jazz players who have learned the high art of true corporate improvisation. Sadly, we have all too often settled for the instant spontaneity of everyone "doing what comes naturally," with strong leaders bullying their way through, organizations lurching from tyranny to chaos and back again, and those within them who feel cowed into submission hiding behind the hope that maybe they're being "humble." All this is, again, an unpleasant parody of what Paul has in mind.

Paul's longest, most sustained appeal for unity is the letter we call 1 Corinthians. The whole letter is a lesson in the habits of mind and heart necessary to attain and maintain a rich, diverse unity. This, again, isn't a matter of "rules"—though, as we have seen, rules may be a good way of pointing people in the right direction and enabling them to check that they're still on track. Rather, it's a matter of learning to think and act in accordance with the Spirit of Jesus Christ in such a way that the things which harm unity are spotted early on and rooted out. Personality cults; sexual immorality; lawsuits; disputes over cultural differences; flirting with pagan practices; a rich/poor divide, especially when it impinges on the Lord's Supper; pride or jealousy over different spiritual gifts; chaotic worship; losing a grip on the heart of the gospel. That just about sums up 1 Corinthians, and at every point Paul is seeking to introduce the habits of corporate life necessary to sort it all out, as well as the theological teaching which will undergird it all—particularly the upside-down wisdom of the cross. This permeates a good deal of the letter from the very beginning, and the spectacular hope of the resurrection, which, it gradually becomes clear, dominates one topic after another until its full statement in chapter 15.

Of course, 1 Corinthians wasn't the end of the story. Second Corinthians tells us, sharply and poignantly, that it all went horribly wrong, and that Paul himself had to model the self-abasing pattern of the cross in order to reestablish the church in Corinth, and his apostolic relationship to it, on the basis of Jesus Christ himself, crucified and risen. That shows, all too clearly, that the habits of the heart are not easy to learn, and that every Christian community and every Christian leader is called to learn them more and more deeply. It also shows that, whether or not people are learning those habits, circumstances may very well push them in a direction where they are forced either to do so more deeply or to lose the plot entirely.

Anyway, it is within this complex of pastoral and theological issues that we find one of Paul's greatest statements on the unity of the one body of believers. Having challenged his readers at the start of the letter (1.13) as to whether Christ himself was divided—as their own divisions would imply—and having warned against those who destroy the unity of the church, which is after all God's new temple (3.16–17), he returns to the theme as the letter slowly builds to its climax. As the body is one, with many members, so it is with the Messiah.

SIX

The most obvious mistake to make, as we read Paul's description of the church as "the body of the Messiah" in 1 Corinthians 12, is to suppose that the image of a human body is simply a convenient metaphor plucked at random to make the point about diversity of gifts and unity of purpose. From that point of view, he might as well have described an elephant, whose body contains even more diverse bits and pieces, or a ship's crew with their different functions, or indeed a car (all right, in his world, a chariot). There were many other ways in which the diversity-in-unity, and the unity-in-diversity, could have been articulated. Why a human body?

Well, for a start, Jesus the Messiah was and is a human being. It's appropriate to think of those who belong to him in the same way. But that answer only scratches the surface. The real answer, as we find elsewhere in this letter and elsewhere in Paul's writings, is rooted in his vision of the church precisely as the renewed, redeemed humankind. There is an *appropriateness* about this metaphor; or, if you like, this is not only metaphor, but also metonymy. The construction, and proper operation, of a new way of being human is exactly what it's all about. A human body isn't just an illustration drawn at random. It is a signpost directly into the heart of what's going on.

The particular issue at stake is that of "spiritual gifts"—tongues, prophecy, special words of knowledge, particular sudden gifts of special faith, and so on. Paul will declare in the next chapter that these things are nothing without love, and that they will be abolished while love will go on. That is part of the point of the present chapter as well: don't worry so much about which gift you have or haven't been given, but recognize that all the gifts come from the same source (12.4–11) and are mutually interdependent, just like the foot, the hand, and the eye (12.14–26). The challenge to live as a single body is the challenge to live as the New Human. When the Spirit of Jesus the Messiah comes to dwell in Christians, individually and corporately, this happens so that they can be—all together—the place where his genuinely human life actually and physically continues within the life of the present world.

No wonder the unity of the church is so contested and difficult to maintain, whether in Corinth in the first century or in the confused world of the twenty-first. No wonder there are so many low-grade parodies of this "unity," both in the forced conformism of ecclesial totalitarianism and the forced jollity of the like-minded small group. Both of these are ways of avoiding the real challenge, which is to allow the central Christian virtues of faith, hope, and love, and the fruit of the Spirit which is love, joy, peace, great-heartedness, kindness, generosity, faithfulness, gentleness, and self-control, to have free course in our relationships one with another, and to discover, as they work their way into our lives, the corporate virtues of mutual submission and mutual recognition of God-given gifts of leadership, teaching, and so on.

That is precisely what Paul insists on in another passage that deserves to stand beside 1 Corinthians 12. Here, in Ephesians 4.1–16, it becomes apparent that the unity for which Christians must work is not merely pragmatic, a recognition of differences in which we all shrug our shoulders, do our own thing, and allow other people to do theirs, but a deep, rich, many-sided unity which enables the church to grow toward maturity, leaving behind—as in 1 Corinthians 13, but now as a present task!—the immature babyhood which might otherwise remain as a permanent and vulnerable state:

> So, then, this is my appeal to you—yes, it's me, the prisoner in the Lord! You must live up to the calling you received. Bear with one another in love; be humble, meek, and patient with each other in all your thinking. Make every effort to guard the unity that the Spirit gives, with your lives bound together in peace. There is one body and one Spirit; you were, after all, called to a single hope which goes with your call. There is one Lord, one faith, one baptism; one God and father of all, who is over all, through all and in all. But grace was given to each of us, according to the measure the Messiah used when he was distributing gifts. That's why it says,
>
> > When he went up on high
> > he led bondage itself into bondage
> > and he gave gifts to human beings.
>
> When it says here that "he went up," what this means is that he also came down into the lower place—that is, the earth. The one who came

down is the one who also "went up"—yes, above all the heavens!—so that he might fill all things.

So these were the gifts that he gave. Some were to be apostles, others prophets, others evangelists, and others pastors and teachers. Their job is to give God's people the equipment they need for their work of service, and so to build up the Messiah's body. The purpose of this is that we should all reach unity in our belief and loyalty, and in knowing God's Son. Then we shall have a mature and genuine human life, measured by the standards of the Messiah's fullness.

As a result, we won't be babies any longer! We won't be thrown this way and that on a stormy sea, blown about by every gust of teaching, by human tricksters, by their cunning and deceitful scheming. Instead, we must speak the truth in love, and so grow up in everything into him—that is, into the Messiah, who is the head. He supplies the growth that the whole body needs, linked as it is and held together by every joint which supports it, with each member doing its own proper work. Then the body builds itself up in love.

There is so much detail here that we might get bogged down. Let me highlight the key elements for our present purposes.

First, this majestic passage stands foursquare on what Paul has said earlier in Ephesians, and tracking this sequence of thought will make it clear what purpose he supposes this hard-won virtue of unity will serve. Chapter 1 concludes with a statement of Jesus's present position as the one spoken of in Psalms 2, 8, and 110—the Messiah who is also the New Human: "God has put all things under his feet," making him sovereign over every other authority, power, dominion, and name (1.22, 21). But this is not simply a matter for Christians to celebrate. They are to share in this identity:

God has "put all things under his feet," and has given him to the church as the head over all. The church is his body; it is the fullness of the one who fills all in all. (1.22–23)

Here is the to-and-fro, the paradox we noted earlier in connection with the Temple: the living God fills heaven and earth, and yet he chooses to dwell particularly in one place. And that place is no longer a building, in Jerusalem or anywhere else. It is a family, the family of those who belong to the Messiah. They are the living expression of the fact that he is the world's rightful sovereign: the royal community of the King. But if they are the *royal* community, they are also the *priestly* community, as the notion of priesthood and that of Temple come together at the end of Ephesians 2:

> You are no longer foreigners or strangers. No: you are fellow citizens with God's holy people. You are members of God's household. You are built on the foundation of the apostles and prophets, with King Jesus himself as the cornerstone. In him the whole building is fitted together, and grows into a holy Temple in the Lord. You, too, are being built up together, in him, into a place where God will live by the Spirit. (2.19–22)

How easy it has been for Western Christians to forget this vocation altogether. (It has helped that many have suggested Paul didn't write Ephesians, a claim that has called the letter's authority into question. That, I believe, was originally at least in part a tactical move to justify abandoning this breathtaking and demanding vision.) Or, if we don't forget this vocation, we domesticate it by speaking in exalted terms of the church—pretending, for instance, that the label "church" refers only to the ultimate eschatological or "heavenly" community—while retreating into subgroups and sub-subgroups where we can maintain an appearance of "unity" without any of the work or the cost.

But virtue is *always* the result of work and cost. Paul's appeal for unity (in chapter 2, the unity of Jews and Gentiles within the one church; in chapter 4, the unity of all Christians with their enormously varied ministries) is nothing if not an appeal for virtue. Here, he declares, is the goal: "mature humanity" (4.13), growing *eis andra teleion,* "into a perfect Human," "measured by the standards of the Messiah's fullness." And here are the things which you must work at. They don't happen by accident; they happen because people who might well have done it differently, left to themselves, have made the clear-eyed choice to "make every effort" (4.3) to cultivate the multiple virtues which together contribute to that maturity. The wide range of different ministries which God gives to his church is meant, not to pull the church apart in pursuit of every new personality or initiative that comes along, but to "build up the Messiah's body," to enable it to grow into a rich, diverse unity. Every single Christian is to exhibit the virtues; every single Christian is to be obedient to his or her unique, distinctive, unrepeatable vocation. There lies the challenge.

Here again, as with the cultivation of the "fruit of the Spirit," there are powerful forces driving us in the opposite direction, toward false teaching, trickery, and deceit (verse 14). That is why, to repeat, unity is a virtue—the corporate virtue in which the very different members of the body "grow up in everything into him . . . who is the head, the Messiah." And, of course, as with the three virtues and the ninefold fruit, the key to the one body is love (verse 16). "Copy God," Paul urges at the end of the next passage, "like loving children imitating your father." Here, unusually but very strikingly, Paul urges his hearers not only to reflect on God's love but to look and see how it's done and then do it themselves. "Conduct yourselves in love," he continues, "just as the Messiah loved us, and gave himself for us, as a sweet-smelling offering and sacrifice to God" (5.1–2). This is what "royal priesthood" looks like in the present time: a community that together learns the lessons of holiness (4.17–5.20), and that learns as well what it means to reflect God's character and actions to one another.

The challenge to strive for corporate virtues is after all precisely what we should expect if the key individual virtue, and the firstfruit of the Spirit, is love. The thought of two or three Christians, or two or three hundred or thousand Christians, all trying to practice "love"— while remaining determinedly in their own hermetically sealed worlds of private spirituality and virtue!—is of course a contradiction in terms. The Christian virtues, unlike the classical or cardinal virtues expounded by Aristotle and others, are designed to produce, not grand isolated heroes, leading a nation in politics and war, but integrated communities modeling a life of self-giving love.

With that, we glimpse a truth which I hinted at near the start of this book and must now return to explore. If the Christian community is genuinely learning the corporate virtues required for a multifaceted unity, then this has, in and of itself, an apologetic value over and above that of simple difference ("Fancy that! Those Christians are living in quite a different way from the rest of us!") and attractiveness ("Well, but their way of living looks really good!"). Precisely because the Christian virtues look upward to the God who made the whole world, and made all people in his image, and outward to that world and all people within it, they cannot be the private preserve of an enclosed community. It isn't a matter of turning our back on the great traditions of virtue developed by pagan and non-Christian philosophers down the centuries. It should be a matter of demonstrating that what they were striving for is fully comprehended within, but also transcended by, this new vision of virtue, which is a vision of Jesus Christ himself.

This can't be, then, merely a matter of adding a few new virtues to a lengthening list, or even of insisting that these new ones are more important. With the addition of the Christian virtues, and their privileging, something has happened to virtue itself, something which points us to the very heart of the challenge which the Christian faith offered, and must still offer, to the world around. Here, these virtues declare, is the new way of being human—not only some new and previously unheard-of virtues, but a new definition of virtue itself, a whole new way of humanity which offers itself as the genuine article to a surprised and suspicious world. Does this, or does it not, commend itself? Thus the one unified body of Christ, striving after the virtues and working hard to bring forth the fruit of the Spirit, must be the missionary body which sets forward the purpose of God, to sum up all things in heaven and on earth in the Messiah. That is what it means, in the present time, to live as the royal priesthood.

7. VIRTUE IN ACTION:
THE ROYAL PRIESTHOOD

ONE

There are, no doubt, many avenues of inquiry that now open up before us. Whole worlds of moral and ethical investigation invite fresh exploration. But this book isn't the place for that. What I want to do, to push home the main point I have been making throughout, is to show what it means to develop the virtues, in the present time, which genuinely anticipate those of the "royal priesthood." We are designed to be, in the end, fully renewed, image-bearing human beings. What will be the character strengths that go to make up that kind of life, and how can we develop them here and now? These, rather than the details of "ethical" or "moral" questions on the one hand, or the fine-tuned study of character traits on the other, constitute the big picture which we must set out.

The present chapter will therefore address three questions, each of which will be spread over two sections. First, what does it mean in the present to behave as the royal priesthood, and what are the habits of heart, mind, and life which contribute to that? Second, how does this vocation not only engage the wider world, by holding before it a vision of a new way of being human, but also visibly upstage the classical (and modern) tradition of a secular virtue ethic, retaining the best emphases within that tradition but transforming them within the new framework? Third, how does this larger vocation give shape and body to the particular habits which generate specifically Christian behavior and help us to avoid specifically pagan behavior? How, in other words, does following Jesus in the vocation to royal priesthood both necessitate and generate a life of genuine Christian holiness?

The first of these questions grows directly out of the study we have made of key parts of the Bible. We have seen that the command to humanity in Genesis 1, and the promise of renewed humanity in the New Testament, both highlight the dual vocation to be "rulers and priests." This, I suggest, is the vocation that shapes the church's two primary tasks: worship and mission.

Worship and mission are conjoined twins. They share a heart: the heart that loves God the triune creator and that loves, for his sake, the world he made and (particularly) the creatures that bear his image. This is the heart that can be trained in the practice of virtue. The frustrating thing, when you recognize this, is to realize how many people regularly attend the training ground but do not take part in the training itself. . . .

Take worship first. To worship the living God, the God we know as Father, Son, and Spirit, is to give voice to our faith, to celebrate our hope, and above all to express and articulate our love. Just as a man in love will enumerate to his beloved the hundred and one things about her that he finds so delightful, so Christian worship consciously stands in the presence of the living God and declares who he is and what he's done that has so swept us off our feet. Just as a couple in love will go back over the story of their first acquaintance, courtship, and mutual discovery, telling and retelling the narrative of "how it all happened," so the worshipping heart will naturally want to tell and retell the story of God and the world, of God and Israel, of God and Jesus, of God and one's own personal story. This is a major element in Christian worship.

Notice that I said that these things happen "naturally" at first. What happens when they are left that way?

The answer is all around us in the contemporary, or even postmodern, Western church, which has somehow got stuck with the "romantic" picture of "falling in love with Jesus" or "having Jesus as my boyfriend." That's fine as far as it goes. The Bible and significant strands in both Jewish and Christian devotion have expressed the worship of God in language taken directly from the romantic and indeed erotic relationship of two human lovers. But, as all romantic and erotic lovers know, things don't keep their initial buzz. And, as I've constantly had to say to puzzled young people exploring love, sex, and marriage, the excitement of romance is like the excitement of striking a match. It's sudden, sparky, and dramatic—and it doesn't last long. The question is, What are you going to do with the match once you've struck it?

The answer—which has obvious resonances with Christian worship, beyond the metaphorical meaning!—is that you will use the match to light a candle. A candle isn't as exciting as a match, at least to begin with; but it can be far more beautiful, far more evocative, and far more long-lasting. Human couples need to learn that lesson, to prevent them supposing that when the match goes out, something has gone dramatically wrong and they must look for another match to strike as soon as possible. To learn this, indeed, is part of the road to the virtue of chastity. In the same way, those who have found their hearts warmed with the love of God need to learn that the virtues of faith, hope, and love, as expressed in worship, are to be worked at, thought through, figured out, and then planned, prepared, and celebrated with a new depth that will stir passions which the "matches" of quick, romantic attraction could not reach. Just as the couple preparing to celebrate their fortieth wedding anniversary may well take considerable thought over what to do and how to do it, so that both partners will receive the maximum delight from the occasion, so the church that cherishes a mature, deep, and long-lasting love for God will want to think carefully about how to worship him—not because that worship isn't "coming naturally" but because what they're interested in is the "*second* nature," the developed and sustained virtues, of a love that has thought through why it is worshipping this God and has figured out ways of doing so which express that deeply and richly.

That, of course, is the difference between liturgy and spontaneous worship. There is nothing wrong with spontaneous worship, just as there's nothing wrong with two friends meeting by chance, grabbing a sandwich from a shop, and going off together for an impromptu picnic. But if the friends get to know one another better and decide to meet more regularly, they might decide that, though they could indeed repeat the picnic from time to time, a better setting for their friendship, and a way of showing that friendship in action, might be to take thought over proper meals for one another and prepare thoroughly. In the same way, good Christian liturgy is friendship in action, love taking thought, the covenant relationship between God and his people not simply discovered and celebrated like the sudden meeting of friends, exciting and worthwhile though that is, but thought through and relished, planned and prepared—an ultimately better way for the relationship to grow and at the same time a way of demonstrating what the relationship is all about.

In particular, Christian worship is all about the church celebrating God's mighty acts, the acts of creation and covenant followed by the acts of new creation and new covenant. The church needs constantly to learn, and constantly to be working on, the practice of telling and retelling the great stories of the world and Israel, especially the creation and the Exodus; the great promises that emerged from those stories; and the ways in which those promises came to their fruition in Jesus Christ. The reading of scripture—the written account of those stories—has therefore always been central to the church's worship. It isn't only that people need to be reminded what the stories say (though that is increasingly important in an age where otherwise "educated" people simply don't know the Jewish and Christian stories at all). It's that these stories should be rehearsed in acts of celebration and worship, "telling out the greatness of the Lord," as Mary sang in the Magnificat. Good liturgy uses tried and tested ways of making sure that scripture is read thoroughly and clearly, and is constantly on the lookout for ways of doing it even more effectively—just as good liturgy is also eager to discover better and better ways of singing and praying the

Psalms together, so that they come to be "second nature" within the memory, imagination, and spirituality of all the worshipping faithful, not just of a few musically minded leaders. It's interesting to study the scriptural account of the early church at worship in the Acts of the Apostles, which describes the first Christians drawing on the Psalms and other scriptures to celebrate God's love and power and to be strengthened and sustained in mission. Because the early Christians were attempting to live as the true Temple, filled with the Spirit, we ought not to be surprised that the major confrontations they incurred were with existing temples and their guardians—the Jewish Temple in Jerusalem, and the whole culture of pagan temples in Athens and elsewhere. That's what you'd expect if a new royal priesthood was being called into existence.

In particular, of course, a church that is learning the habits of the royal priesthood will celebrate the sacraments—those occasions when the life of heaven intersects mysteriously with the life of earth, not so that earth can control or manipulate heaven (that would be magic, not faith) but so that the story of heaven may become concrete, physical reality within the life of earth, catching up human beings within a world where all sorts of things make sense that don't otherwise, and all sorts of other things that might have appeared to make sense do so no longer.

All of this life of worship is something to be *learned*. Communities can grow into liturgy and the sacraments, and can take delight in discovering that these things can become, as it were, habits of the community's heart as well as of the individual's. Shared worship is part of what it means when we compare Christianity to a team sport. It is *together* that we are God's people, not as isolated individuals.

That being-togetherness does not, of course, mean uniformity. What counts is precisely the coming together of people who are quite unlike one another in everything except their commitment to the God we know in scripture and ultimately in Jesus. That unlikeness carries forward into the multiple vocations to which God calls us—vocations which, as we saw in the previous chapter, are nevertheless designed as gifts to enable the whole community to grow to a mature unity. And it is precisely in shared worship that this differentiated unity is expressed and learned.

This is where, ironically, we meet the opposite objection to the one we met earlier. The normal Protestant objection to virtue, as we've seen, is that it's just hypocrisy, "putting it on" when you don't yet fully mean it. The standard answer is that this is the only way to acquire the deep-rooted characteristics of faith, hope, love, and all the rest. If we wait to start practicing these things until we "mean them" from the bottom of our hearts, we will wait a long time and probably mess up a lot of lives, including our own, in the process. But now we face the opposite problem: the charge that liturgy and other aspects of formal worship have become "just a habit," implying that because worship is a habit you don't really mean it. At one level, the two charges cancel one another out. If you're just putting it on, it isn't a habit; if it's a habit, you're not just putting it on! But there's a serious point underneath this second problem. Virtue, whether individual or corporate, is never something that can be taken for granted. Once the habit is formed, by many conscious choices and decisions, it has to be maintained in good running order. Here is the difference between "authenticity" and "spontaneity." Spontaneity objects to all habits: things ought just to *happen*! Authenticity, on the other hand, doesn't mind habits, so long as they don't become hollow. Fair enough. It would be good, frankly, to think that many of today's Christians were anywhere near the danger of forming habits of worship so strong that they could become "just a habit." That is perhaps a problem that is dying out. But if and when the danger is present, the warning is justified.

When human beings worship God the creator, articulating their praise and adoration because of who he is and what he's done, they are, whether or not they realize it, summing up the praises and adoration of the whole creation. That is another reason why the *physical* expression of worship, in liturgy and especially in the sacraments, remains important. We shouldn't expect to worship as disembodied souls who happen to be temporarily resident in these strange things called physical bodies, and then to be able to do our job as God's royal priesthood, picking up creation's praises and presenting them before God's throne. Remember: that is what we are called to do and to be. Don't be surprised if the body language of worshippers expresses something of what is being said and done. No doubt this, too, can become a hollowed-out habit, to be challenged from time to time in the name of authenticity. But to frown on the physical expression of worship (gestures of hand and arm, of head and knee, whatever)—as though all such things were signs of hypocrisy or the attempt to put God in our debt—would be as ridiculous as to suppose that such expressions were all that was required, without the devotion of the heart and mind. As we have seen frequently in this book, the church is called to be the new Temple, the place where the living God dwells by the Spirit. This is a whole-person vocation.

The life of worship, then, is itself a corporate form of virtue. It expresses and in turn reinforces the faith, hope, and love which are themselves the key Christian virtues. From this activity there flow all kinds of other things in terms of Christian life and witness. But worship is central, basic, and in the best sense habit-forming. Every serious Christian should work at having worship become second nature. Expressing the love of God in this way will then flow "naturally" across from the first conjoined twin to the second, reinforcing the life of mission. The Temple is there because God's filling of the house with his presence is to be a means, as well as a sign, that God intends to fill the whole world with his glory. Worship must lead to mission. The priests are also royal.

TWO

If you want to see what it looks like for God's renewed people in Christ to be "royal," to be "rulers" in the sense indicated by the vocation to be a "royal priesthood," don't look at the fourth and fifth centuries, when the Roman emperors first became Christian. That raises questions and challenges at other levels, but to begin there would be to miss the point. Look, instead, at what the church was doing in the first two or three centuries, while being persecuted and harried by the author-ities—and announcing to the whole world that Jesus, the crucified and risen Messiah of Israel, was its rightful Lord. *That* is what it means to be "rulers" in the sense we're discussing here: to be agents of *that* King's reign, the reign of the Prince of Peace, the one through whom tyranny itself (not to mention any individual tyrants) was overthrown with the destruction of its most vital weapon—namely, death—and the one through whom therefore was brought to birth a new world in which order and freedom at last meet. (We shouldn't forget that death is the last weapon, not only of the tyrant, but also of the anarchist.)

Look, particularly, at the Acts of the Apostles, where the church is explicitly commanded by the risen Lord himself to witness to him as king and to the reality of his kingdom (Acts 1.7–8). The commu-nity that lives as the renewed Temple is also to live as the rulers-in-waiting, as people who can declare that they must obey God rather than human authorities (Acts 4.19; 5.29). Those early Christians were not disobeying the laws of the land; they were merely giving allegiance to the God who had revealed himself in a fresh way. (This must have been particularly frustrating, of course, for those traditional Jews who thought they were the divinely appointed channels of God's wise or-der.) Jesus's followers will continue to serve the God of their ancestors, and to tell the story of his mighty work. But they will tell this story with a different climax (as, for instance, in Acts 7 and 13). Instead of the story's climax coming with the presence of the high priest in the Temple (as expressed in the book called Ben-Sira, or Ecclesiasticus, written around 200 BC), or with the coming of a future warrior-messiah who would lead the armies of Israel in a mighty battle against the Romans (as the Essenes seem to have hoped), or with the intensi-fied keeping of Israel's ancestral Law (as the Pharisees had wanted), the climax would be Jesus himself, the true King, rejected but now ex-alted, claiming a divinely given sovereignty of which the apostles were the witnesses and agents.

And this sovereignty would not stop with Israel. Already in those early centuries, it spread throughout the world, in one paradoxical confrontation after another. Paul and his companions reminded magistrates of their duty under Roman law (Acts 16.35–40), confronted the most famous pagan court in the Greco-Roman world (Acts 17.22–34), gained a favorable verdict before Seneca's adopted brother Gallio and an implicit vindication from the town clerk in Ephesus (Acts 18.12–17; 19.35–41), reminded a Roman tribune of his legal position (22.25–29), announced God's coming judgment to one Roman governor and his present legal standing to another (24.25–26; 25.6–12), and ended by using his Roman citizenship to gain a safe passage to Rome, to which he had long believed God intended him to go to announce God as King and Jesus as Lord (25.11; 28.30–31; Romans 1.13–15). This is one part, at least, of what it means to be "rulers," calling the world's rulers to account before Jesus for their proper performance of their subordinate duties.

More particularly, the early Christians were becoming the agents of God's sovereign rule through their work in announcing Jesus as Lord. As they did this, and as the power of the gospel transformed people's hearts and lives, they saw communities spring up that gave allegiance to Jesus and celebrated his lordship. "Celebrate in the Lord always!" Paul exhorted them. "I'll say it again: celebrate! The Lord is right here, near at hand!" (Philippians 4.4–5). These communities—though not of course without the many problems which we glimpse in the mirror of Paul's correspondence—were, not least, communities of mutual love and support, communities in which people welcomed one another across the traditional boundaries of race, gender, and class, and looked out for one another's needs, taking special care of the poor. They were the communities, in other words, in whom Jesus's challenge to the rich young man in Mark 10 were being fulfilled, as people pooled their resources in order to look after those who had made common cause with Jesus and his people (Acts 2.43–47; 4.32–37). This was not straightforward, as Acts itself testifies (5.1–11), but the principle extended into the wider church, not least in the command to love. We see this, for instance, in 1 Thessalonians 4.9–12, where the command to love means "make sure you earn what you can and give what you can to those in need," and in particular in Paul's pet project, the substantial collection of money from the Gentile churches around the Aegean coastline to support the church in Judea following the famine (Acts 11.27–30; 1 Corinthians 16.1–4; 2 Corinthians 8–9; Romans 15.25–29).

How exactly does this play into the idea of the Christians being "rulers" in God's new world? Paul answers that question by gathering it all together in Ephesians 3, and declaring that this mission of generating and sustaining Jew-plus-Gentile churches on Gentile soil, binding together in love a surprised new family that was discovering a different way to be human, was a direct sign to the powers of the world that God was God, that Jesus was Lord, and that the time had come for the world's present rulers to be confronted with their rightful master. After all, Alexander the Great had seen himself as the true world ruler because he had brought together Greeks and barbarians into a single empire. The various Roman emperors, following Augustus—the first and possibly the greatest to bear that title—saw themselves as the true rulers of the world because they united in their empire people of many different nations. Paul saw the achievement of Jesus, drawing together the two archetypal divisions of humankind, Jew and Gentile, into one, as signaling not only that the new Temple had thereby been built, but also that the new Lord had been announced. Being "rulers" meant, for the early Christians, living together in the way that declared to the world that Jesus, the crucified and risen one, was the world's true sovereign.

It is enormously important, both for our historical understanding and for our contemporary reflection, that we consider the way in which the early Christians thus understood themselves to be living, at the same time, both as model citizens of their various countries and as people owing allegiance to the new Lord. The virtue which they were to develop was not entirely discontinuous with the virtues of the pagan world around them. Indeed, Paul can appeal to the moral standards of surrounding paganism to show the Corinthians just how badly they are themselves behaving: "Look," he says, "even the pagans don't do *that*!" (1 Corinthians 5.1). And he can assume that there are all kinds of standards in common: "Hate what is evil," he says, "and hold fast to what is good" (Romans 12.9). The church is to behave wisely toward outsiders (Colossians 4.5), seeking peace (Romans 12.14–21), obeying the authorities (while remembering that they, too, answer to God— something many pagan authorities preferred to forget) (Romans 13.1–7), and holding their heads up within their own communities (Philippians 1.27). Indeed, it is in Philippians that we find Paul giving a strong nod of approval to the wider world of pagan virtue:

> For the rest, my dear family, these are the things you should think through: whatever is true, whatever is holy, whatever is upright, whatever is pure, whatever is attractive, whatever has a good reputation; anything virtuous, anything praiseworthy. (Philippians 4.8)

This doesn't mean that Christians should go along with everything the world *does*. The next verse insists, as we saw in an earlier discussion, that Paul's own way of life, radically different from that of the world around, must be the model for that: he calls his readers to do "what you learned, received, heard, and saw in and through me." However, there are many things out there in the wider world which, because of God's goodness in creation, really are true, holy, upright, pure, attractive, well-reputed, virtuous, and praiseworthy. Christians should not be mealymouthed about this. We should be the first to give praise where praise is due, and, equally, to "think through" these things, to ponder them, to inquire how they work and the effect they have.

What then are the particular Christian virtues of being "rulers," "kingdom-people," practicing in the present time for the royal priest-hood which is promised us in the new world? The answer comes once more, unsurprisingly, in the character which Christians are to develop, the character of love, gentleness, meekness, and so on. These are the things which, according to Jesus in the Beatitudes, will characterize those who are to be set over God's world. These are the things which Jesus himself exemplified throughout his life and supremely in his giving of himself to death. These are the things which the early Christians busily set about practicing, not least in looking after the poor and sustaining communities of mutual support. This may not be everybody's idea of "kingship" but it does begin to look as though the redefinition of royalty which was put into effect throughout Jesus's life, and particularly in the great narrative sequence extending from his riding into Jerusalem on a donkey through to his death on a Roman cross, had taken hold of the imagination and life of his followers. If this is what it meant for him to be King, they would find and follow similar paths to take up their own royal responsibilities, to practice in the present the virtues of the royal priesthood.

The fundamental habits of this new, strange, upside-down "royalty" are therefore becoming clear—and they are the very things which Jesus and Paul were urging. They are the virtues, hard initially but second nature after long practice, which generate communities in whose life the lordship of Jesus is apparent, a life which by its very nature doesn't stay as a hidden property within those communities but of necessity spills out into the world around as people see human life lived in a radically different, and often compellingly attractive, way. Here, again, the life of Christian virtue is a team sport.

It is in this context, too, that the church gains the platform and the moral right to speak publicly about Jesus and announce him as Lord, explaining how he died for the sins of the world and rose again. In other words, at the heart of the calling to be a royal priesthood lies the task of *evangelism:* proclaiming Jesus, persuading people to consider him, inviting people to give him their allegiance and discover through him, and through the company of his followers, a whole new way of being human, a life (in fact) of faith, hope, and love, of kindness and gentleness, of forgiveness and generosity, of patience and chastity. Evangelism, too, has something of the character of virtue. It must have seemed very strange for the early apostles to tell unsuspecting strangers that a crucified Jew was actually the Lord of the world—a strangeness which continues to be felt to this day in every culture, both those where the name of Jesus is well known and those where it isn't. But telling people the good news is habit-forming, and the habit is, like all Christian virtues, one that genuinely anticipates in the present time the life of the age to come, where celebration of Jesus's rescuing, healing lordship will be unstinted and unending. At that point, of course, the royal and priestly vocations join up once more.

But the notion of reflecting God's image once more into the world—the image of the generous, loving creator, filling his world with beauty, order, freedom, and glory—must go wider than community-creation on the one hand and evangelism on the other. The "royal" vocation of Jesus's followers must give rise to the hard-won virtues of seeking, generating, and sustaining justice and beauty in a world where both have been at a discount for too long. This is a large topic, in need of much fuller exploration than we can give it here, but the line that runs forward from Aristotle's insistence on "the beautiful and the just" at the start of his *Nicomachean Ethics* is one which Christians should celebrate and advance.

Consider justice. One of the greatest books in the New Testament (Romans) is about God's restorative justice. Those who are called to reflect God's image through their own work must give attention to the task of working out, in a highly contested contemporary world, what that restorative justice ought to look like and how we might help bring it about. This will mean engaging with political debates and processes of various sorts, campaigning on key issues, and highlighting oppression and injustice wherever they occur. The Western world has supposed, for two hundred years and more, that splitting off questions of social justice from questions of God and faith would give us a more just society. The revolutions, totalitarianisms, and all-out wars of that period have proved us wrong. But to put God and human justice back together again will require a sustained effort, not only by individuals but by the church as a whole, developing the corporate virtues of justice-work that will become habits of the church's heart and will appeal to the conscience of the wider world.

Similarly with beauty. If the Temple in Jerusalem, the place where God's own glory was to dwell, was seen as the "little world," the microcosm where the world's beauty was to be concentrated, then part of the virtue of the royal priesthood, the new and living Temple, ought to be the cultivation and celebration of beauty at every level. This calls for the "royal" virtues of bringing that delicately balanced combination— order and freedom—to birth, as art has lurched from the overordered world of cubism to the multiply disordered and deliberately chaotic world of much recent pop art. How can we work in the present time to anticipate the future of God's remade world, where the horrors of today's world will at last be overcome? That is the challenge, as we seek to generate fresh expressions of beauty. Today's aesthetic world lurches to and fro between the brutalism that, starting with an architectural style, has spilled over into all manner of sheer tawdry ugliness, and the sentimentalism that, wishing still to glimpse the loveliness of creation, cannot find a way to express that without collapsing into kitsch. The virtues of the royal priesthood are called for to declare, in art as well as word, the hard-won victory of Jesus over the evil that has corrupted and defaced the world, and to declare the new creation, launched in the resurrection, of a world full of freedom and glory.

Freedom itself must be generated, protected, and celebrated. But thinkers from St. Paul in the middle of the first century to Bob Dylan in the middle of the twentieth, and beyond, are still asking what "freedom" actually means. In a Christian sense it clearly doesn't mean the random whizzing about of the subatomic particle, however much some eager political or psychological rhetoric may go on about the total removal of constraints. (Removing constraints is what the governments did to the financial markets in the years before the recent economic crash. Not a good omen.) For an actor to be "free" to play Hamlet, other actors must be involved, each of whom will curtail their own "freedom" in search of the higher "freedom" of being constrained by, but finding new meaning again and again within, Shakespeare's play. For musicians to be free to play the blues, the guitar must be in tune, the pianist must be practiced if not perfect, serious if not necessarily completely sober, and the drummer and bass player must discover their "freedom" within the quite severe constraints of a time signature. And for the ordinary citizen to be "free" politically there must be forces of law and order that can hold back chaos and riot, defend property and life, and prevent the malicious and the violent from doing whatever they fancy.

We willingly accept constraints like these. We recognize that a "freedom" which consists merely of random or spontaneous activity is not necessarily genuine freedom, but may be merely chaos. We seek a freedom which consists in a glad, integrated, thought-out choice of a life-path and which includes taking responsibility for working that path out, paying its way, and living with its consequences. And the Christian, called to reflect God's generous and creative love into the world, must develop the civic as well as personal virtues that will support and sustain this freedom, this giving to human beings the chance to be genuinely human. How that works out will be complex and demanding, with many odd twists and turns. Like all the great slogans, "Freedom!" raises a question rather than providing answers. But it is a Christian slogan as well, and those called to be royal priests must work at the virtues required to create conditions for it and enable it to flourish where and when it can. We are going to need this in the days to come, as world population increases, food sources and supply chains present new problems, and the world's climate changes alarmingly. We cannot assume that the whole world will steadily become more and more dominated by Western-style liberal democracy, with people meekly voting every once in a while and doing their own thing between elections.

Freedom, like authenticity, is what we are promised when our desires and longings completely coincide with God's designs and plans for us as fully human beings. God's service, says the ancient prayer, is "perfect freedom." And, as with authenticity, freedom grasped too soon becomes an over-realized eschatology, a failure to realize how much work virtue still has to do to bring it to the goal. But the point of virtue is to work at anticipating the future in the present, and glimpsing and grasping the true freedom we are offered in Jesus Christ is a vital element within that. Otherwise, the slogan of "Freedom!" becomes just an excuse for license, as Paul saw already in Galatians 5. To accept appropriate moral constraints is not to curtail true freedom, but to create the conditions for it to flourish.

Royal priests are, in short, to work at revealing the glory of God to the world. That is the task of the renewed Temple. But if, as in John's gospel, the glory of God is revealed when Jesus of Nazareth goes to the cross as the supreme act of love (John 13.1; 17.1–5), then we should expect that God's glory will be reflected out into the world when Jesus's followers learn the habits of mind, heart, and life that imitate the generous love of Jesus and thus bring new order, beauty, and freedom to the world. It is hugely important that we see these habits precisely as *virtues,* not simply as "principles" to be "applied" or "values" to be "embraced." We do not start, as it were, with the Platonic form of justice, beauty, and freedom, so that, possessing that great and awesome knowledge, we might come down to earth with a grand plan for how these noble ideals should trickle down into reality from their Platonic ideal existence. We are given, rather, the promise that the earth shall be full of the knowledge and glory of God, as the waters cover the sea; we are given the resurrection of Jesus to be the start of that project; and we are given the Holy Spirit to enable us to anticipate the former by implementing the latter. To begin on those tasks does not mean we know it all and can see exactly what needs doing (as we might imagine if we thought of principles and values). It means that we are committed to taking the difficult first steps toward acquiring the corporate habits that will be justice-generating, beauty-producing, and freedom-enhancing, and to continuing the many-sided debates as to what exactly those phrases will mean. And, once again, every follower of Jesus will have his or her own unique and interestingly different vocation within this complex overall project.

The task of being God's royal priesthood in the present, then, is all about worship and mission—a worship and mission which share a heart, the heart that is learning to love God the creator and God the recreator and discovering how to develop the habits that will reflect God's love into the world and the world's grateful love back in return. We must now look further at how this might work out in practice.

THREE

I once had a student, studying theology, who spent his whole summer vacation working in a sub-Saharan African country. When he came back, the head of the college asked him what he wanted to do when he graduated. He replied that he was hoping to work in international development, bringing help and wisdom to the poorest parts of the globe. The head of the college at once asked him why, in that case, he was studying theology rather than politics and/or economics.

The student didn't miss a beat. "Because theology is much more relevant," he replied.

He had seen, firsthand and over some months, the way in which the church had gone about its business in the country where he had lived. "Liberation theology," as it was then known, wasn't any longer an abstract exercise, a seemingly exciting, flaky, and slightly dangerous sub-branch of systematic theology created to keep left-wing students from getting bored with the study of ancient dogmas. It was about churches, themselves poor and living among the poor, that were working out from day to day what it meant to call Jesus Lord and to make that lordship a living reality in their wider communities.

I was proud of that student, both for his experience and for his answer. But as I reflected on the exchange, I wondered how we had got to the point, in the Western world, where it could be assumed that theology was irrelevant to the real needs of the real world. As I pondered this, I realized that though theology as a topic might seem remote (it isn't, in fact, but those who control our news media have no idea what it is, so they routinely discount it), the practical life of the church reaches out into numerous areas of "ordinary" life in the Western world, unobtrusively and without a blast on the trumpets. This

fact needs highlighting and celebrating as an already flourishing reality. In England, the government's own statistics show that the solid
majority of those who give of their time, money, and energy to voluntary service in their communities—working with the elderly, the
handicapped, the dying, the very young, and so on—are practicing
Christians. Many of them will say that they're not very good Christians, meaning that they're aware of their own moral failures, of many
things in the Bible they don't understand, and so on. But something in
the lifeblood of the church has stirred them to offer help where help is
needed, and they do it gladly, finding (not surprisingly) such a strong
personal fulfillment in doing so that it keeps them coming back even
when they themselves are getting old and tired. (I know one couple
who went on taking "meals on wheels" to "elderly" people around the
town until they themselves, well into their eighties, were older than
most of the people they were visiting!)

The habit of practical service—the outward and visible sign of the
virtue of love—goes back to the early church. One of the most striking
passages in Rodney Stark's remarkable book *The Rise of Christianity* is
his description of how Christians in ancient Turkey would react when
their town was struck by plague. The rich, the well-to-do, and particularly the doctors would gather up family and possessions and leave
town. They would flee to the hills, to fresher and less polluted air, or to
friends or family in towns some distance away. But the Christians, often among the poorest, and many of them slaves, would stay and nurse
people, *including those who were neither Christians, nor their own family members, nor in any other way obviously connected to them.* Sometimes such people got well again; not all diseases were necessarily fatal.
Sometimes Christians would themselves catch the disease and die
from it. But the point was made, graphically and unmistakably: this
was a different way to be human. Nobody had ever thought of living
like that before. Why were they doing it? And the Christians, called
upon to explain the habits of the heart which made it "natural" (*second*
nature, of course) to do such things, would talk about Jesus, and about

the God they had discovered through Jesus, the God whose own very nature was and is self-giving love. Stark suggests that this kind of behavior was one of many contributory reasons for the rapid spread of Christianity, despite the best efforts of efficient Roman persecutors, leading up to the time when, by the start of the fourth century, nearly half the empire was Christian and the emperors decided it was better to join what seemed to be the winning side.[1]

All this ties in with Paul's exhortations in Romans 12 and Philippians 4: that Christians should practice the art of living as good citizens, celebrating what can be celebrated in the wider world and grieving over what has brought sadness into people's lives. The generous creator God is not honored, is not reflected into his world, by a church that stands aloof, secure in its own holiness, and looking down on the best that the rest of the world can do as so much unspiritual, un-Christian, or ungodly rubbish. (That doesn't mean there isn't a lot of rubbish out there, just as there is within the church itself.) Precisely because the greatest Christian virtue is love, modeled on that of the creating and life-giving God, the individual Christian and the church as a whole must develop the settled habits of looking out for what's going on in the surrounding world, rejoicing with its joy, weeping with its grief, and above all eager for opportunities to bring love, comfort, healing, and hope wherever possible. And with all these it may bring faith, not necessarily by speaking of Jesus all the time (though there will be such opportunities), but by *living* Jesus in public. The world, and sadly some in the church too, may well sneer at the "do-gooder." Sometimes the sneering may even be earned: blundering self-righteousness is always possible, and must of course be avoided. But the abuse doesn't invalidate the use. It may well simply demonstrate that the work that needs doing is best done through *habit*. Through virtue. Through the ninefold fruit of the Spirit. Through the conscious choices of a whole community, and individuals within it in pursuit of their own particular vocation, to develop, acquire, and sustain the habits of the royal priesthood.

FOUR

If the Christian *life* of virtue has an outward look toward the wider world, what about the Christian *theory* of virtue?

This question has been, in reality, one of the subtexts of this whole book. I trust that the rest of the exposition will stand up without the discussion to which we now turn. But since part of what I've been saying is that the habits of Christian virtue must be outward-looking, must reach out beyond the confines of the church, and must act in the world to bring healing and hope, it would be odd if we were then to retreat, and declare that what the Christian says about Christian virtue has no point of contact with what the pagan says about pagan virtue, as though they were two quite separate things, neither overlapping nor impinging on one another.

On the contrary. If the Christian claim is that in Jesus Christ, and by the Spirit, the creator God has launched a new way of being human, we should positively expect that there will indeed be an overlap, an interplay: perhaps a partial confrontation, possibly a partial convergence.

This brings us, at two levels, into the huge area which theologians have loosely labeled "nature" and "grace." One of the primary questions the study of that area raises is this: Is it possible for a human being, unaided by divine grace—that is, in a state of pure nature—to attain virtue? Paganism itself would have been divided over this question, since for some pagans—for Stoics, at least—a divine power was at work in all human beings, so that all human life, not least all moral effort, would have been understood to have some kind of divine subcurrent flowing through it. But for Paul and the early Christians, thinking in a Jewish mode about creative and life-giving God, something much more explicit was called for. Yes, pagans could articulate and respect, and sometimes even live up to, noble ideals; but faith, hope, and love, the full fruit of the Spirit and the unity of the one body—these were further gifts, available only by the grace of Jesus Christ, going beyond what paganism could do. Without that grace, even the zealous follower of the Jewish Law would end up in the same place as the puzzled pagan moralist: "The good I want I do not; the evil I do not want is what I do" (Romans 7.19; but this is not the place to explain or justify this interpretation of that vexed passage). For grace to have the desired effect, Paul concluded, it isn't enough simply to add a bit on to nature. It isn't that nature, morally speaking, is good but incomplete and merely needs supplementing—topping up, as it were. No: nature needs to be put to death and to come to life on the other side: "Those who belong to the Messiah have crucified the flesh with its passions and desires" (Galatians 5.24). As long as the cross remains a stumbling block to Jews and folly to pagans, so the work of grace in producing the moral life envisaged by the New Testament will be a matter not merely of supplement but of crucifixion and resurrection. But in that resurrection there really will be an affirmation of the created order, and with it a reaffirmation of the way of life built into creation itself, glimpsed by paganism at its best but unattainable within that framework.

There is, as I hinted much earlier, a parallel here with what Paul says about the Jewish Law. The Jewish Law looks on at God's achievement in Christ and by the Spirit and applauds it, even though the Law itself, being "weak because of the flesh," is unable to produce that result (Romans 8.3–4). In the same way, the work of grace will produce a kind of human life which the serious pagan ought to acknowledge as genuinely and fully human—and which the Christian ought to see, in retrospect as it were, as the goal toward which the paganism of Paul's day had been pointing, however impotently.

Which brings us to another question: Is there a complete disjunction between the *theory* of virtue, as (for instance) in Aristotle or Seneca, and the theory we have seen developing in the proclamation of Jesus and the teaching of Paul? No. I suggest that, at the level of theory, we witness something very similar to what we have just seen at the level of practice. For Aristotle, we become virtuous by doing virtuous deeds: "second nature" develops, and we grow into the full attainment of that which, glimpsing the "goal" of complete human flourishing, we have begun to practice. So for Paul, taking 1 Corinthians 13 as the obvious example: here is the goal, the state of being *teleios,* complete; here are the qualities of character which contribute to it; here are the steps you must take to practice that quality of character. Or take Colossians 3 or Ephesians 4: here is the state of perfect, mature humanness; here are the qualities of character you must "put on," clothing yourself with them and learning how to practice them. It is only, I suggest, the somewhat frantic cult of spontaneity, and the more reflective but still insistent culture of "authenticity," which has prevented readers of Paul over the last two centuries from recognizing what is going on. What Paul is arguing for is a Christian form of the ancient pagan theory of virtue.

But it has indeed been thoroughly Christianized. It has itself, at this second level, been put to death and brought to new life. This is all about nature and grace again, but now in relation to the theories themselves; it isn't a case of Aristotle being topped up by Paul. Aristotle's tradition led ultimately to pride. Indeed, even some of his supporters have recognized a serious problem in his view that the fully virtuous person will have, as a kind of super-virtue, a pride in his own achievement.[2] For Paul—and this was one of the most painful things he had to work out, as we see in 2 Corinthians—the Christian life of virtue was shaped by the cross of Jesus Christ, resulting in a quite new virtue, never before imagined: humility. Just as the Christian practice of charity resulted in a way of being human that nobody had imagined before, caring voluntarily for people with no obvious claim on one's attention, so humility cut across not just all previous ideas of what virtue would look like, but across the ancient pagan theory of virtue itself, saying, in effect, that one of the highest virtues was the state where one was no longer conscious of one's own virtue. As C. S. Lewis said in another context, it is as though you met the sea-serpent and discovered that it didn't believe in sea-serpents.[3] The Christianly virtuous person is not thinking about his or her own moral performance. He or she is thinking of Jesus Christ, and of how best to love the person next door.

These questions are not, though, simply a matter of detached theory. They are severely practical. They directly affect two other questions, both urgent. First, can we use ancient non-Christian traditions to help us in our moral quest, or must we only use the scriptures? Second, can we address our non-Christian contemporaries on moral questions, or can we merely say to them, "Look at us: because we're Christians we do it differently"? If there is no major distinction—if we can read Aristotle and Paul side by side, shrug our shoulders, and learn from both with equal profit, and if we can contribute our two cents' worth of wisdom to today's questions of public morality along with everyone else—then we have clearly taken a large step away from the world of the gospels and the epistles. On the other hand, if there is *no* overlap, *no* point of contact, then we are in a closed world. We are sealed off from learning anything new from the outside but also, more worryingly, sealed off from being able to give anything. Why should the world take any notice of us? If I stand up in Parliament and say that because I live in a world shaped by the faith and life of the Christian church I don't believe in euthanasia, those in that place who don't share that faith will smile and say, in effect, Very well, but since *we* don't start from that Christian premise, we won't take any notice. Is there no continuity between Christian morality and that of the wider world? If we claim that Christian faith produces genuine humanness, must there not be many areas of massive overlap on which we can work toward agreement?

A good deal of Christian theology down through the centuries has worried away at questions on this borderland, sometimes moving toward saying that the world is basically good but in need of some help and advice, and sometimes moving toward saying that the world is basically bad and in need of rescue and a complete makeover. It has proved difficult to say what many have wanted to say: that the world is a rich and strange mixture of good and bad and that the death and resurrection of Jesus Christ *both* passes judgment on its utter and rebellious wickedness *and* reaffirms—the other side of that judgment—its inherent, God-created goodness. But something like this, I believe, is necessary. I hope I have indicated one way at least in which we can do this in the sphere of moral discourse.

There is much more that could be said at this level, but not here. I hope that among the effects of this book will be that I have alerted virtue theoreticians to the wealth and depth of material in the New Testament, which they have normally ignored by going straight for the major subsequent exponents, such as Aristotle and Aquinas. And I hope, conversely, to have alerted New Testament ethicists to the fact that Jesus and his first followers can be understood within the context of ancient pagan theories of the moral life, not in terms either of straightforward borrowing or simplistic "topping up," but in terms of a transformation of the theory itself. The early Christians believed that they were the true Temple of God, filled with God's glorious presence by his Spirit and called to reveal that glory to the world. They therefore saw themselves standing in a relation to all other temples, Jewish and pagan, as the reality stands to the parodies. (Imagine suddenly meeting a public figure you had previously known only through grisly caricatures in popular newspapers!) In the same way, the early Christians seem to have believed that their way of glimpsing the ultimate goal of human life, and their way of "practicing" it in the present time, was the reality for which the ancient pagan "goal" of happiness, and the virtues which anticipated and cultivated it, were at best a fine parody. Whether we go on, with Augustine, to declare that pagan virtues are therefore, ultimately, merely "splendid vices," leading people toward pride and so away from the God revealed in Jesus Christ, or whether we hold out the possibility that, by the pagans' grasping at such possibilities of moral life as they knew, they were in fact responding already, as best they could, to God the creator, is a further question beyond the scope of this book. There may be some to whom Jesus might say, as he did to the scribe, "You are not far from God's kingdom" (Mark 12.34). "Not far," of course, indicates that there is still a short but significant step to take.

FIVE

I have suggested that part of the inner dynamic of virtue itself, seen from a Christian point of view, is precisely to point away from itself, and outward to God in worship and to the world in mission. That is what it means to be a royal priesthood. I now want to show how Christian holiness is not a separate idea from worship and mission, but belongs organically and intimately within that picture.

All this is contained in the idea of being remade in God's image. The point of a mirror isn't that it's useful or beautiful in itself, but that it reflects the face of one who looks into it. The point of an *angled* mirror is that it reflects one thing to another: in this case, God to the world (mission) and the world back to God (worship). I now propose that the New Testament's vision of Christian virtue, of the holiness to which Jesus's followers are called and for which they are equipped by the Spirit, can be understood (and is perhaps *best* understood) as a function of that dual role. It isn't, in other words, that there are two separate things going on—first a call to holiness and second a call to worship and mission. (Or even three separate things, if worship and mission are likewise separated, as sadly they often are.) Rather, the call to holiness comes precisely because it is as genuine human beings that we will be able to sum up the praises of creation, and as genuine human beings that we will be able to bring God's justice, freedom, beauty, peace, and above all rescuing love to the world.

This, I take it, is the line of thought which Paul envisages when he insists that holiness must be aimed at mission:

> Do everything without grumbling and disputing. That way, you will be blameless and pure, unblemished children of God in the middle of a twisted and depraved generation, among whom you shine like lights in the world, holding out the word of life. That's what I will boast of on the day of the Messiah, since it will prove that I didn't run a useless race or work to no purpose. (Philippians 2.14–16)

The world is dark; you are to shine God's light into it. Here Paul is drawing together various strands of Jewish expectation, of Israel's call to be the light to the world (Isaiah 49.6, God's call to his "servant," who has just been anxious, in verse 4, that he might have been working to no purpose). In particular, Paul is echoing Daniel 12.3, where the prophet declares, "Those who are wise will shine like lights in the sky, and those who turn many to righteousness, like the stars for ever and ever." Interestingly, one of the ancient Greek translations of the phrase "those who turn many to righteousness" decided on a paraphrase, rendering it "those who are powerful in my word." Paul may be echoing that version in the text quoted above, where he speaks of "holding out" (or perhaps "holding fast to") the word of life. The point is this: those who follow the crucified and risen Jesus and hail him as Lord (2.11), those who "work out" what their own "salvation" is going to mean, as opposed to the various forms of "salvation" offered by the pagan world around them (2.12), those in whose lives the living God is now at work to accomplish his good pleasure (2.13)—these people are to be holy *for the sake of the mission in which Israel's call to be the light of the world is at last realized.* With this, "the glory of God the Father" (2.11), which is displayed when people hail Jesus as Lord, is unveiled before the nations as Isaiah had promised (60.1–3), no longer hidden in the Temple. The holiness of Jesus's followers is part of the necessary equipment for them to be the royal priesthood.

The early Christians clung to this vocation in the teeth of harsh evidence that the light would not be well received by the dark world. This is a major theme in the Gospel of John. Nevertheless, they were to continue with the project. Their holiness would be a sign to the world that there was indeed a different and better way to be human, even if the only effect would be that the world would be without excuse when God finally put everything to rights. Peter conveys the same message. Immediately after declaring that Jesus's followers are a "royal priesthood," formed to proclaim the powerful deeds of the one who called them from darkness to light, he continues:

Beloved, I beg you to hold back from the fleshly lusts which are fighting a war against your real selves. You are, after all, aliens and exiles!
Maintain good conduct among the pagans, so that when they sneer
at you as though you are evildoers they may see your good behavior
and give God the glory on the day when he visits in judgment. (1 Peter
2.11–12)

The point is repeated in the following chapter:

Always be ready to explain yourselves to anyone who asks you about
the hope that is in you, but do it with gentleness and reverence, maintaining a good conscience, so that when you are spoken against, those
who are reviling your good behavior in Christ may be put to shame.
(1 Peter 3.15b–16)

The whole sequence of thought we're exploring is exactly that of
Ephesians 4 and 5. After the great opening of that section (4.1–16),
urging the church to work hard for unity and to see the varied ministries within it as contributing to the state of "completeness," of maturity in Christ, Paul goes on to emphasize the necessity of a radical
break with the pagan pattern of life. That is the setting in which Jesus's
followers are to

take off your former lifestyle, the old humanity. That way of life is
decaying, as a result of deceitful lusts. Instead, you must be renewed
in the spirit of your mind, and you must put on the new humanity,
which is being created the way God intended it, displaying justice and
genuine holiness. (Ephesians 4.22–24)

The point of this, as of Philippians 2, is that Paul's listeners are instead to live as light in the midst of darkness, as resurrection people
in a world of death (Ephesians 5.8–14). To this end they will need
to deploy all the regular means by which Christian character can be

fostered, avoiding the obvious causes of corruption, such as sexual immorality and drunkenness, and embracing the life of forgiveness, kindness, and above all grateful worship (4.25–5.20).

The same point is likewise made in Romans. Those who are to be God's agents in the final putting-to-rights of all creation—those for whom creation itself has been longing, since only when they are revealed as true human beings will creation itself be renewed—are those who must learn to "put to death the deeds of the body" (8.13) so that they may live. If they are to be the royal priesthood, ruling over God's new world (Romans 5.17), they must be people through whose lives shine a genuine humanness, reborn in Christ after judgment has been passed on their own sin. God's work of rescuing, restorative justice must happen *in* us in order that it can happen *through* us. That is the inner logic which links personal conversion, faith, and sanctification with the wider task of the church in the world.

From all this—and there is of course much more besides which we could have explored—it should be clear that the New Testament envisages the holiness of God's people as a major factor in their larger vocation to be the lights of the world. From this there emerge those particular features of Christian behavior, those particular virtues which nobody (except, in some cases, the Jewish people) had thought of as virtues before, and which, according to Jesus and the early Christians, were the secret clues to that genuine humanness through which the creator God would be made known in his world and the world would be summoned to worship. I return to the earlier-quoted list of these characteristics offered, almost as a throwaway line, by Simon Blackburn: humility, charity, patience, and chastity. These are all on display, again and again, in the pages of the New Testament, and they contributed materially to the sheer puzzlement of ancient paganism when faced with the early Christians: Why would anyone want to behave like that? The Christian answer was, and is, that these virtues exemplify and model genuine humanness; that this genuine humanness was lived out by Jesus himself, whose life is given to his people by his Spirit; and that in Jesus, and indeed in all who share his way of being human, one can see the genuine reflection of the creator God, so frequently parodied in paganism but so clearly redisplayed in the death and resurrection of Jesus. This composite of virtues is what the Proper Man looked like. This is what his followers must look like.

It is thus more or less impossible to speak of God with any conviction or effect if those who profess to follow Jesus are not exemplifying humility, charity, patience, and chastity. These are not optional extras for the especially keen, but the very clothes which the royal priesthood must "put on" day by day. If the vocation of the royal priesthood is to reflect God to the world and the world back to God (the world, that is, as it was made to be and as, by God's grace, it will be one day), that vocation must be sustained, and can only be sustained, by serious attention to "putting on" these virtues, not for the sake of a self-centered holiness or pride in one's own moral achievement, but for the sake of revealing to the world who its true God really is. The church has been divided between those who cultivate their own personal holiness but do nothing about working for justice in the world and those who are passionate for justice but regard personal holiness as an unnecessary distraction from that task. This division has been solidified by the church's unfortunate habit of adopting from our surrounding culture the unhelpful packages of "left-wing" and "right-wing" prejudices, the former speaking of "justice" and meaning "libertarianism" and the latter speaking of "holiness" and meaning "dualism." All this must be firmly pushed to one side. What we need is integration.

The high calling of Christian morality is therefore the necessary handmaid of the still higher callings of Christian worship and mission. The virtues which constitute the former are the vital components of the latter. The only way for worship and mission to become second nature to the followers of Jesus is for the virtues, the Spirit's fruit, the passion for unity, and the celebration of the multiply varied vocations within the one body all to become second nature as well. Otherwise, worship will be a sham and mission a mere projection of ideologies. Reflecting God's image means learning the disciplines of a God-reflecting human life.

SIX

So what are those disciplines, and how can we learn them? This points us forward to the final chapter in this book. First, though, some preliminary words are in order about the way in which the earlier-named strikingly *different* Christian virtues—humility, patience, chastity, and charity—have developed over time.

Humility, in the Western world at least, has gradually come to be accorded a grudging respect. True, some philosophers (notably Nietzsche) have pooh-poohed it, dismissing it as a weak, spineless thing, the cause or sign of human degeneracy rather than true nobility. Humility can easily be parodied on the one hand and pretended to on the other, and neither makes a pretty sight. False humility is as unattractive as over-the-top fawning. (Only twice have I received regular messages from correspondents signing themselves "Your humble servant," and it was clear that actually neither of them had any intention of doing what I suggested.) But our culture has shifted noticeably from the ancient world, where self-advertisement was the expected norm—where, for example, Cicero could congratulate Rome on its good fortune in coming to new birth while he was consul, and where Augustus could write a book about his achievements and have the whole thing carved in stone by the banks of the River Tiber for all to read to this day. We don't like it when people start off down that road these days, and we tend to pull them up sharply. "Showing off" has had a bad press, especially in England; as cultural critic George Steiner has commented, the phrase "Oh, come off it!" is a particularly English expression, hard to translate into an exact and equally devastating equivalent in other languages. To that extent, something of the Christian virtue of humility has remained, at least in outline, within post-Christian Western culture.

However, we have revived something of the ancient pagan alternative in our passion for the heroes and heroines of sport, popular music, and other similar attractions. We expect them to fulfill the role of "celebrity" in being both superhuman in some respects and more or less subhuman in others (in their undisciplined use of drugs, alcohol, fast cars, and sex). They reflect, in fact, an image which is well known to students of the classical world: the gods and goddesses of ancient Greece and Rome, who were powerful, dazzling, capricious, licentious, and unusually helpful to people they liked and dangerous to people they didn't. And when, within a would-be "Christian" culture that has forgotten its roots, as ours has, preachers and teachers of the gospel are treated in the same way as other "celebrities," their now-routine fall from grace, usually through financial or sexual misdemeanor, is simply a sign that all along they were deeply out of tune with the core message. This applies equally to the televangelist who has embezzled millions in church funds and to the parish priest who has sexually abused children. They have enjoyed a status in their communities which has encouraged them to a kind of humanness that reflects, not the generous and self-giving love of the creator God, but the self-glorifying and self-gratifying lust of the pagan gods and goddesses.

The same holds true for patience. Patience is one of the places where faith, hope, and love meet up. Those who believe in God the creator and in the eventual triumph of his good purposes for the world will not be in a hurry to grasp at quick-fix solutions in their own life or in their vocation and mission—though they will not be slow to take God-given opportunities when those arise. In particular, they will not be in a hurry to force ideas and solutions on other people. Not for nothing is patience the first thing that Paul says about love (1 Corinthians 13.4).

Here again our culture is pulled two ways. We applaud patience but prefer it to be a virtue that others possess. When a well-known bank, introducing credit cards to an unsuspecting public in the early 1970s, declared that their piece of plastic would "take the waiting out of wanting," it struck two very different chords among its hearers. Some—the majority—decided that that's what they'd always wanted, and signed up. Others, who appeared at the time to be "living in the past" and to be "out of date," warned that this slap in the face to the virtue of patience would bring its own dire rewards. A generation

later, with levels of personal debt in the Western world at unprecedented, astronomical levels, not least among young people, the second
group have been proved right again and again. This is not to say that
there is not a responsible use of credit cards and similar schemes. It is
only to say that when a society as a whole decides that patience is out-
moded, something about its genuine humanness takes a severe blow.
And when humanness deteriorates, the results are corruption (in the
sense of something decaying or going bad) and slavery.

Patience is needed for the pursuit of *all* the virtues, of course. Part
of that same have-it-all-now culture, as applied to Christian living,
declares that now that you're a Christian, indwelt by the Spirit, you
ought to be instantly holy. You want to be like Jesus Christ—pray this
prayer, have this experience, and it's all yours! No, replies Patience,
with Humility standing close beside: we shall learn the present lesson this week, the next one the following week, and so on. We shall
practice the virtues, step by step, "putting them on" with conscious
thought and effort, even though the clothes don't seem to fit us very
well at the moment. We won't be distracted, either by the glittering offers of instant fix-it spirituality or the sneering charges that we're just
putting it on, just being hypocrites.

And then there is chastity. It comes as a surprise to many people to
discover just how much the ancient Christians (and the ancient Jews)
were seen as out of step with the surrounding culture in this area. Just
about everybody in the ancient world took it for granted that people
had, to put it straightforwardly, as much sex as they could get. Marriage (between a man and a woman) was one thing, and many either
wanted to stay faithful or were afraid, for whatever reason, to stray.
The main problem with adultery, though, was not the moral lapse
but the jealous spouse. Unmarried sexual liaisons were common and
expected, and in a world where abortions were often procured, and
unwanted children abandoned to wild beasts, some of the residual
problems were easily dealt with, leaving the main difficulty that of the
family trying to marry off a daughter with a "past." Other taboos ex-
isted in various times and places. In ancient Athens, for example, there

was a carefully graded scale of what was acceptable when a man was conducting homosexual friendships with younger men. But nobody thought that homosexual behavior, including lifelong quasi-marital partnerships, was particularly unusual, let alone reprehensible in and of itself. Indeed, Plato (in *The Symposium*) celebrated such partnerships as the highest form of love. Other quite different forms of sexual activity, such as sex with animals, was something at which most people shrugged their shoulders. A good deal of all this behavior took place in and around pagan temples, but it was by no means confined to them.

The early Christians shared the view of Jews, ancient and modern, that this kind of behavior was dark and dehumanizing, distorting the very essence of what it means to be human. Sex was given, they believed, for the mutual and outward-looking delight of husband and wife (outward-looking because, like God's love, the love of spouses generates new creation, both in the procreation of children and in the creation of a warm, secure, and hospitable home). That, rather than arbitrary prejudice or fear-driven repression, is why they rejected the all-too-familiar way of their world. They believed themselves called to shine into this darkness the light of a different way of being human.

The striking contrast of their belief and behavior with their milieu at this point goes back solidly to Jesus himself. Jesus warned, in a passage we looked at earlier, against the kind of unclean behavior which emerges unbidden from the deep recesses of the human personality. The terms in which he issues that warning, echoing and endorsing central prohibitions from the Old Testament, make it clear that, despite popular impressions to the contrary, he is firmly endorsing the ancient Jewish prohibition on sexual relationships of any sort outside the lifelong marriage of a man and a woman. The whole New Testament insists that the point of Christian living is the remaking of humans in God's image; and when we trace that idea to its root, it is clear that the image-bearing pair are male and female, called to leave others and cleave to one another. Not for nothing have theologians from that day on seen that human union as a sign of the unbreakable commitment of the creator God to his creation. We should not be surprised that, when heaven and earth finally come together at the end of the book of Revelation, the image used is that of a marriage. That is the *telos,* the goal of all our existence. Virtue grasps that goal by faith and learns the lessons of living in the present in such a way as genuinely to anticipate that future, by fidelity within marriage and abstinence outside it.

Western culture, comprised largely of at least nominally Christian nations, has been partly colonized by the Christian vision of marriage and sexuality, but mostly not. Attempts at enforced abstinence have come and gone, to be replaced, again intermittently, by virtually enforced indulgence (think of the seventeenth century, with the Restoration following the Puritans; or the rebellion after the First World War against supposed "Victorian" standards, though history reveals that a good deal of nineteenth-century Europe was just as sexually unrestrained as any other time). Street-level Freudianism, which assumes that sex is at the bottom of everything and thus you can't resist it so you shouldn't try, and street-level Darwinism, which insists that what matters is the life-force that leads us to propagate ourselves so we'd better get on with it, have together created a climate where, in the popular mind, any serious call for restraint either in the mode or in the particular circumstances of sexual expression is met, not with serious argument, but with scorn. "Ha!" exclaimed one correspondent to a popular paper the other day. "All this talk of Abstinence by some misguided right-wing lunatics. Pretty soon biology will kick in and then they'll be at it like everyone else." In other words: biology rules, we have urges we can't control, and it's unhealthy and unnatural to resist. Multiple sexual partnerships, and now even multiple quasi-contractual relationships ("polyamory," with three or more people entering into multidirectional sex-sharing agreements), are making their way into "accepted" behavior. Easy contraception and abortion have opened the floodgates to a fresh round of sexual license over the last few decades—a license that even the AIDS crisis has done little to check.

Yet Christians have always insisted that self-control is one of the ninefold varieties of the Spirit's fruit. Yes, it's difficult. Yes, you have to work at it and discover why certain temptations, at certain times and places, are hard to resist. That's because chastity is a *virtue:* it's not first and foremost a *rule* which you decide either to keep or to break (though certain rules are clear enough scripturally); it's certainly not something you can calculate according to a *principle,* such as the greatest happiness of the greatest number (not least because the overwhelming short-term happiness of most sexual congress would tip the scales artificially); and in particular, as Jesus himself indicated, it won't be generated by going with the flow of *what comes naturally.* This is where the genuine celibate, like Jesus himself, and like a great many unsung heroes and heroines both in monastic communities and in plenty of less obvious places, have discovered the joy of a "second nature" self-control which much of our culture, like most of the ancient world, never even imagines. By contrast, as those of us who care pastorally, or in families, for people who have embraced the present habits of society will know, the bruises and wounds caused by those habits are deep, long-lasting, and life-decaying. The church is often called a killjoy for protesting against sexual license. But the real killing of joy comes with the grabbing of pleasure. As with credit card usage, the price tag is hidden at the start, but the physical and emotional debt incurred will take a long time to pay off.

Here Patience and Humility, standing on the sidelines, come into play once more. The frantic urge toward sexual intimacy is part of the drive to express yourself, to push yourself forward, to insist that this is who you are and this is how you intend to behave. No, says Humility; you don't discover your true self that way. You find it by giving yourself away. Precisely, agrees Patience: taking the waiting out of wanting is shortchanging yourself and everybody else. The virtues are linked together, just as Aristotle said regarding his list of four (courage, temperance, prudence, and justice). If you want one of them, you'd better develop all of them.

And so, of course, to charity, which as we noted is described by Paul as the virtue which you need to put on over and around all the others, like the belt which keeps the rest in place (Colossians 3.14). Love (the normal, if imprecise, word we use because "charity" has shrunk) is the thing that will enable patience, humility, and chastity to stay in place, because love respects the other person and wants the best for him or her. And love in turn is sustained, as in Paul's famous passage, by faith on the one hand and hope on the other, all together looking at God the creator and recreator and at his promises, made sure and certain in Jesus Christ.

Western society has known something of this love. Forgiveness is held as a virtue by many in our world, in a way which is quite foreign to some other worldviews. (I recall the shock on being told by a friend in the Middle East that forgiveness had never been seen as a good thing there.) We know we don't do it, by and large, but we think we *should*. The result of this, unfortunately, is that we have developed a corollary that is neither love nor forgiveness—namely, tolerance. The problem with this is clear: I can "tolerate" you without it costing me anything very much. I can shrug my shoulders, walk away, and leave you to do your own thing. That, admittedly, is preferable to my taking you by the throat and shaking you until you agree with me. But it is certainly not love. Love affirms the reality of the other person, the other culture, the other way of life; love takes the trouble to get to know the other person or culture, finding out how he, she, or it ticks, what makes it special; and finally, love wants the best for that person or culture. It was love, not just an arrogant imposition of alien standards, that drove much of the world to oppose the apartheid regime in South Africa. It was love, not a dewy-eyed anti-business prejudice (though that's what they said to him at the time), that drove abolitionist William Wilberforce to protest against the slave trade. It is love, not cultural imperialism, that says it is dehumanizing and society-destroying to burn a surviving widow on her husband's funeral pyre, or to kill the daughter who has eloped with a man of a different religion or race. Love must confront "tolerance" and insist, as it always has done, on a better way.

It is interesting how all the roads lead back to love. Love is often parodied, but its power shines through nonetheless. The greatest of the virtues, the firstfruit of the Spirit—even the pagan moralists note it as the primary thing which sets Christianity apart.

We must now ask, finally: If this is what it means to be the royal priesthood, worshipping the living God and bearing his love and restorative justice into the world, what are the pathways by which we can cultivate all the necessary virtues? How can we acquire that complex "second nature" which will enable us to grow up as genuine human beings, reflecting God to the world and the world back to God? What steps can we take toward the fully formed character which, when emergency strikes, will know by instinct what to do?

8. THE VIRTUOUS CIRCLE

ONE

We began our investigation with (among other things) two scenes: a pilot landing a plane safely on the Hudson River, and an eager young man asking Jesus for advice on what "good thing" to do in order to "inherit eternal life." Jesus's response to the petitioner was not to give more rules, but to offer a different kind of suggestion altogether: the challenge to a way of life, a character-forming set of actions, which would reflect the generous love of God into the world rather than project one's own moral achievements onto the screen of the watching cosmos. Pilot Chesley Sullenberger's achievement was to have so formed his character, by thousands of small choices and learned decisions over many years, that when the test came he did, by "second nature," what was required. These two scenes are of course quite different, but they have some key features in common.

Now, having expanded Jesus's challenge, and developed from the New Testament the idea of a Christian virtue-based answer to the question "How shall we live?" we come to the final bit of the "how" question. If the initial answer to "How shall we live?" is "by faith, hope, and love" (and all the rest), and the second part of the answer is "by the practice of virtue," the final question now faces us: How then can virtue be practiced? If it isn't, after all, a matter of self-help moralism—making oneself better entirely by one's own efforts—how is it done?

Before we get under way, let us note again the danger that lurks in a too-easy rejection of "moralism" and "effort." Everything that I now say assumes that God the Holy Trinity has acted decisively within history to rescue humans from the mess they've got themselves into, so that all we do ourselves is framed within that act and world of grace. It also assumes, to bring that cosmic story down to human level, that everything a Christian does by way of moral decision-making and acting is itself led and enabled by the Holy Spirit. One of the great Easter prayers in the old English *Book of Common Prayer* asks for two things: first, that God's special grace will put good desires into our minds; and second, that his continual help will enable us to bring those desires to good effect. And the special prayer for the first Sunday after the Epiphany, some weeks earlier, says pretty much the same thing. It asks that God's people may "perceive and know what things they ought to do, and also may have grace and power faithfully to fulfil the same."[1]

I have suggested throughout this book that the New Testament itself answers the first half of each of these prayers in terms, primarily, of a clear list of character traits whose radical novelty is generated from within the life, vision, achievement, death, and resurrection of Jesus himself. These events, taken together, constitute Jesus's followers as the true, image-bearing human beings, the royal priesthood. I have proposed, further, that according to the New Testament the way God the Holy Spirit answers the second half of the prayer is by renewing the individual heart and mind so that we can freely and consciously choose to practice those habits of behavior which, awkward and clumsy at first, will gradually become "second nature."

At that point, there is indeed something we might call "moralism." There is indeed, also, "moral effort." But it is not subject to the suspicion of Pelagianism—that is, of saying that we can pull ourselves up by our own moral bootstraps and that God is content with that. That charge, like so many second-rate theological proposals, is actually based on a simple mistake—namely, the idea that whatever God does we don't do, and vice versa. Life (thank God!) is more complicated than that.

With those preliminary remarks, we turn to business. How does virtue, in this fully Christian sense, happen? It happens, I suggest, as Christians find themselves caught up within a particular circle of activities and practices—the "virtuous circle" of this chapter's title. I have already spoken about some of these practices, but I want now to develop them within a slightly different argument.

Now, there are many people who practice most or all of the things I am talking about here, but who seem to advance very slowly if at all in the life of virtue. Indeed, some readers may be quite disappointed at this chapter for that very reason: surely, they will think, these practices are the things we've done for many years, and if you're talking about a new kind of holiness, we should expect some new things to help us! People in this situation are often like the man in the old Jewish joke who constantly prayed that he would win the lottery. Eventually, he shook his fist heavenward and demanded that God explain why he wasn't answering the man's fervent prayer. "My son," God replied, "you need to come halfway to meet me. You could at least buy a ticket!" Many people expect that virtue will happen to them automatically simply because they take part in the practices discussed here. But the practices aren't like prescribed medicine that will cure you whether or not you understand how it works. The key to virtue lies precisely, as we have seen, in the transformation of the mind. The point is not that the practices are wrong, or inadequate, but that our conscious mind and heart need to understand, ponder, and consciously choose the patterns of life which these practices are supposed to produce in us and through us. As we saw earlier, that is a nonnegotiable part of the process.

Even if consciously chosen, none of these practices, by itself, is sufficient to generate or sustain the hard-won, habit-formed character of which we have spoken. Several of them together may well have that effect; all of them together probably will. As with a bicycle, you need to be able to operate the pedals, the handlebars, and the brakes—and learn to keep your balance!—if the thing is going to work. One of the above by itself won't do.

Also as with a bicycle, it is easier to draw the circle of practices, the virtuous circle, than to describe it; but let me first list the component parts in what seems to me the natural order. We shall then explore them in more detail one by one, and give some examples of what they might look like in practice.

The circle does not include God, Jesus, and the Holy Spirit, because they are not only presupposed by it but also present in it at every point. Thus the circle should be understood as having "grace" as its starting point and "glory"—a life, individual and corporate, filled with the presence of God—as its goal. In light of all I have said so far, it has "justice" and "beauty" among its chief objects. Within those parameters, there are five elements: scripture, stories, examples, community, and practices:

One of the encouraging things about this circle is that it doesn't matter where you break into it—or where, so to speak, it breaks in upon you. One person is drawn in by the example of someone he doesn't even know, but who behaves in a particular way that he finds compelling and attractive. Another finds herself spellbound by sitting in the back of a church as the eucharist is being celebrated one weekday lunchtime, and doesn't know why. Another hears a story on the radio, doesn't know where it comes from, and starts asking questions. But, sooner or later, all three enter the circle, and if they follow it all around, this is what they will find.

TWO

I have put *scripture* at the top for fairly obvious reasons, which are there in Jesus's teaching and elsewhere in the writings of the early Christians. The practice of reading scripture, studying scripture, acting scripture, singing scripture—generally soaking oneself in scripture as an individual and a community—has been seen from the earliest days of Christianity as central to the formation of Christian character.

It is important to stress at this point (lest the whole scheme collapse into triviality) that this has only secondarily to do with the fact that scripture gives particular instructions on particular topics. That is important, of course; but it is far more important that the sheer activity of reading scripture, in the conscious desire to be shaped and formed within the purposes of God, is itself an act of faith, hope, and love, an act of humility and patience. It is a way of saying that we need to hear a fresh word, a word of grace, perhaps even a word of judgment as well as healing, warning as well as welcome. To open the Bible is to open a window toward Jerusalem, as Daniel did (6.10), no matter where our exile may have taken us.

It is, in particular, a way of locating ourselves as actors within an ongoing drama. No matter how many smaller stories there may be within scripture, and how many million edifying stories there may be outside it, the overall drama of scripture, as it stands, forms a single plot whose many twists and turns nonetheless converge remarkably on a main theme, which is the reconciliation of heaven and earth as God the creator deals with all that frustrates his purpose for his world and, through his Son and his Spirit, creates a new people through whom his purpose—filling the world with his glory—is at last to be realized. To be formed by this capital-S Story is to be formed as a Christian. To take the thousand, and ten thousand, decisions to open the Bible *today* and read more of this story, even if we can't yet join it all up in our own heads, is to take the next small step toward being the sort of person who, by second nature, will think, pray, act, and even feel in the way appropriate for someone charged with taking that narrative forward.

We are not yet, after all, at the end of the drama. Bible-readers (unless they adopt one of the well-known strategies for resisting this process) will find themselves drawn in as "characters" on stage. Yes, that may well mean "playing a part," and all the old charges of hypocrisy that cluster around the practice of virtue will come rumbling in here as well. But the more you know the play, the less you will be "playing a part" and the more you will simply be yourself. Sooner or later, you'll be acting naturally. *Second* nature. That's how virtue works.

Of course, within the Bible there are all kinds of far more specific passages which shape and direct the life of faith, hope, and love, and which the Spirit can and does use to stir up God's people to produce fruit. Almost every paragraph in the four gospels will have this effect, if read, pondered, and prayed through slowly and carefully. Likewise, the Psalms will open up the heart and mind of anyone who reads, sings, or prays them with any attention; they will form and reform that heart and mind in a way which, though by no means always comfortable, is always formative of Christian character. Even the genealogies, best read today at a run, can provide a powerful sense of the ongoing purposes of God, with generation after generation living by faith and hope before the next major point in the divine purpose unfolded, like a long-awaited late-blooming orchid. Some parts of the Bible are best drunk like a large glass of water on a hot day—in other words, large quantities at a time—while others, such as many parts of the letters, are best sipped and savored, drop by drop, like a fine wine (always remembering that, especially in a letter, every verse means what it means *in relation to the whole thing,* not on its own). But the point is that reading the Bible is habit-forming: not just in the sense that the more you do it the more you are likely to want to do it, but also in the sense that the more you do it the more it will form the habits of mind and heart, of soul and body, which will slowly but surely form your character into the likeness of Jesus Christ. And the "your" here is primarily plural, however important the singular is as well.

This isn't to say there aren't hard bits in the Bible—both passages that are difficult to understand and passages that we understand only too well but find shocking or disturbing (for example, celebrating the killing of Edomite babies at the end of Psalm 137). Avoid the easy solutions to these: that these bits weren't "inspired," or that the whole Bible is wicked nonsense, or that Jesus simply abolished the bits we disapprove of. Live with the tensions. Goodness knows there are plenty of similar tensions in our own lives, our own world. Let the troubling words jangle against one another. Take the opportunity to practice some patience (there may yet be more meaning here than I can see at the moment) and humility (God may well have things to say through this for which I'm not yet ready). In fact, humility is one of the key lessons which comes through reading the Bible over many years; there are some bits we find easy and other bits we find hard, but not everybody agrees as to which is which.

Some people, it seems, are temperamentally suited to a particular book or type of book which others find opaque. John's gospel is like that: some acclaim it as the very summit of the scriptures, while others, though appreciating some of its great strengths, find it awkward and puzzling. Some people find that with St. Paul as well. Perhaps—and this is where humility comes in—it might just be the case that scripture is so arranged that in order to grow toward a full, genuine humanness, toward the well-rounded virtue of being a royal priesthood, we have to grow into scripture, like a young boy inheriting his older brother's clothes and flopping around in them while he gradually fills out and grows up. Perhaps it's a measure of our maturity when parts of scripture that we found odd or even repellent suddenly come up in a new light; when people who naturally embrace Paul come to love John as well, and vice versa; when people soaked in Revelation suddenly warm to Acts, and vice versa. Perhaps it's another sign of maturity when our sense that scripture is made up of some bits we know and love, and other bits we tolerate while waiting for our favorites to come around once more, is suddenly overtaken by a sense of the *whole thing*— wide, multicolored, and unspeakably powerful. We had, perhaps, been wandering around in light mist, visiting favorite villages and hamlets, and then, as the mist gradually cleared, we discovered that everything we had loved was enhanced as it was glimpsed within a massive landscape, previously unsuspected, full of hills and valleys and unimagined glory.

THREE

Scripture, then, is habit-forming and character-forming. But scripture trains us to listen to and learn from *stories* of all kinds, inside the sacred text and outside, and to discern patterns and meanings within them. And stories of all sorts form and shape the character of those who read them.

For a story to be a story (as opposed to a mere collection of sentences) there must be a plot, with some kind of tension and resolution. We are storied creatures; we naturally love stories because our lives are filled with tension and resolution, and at any given moment there is likely to be more tension than resolution. So we identify with this character or that, with this moment or that, with this or that twist of the plot . . . and we are hooked. We want to know what happens, how it works out. We want resolution, closure, a sense of justice being done, or at the very least some sense of completeness.

So we live within the world of the narrative as creatures in search of an ending, in search of happiness, on the quest for *to teleion,* "the complete." Tracking how situations and characters lead up to that, or away from it, is part of the appeal. And all of this, at a deep level and not merely at the point of liking a particular character or approving or disapproving of a particular style of behavior, is character-forming. Comedy or tragedy, epic or romance, we watch characters developing and unfolding, facing and making choices, and slowly reaping the consequences; and (unless we are deaf in our hearts and souls) we learn how these things work and become sensitive to the same questions and challenges in our own lives.

All of this is true, of course, of any human being in any tradition. But within the Christian tradition there is special reason to pay attention to stories. Many of the great writers in the world have been deeply formed by the Jewish and/or Christian tradition, and their thoughtful words can help us to reflect on that tradition more deeply. But Christians believe that *all* human life is itself a gift of God and, however much it may be distorted, a reflection of God. Thus even stories written by writers who are explicitly atheist—indeed, writers whose words were intended to mock or dismiss God—have a strange knack of making crucial points about what it means to be human, about the importance of love and justice and beauty. Living within the world of stories increases—if we let it—the capacity for discernment.

But of course it is within the world of biblical stories in particular that many have found a special impetus toward acquiring the habits that together make up the virtuous life. The courage of Noah, the faith of Abraham, the hope of Joseph in prison, the leadership of Moses . . . and so on, and so on. Yes: scripture is indeed full of such characters and their stories, and we can and should be urged on by their example.

And yet. As my three-year-old grandson declared, having shown no earlier signs that he was listening in church to the second reading (which happened to be Jesus's parable of the wicked tenants, who beat up the master's servants and finally killed his son), "That's not a very nice story." No: and it wasn't meant to be. Only a small number of the stories that make up the Story in scripture are what we might call "nice." Only a small number, in fact, are told directly as examples. Those that are are important (as Paul notes in Romans 15.4 and 1 Corinthians 10.11), but many of the stories are much more oblique, including the ones we have just noted. Noah, after all, got drunk. Abraham, after all, put Sarah's life and God's promises in jeopardy through cowardice. Joseph was in prison because of his own original big-headedness. Moses didn't want to lead God's people in the first place, and more than once grumbled at God about the way things were going. Even Jesus's own mother, called "blessed" by all generations, was rebuked by her son for misunderstanding him and his vocation. Bit by bit, we realize that scripture was not given so that we can comb it for saintly, virtuous lives that we can copy as they stand. It was written as the story of God, God's people, and God's world; and God's people find themselves caught between God and the world again and again—in scripture as in today's life—in ambiguous and morally compromised situations. Hardly anyone in the entire Bible, Jesus alone excepted, stands out as a character of whom one can say, "Look at him, look at her; just do it the way they did it." (Daniel and his friends come close, but maybe the book of Daniel was written more with an eye to providing "examples for Jews under pagan pressure" than most of the other biblical books, and thus it might be the exception that proves the rule.)

What we find in the biblical stories, then, may be exemplary, but it is exemplary in a far more interesting way than merely offering a set of character templates to pick up and put down on ourselves. It is exemplary, if and as it is, *within the overall ongoing narrative* in which Christians themselves are called to live and play their part, taking forward the Israelites' vocation as God's royal priesthood, not primarily because we can detach particular characters from it and hold them up as models to copy. People still do that with, for instance, Elijah and Elisha, though if either of those men were to burst in upon a typical modern Western church or Christian gathering, there might be dismay, not to say mayhem. A good reader can "learn" from every character in every story, but only by a process of complex discernment, generalization, and carefully filtered application. Even slavishly scriptural preachers are unlikely to recommend that Christian teachers round up their enemies and have them killed on the spot, as Elijah did (1 Kings 18.40); and Elisha's response to the teasing of small boys would be unlikely to get him a second invitation to address the Youth Club (2 Kings 2.23–24). The same kind of process whereby we extract from such stories the bits we can apply to our own situations will also enable us to start with much less promising characters—some of the really third-rate kings, for instance, or the bored priests in Malachi—and think through what is going on in such a way as to find wisdom.

Wisdom, after all, is what we're after: not rules, not templates, but a sense of understanding how the ways of God and humankind work—all set within the great Story of the way of God with humankind, focused first upon Israel and ultimately upon Jesus. Learning to live from within the stories, to live within the plot at the point it has now reached, is the important thing. Examples fit within that.

But, once we've got that point, we will find other examples, of all kinds of things, all over the place. This brings us around the circle to the next category.

FOUR

Having recently advised against looking for examples too soon in scripture, I should point out that there are some obvious places where we are told to do just that. Paul provides a striking instance:

> I hope in the Lord Jesus to send Timothy to you soon, so that I may be encouraged in my turn by getting news about you. I have nobody else of his quality: he will genuinely care about how things are with you. All the rest, you see, are looking after their own interests, not those of Jesus the Messiah. But you know how he has proved himself; like a child with a father he has slaved with me for the sake of the gospel. So I'm hoping to send him just as soon as I see how it will turn out with me. And I trust in the Lord that I myself will come very soon as well. (Philippians 2.19–24)

Here, close up, we see how it sometimes works. Timothy is an example to be followed because he is doing exactly what, a few verses earlier, Paul said that Jesus himself did, and a few verses later will declare that he too has done. Timothy has looked not to his own interests, but to those of Jesus and the gospel. More: he is a good example of the apprentice, working alongside the master craftsman and learning his trade. There are no doubt other things to be said about Timothy as well, but this is a start. In these respects at least he is an example to copy.

Other New Testament writers draw attention, in a similar "exemplary" way, to characters from the distant past. Here is James, selecting from the Elijah story as modern preachers will do, noting the fact that he is exemplary in the highlighted respect though perhaps not in everything:

> The prayer of a righteous person is very powerful in its effects. Elijah was a human being with the same passions we've got, and he prayed fervently that it wouldn't rain, and it didn't rain on the earth for three years and six months. Then he prayed again, and the heaven gave rain and the earth brought forth its fruit. (James 5.16b–18)

And here is the letter to the Hebrews, holding up a dozen examples, with Jesus himself as the climax of them all:

> What about us, then? We have such a great cloud of witnesses all around us! What we must do is this: we must put aside each heavy weight, and the sin which so easily gets in the way. We must run the race that lies ahead of us, and we must run it patiently. We must look ahead, to Jesus: he is the one who carved out the path for faith, and he's the one who brought it to completion. He knew that there was joy spread out and waiting for him. That's why he endured the cross, making light of its shame, and has now taken his seat at the right hand of God's throne. He put up with enormous opposition from sinners. Weigh up in your minds just how severe it was; then you won't find yourselves getting weary and worn out. (12.1–3)

The writer knows very well that there is much more to say about Jesus than this—Jesus the Son of God, superior to angels, Jesus the high priest after the order of Melchizedek, Jesus the one who offered his own blood to make atonement. But also . . . Jesus the example of virtue, looking ahead and bringing one's life into line with the vision of "perfection" (11.40) that we glimpse. Negative examples are likewise offered in Hebrews: consider Esau, who sold his birthright for a single meal and wasn't able to reverse the decision afterward (12.16–17).

The same writer can invoke examples from much closer at hand, drawing attention to the leaders within the community itself: "Remember your leaders, who spoke God's word to you. Look carefully at how their lives came to complete fruition, and imitate their faith" (13.7). This is virtue language: see where they ended up, not (we assume) in terms of their death, but in terms of the fully formed character which they developed. So copy them, particularly their faith, and you will find the same character growing in you as well.

Scripture is thus full of stories which, even if not written primarily for this purpose, can serve as examples of people who developed the character of virtue. The New Testament holds out in particular the stories of the eleven disciples who, traveling around with Jesus, learned from him a whole way of life which they then modeled for others. Paul, as we've seen, uses himself as an example, specifically in his imitating of Jesus Christ (1 Corinthians 10.31–11.1; Philippians 3.4–17).

But of course part of living within the story of God's people is that there are now countless others to whose example one may also appeal. The phenomenal success, in human terms alone, of St. Francis of Assisi can be put down in large measure to the power of example: people suddenly saw, in the middle of an apparently corrupt and careless church, someone living (as he and they supposed) as Jesus had lived. The sight was sufficiently compelling to make a lot of other people decide to live like that as well, to make the many large choices necessary to embrace the life of poverty, chastity, and obedience. This follows the line already set by the Desert Fathers and Mothers of the early centuries, who abandoned the corrupt life of their cities and set out for the wilderness to live in solitary prayer—and who inspired considerable numbers to imitate them. We may suspect that there is something more than mere imitation going on here. One recent writer speaks of "cascading grace": when God does something in one person's life and through his or her work, other people see it and think, "Do you suppose that could happen here?" and a spark turns into a flame—often a flame of a subtly different color. Imitation need not be slavish. Led by the Spirit, it can be a means toward something quite new.

I suspect that many of my readers, in fact, are reading this book not least because they themselves have had Christian leaders to whom they have looked up as examples. Christian leaders have been warned from the beginning that they were to act as examples (1 Timothy 4.12; Titus 2.7; Hebrews 13.7; 1 Peter 5.3; and other similar places), and whether we like it or not (and many of us leaders are anxious about it), Christian folk—like our own blood-children—will tend to copy us.

Each century since the time of Jesus has provided particular examples of people whose characters were so formed by persistent attention to the patterns of virtue that, when the moment came, they were ready for it; and they now serve as among our most striking examples. Several twentieth-century martyrs from countries and cultures all over the world are displayed in effigy on the western front of Westminster Abbey. I will mention only one.

Maximilian Kolbe was a Polish Roman Catholic priest who was seen to the Auschwitz death camp with his people. One day one of his fellow prisoners was being threatened with death for attempting to escape. The man began to weep: he had a wife and children he was concerned for. Kolbe stepped forward and offered himself in the man's place. He went to his death calmly. The punishment was intended to be death by starvation, but when Kolbe was still alive after two weeks, he was killed by a lethal injection. The point is this: he wasn't acting spontaneously or in obedience to a rule. He was doing something that came naturally, as the climax of a life spent in giving himself away, in following Jesus in the work of his pastoral ministry, and in the daily sacramental life. Like Chesley Sullenberger, he didn't have time to think, but he didn't need to. The thinking had been done a long time before, and the second-nature habits of self-giving love had been ingrained in him as a result. The moment came; the decision was made.

Another, more recent example. I was at a huge service in an enormous church, with wonderful music, flowing robes, and a crowd of thousands that only just fit into the large building. Suddenly, about ten minutes into the service, some men pushed their way roughly past the ushers at the doors, injuring one of them, and ran into the church shouting slogans. The disruption was caused by a protest group that had recently acquired a national reputation for behaving outrageously in pursuit of their cause (which, by the way, had nothing directly to do with the church or any of the people there).

The protesters reached the front of the church, shouted some more slogans, waved their placards, and then simply stopped. Clearly they hadn't decided what they would do next, if they managed to get that far. But nobody in the church had any idea what to do next, either. The ushers were clearly frightened and unsure how to proceed. Nobody wanted a scene (except perhaps the protesters, who would have loved to be carried out by the police, shouting more slogans as they went). The service had been massively disrupted as it was. Scuffles, and the violence necessary in restraint, would have soured the atmosphere even more. As all of us wondered what would happen next, one of the senior clergy walked quietly across toward the leading protester and had a short, quiet conversation with him. He then walked over to the presiding cleric for another brief conversation. A moment later the presiding cleric spoke to the congregation, informing them that "our unexpected guests" had agreed to state their case for three minutes and then leave the building quietly.

How was it done? I was in awe of the man who had stepped forward and spoken with the protester. I wouldn't have known what on earth to say. I would have been frightened what the group of protesters might do if I approached, and worried that I would make matters worse by words or action. Apparently, as I discovered later, he pointed out that they had made their protest and that if they continued much longer they would alienate more people than they influenced. But how had he been able to do that so calmly?

Then I remembered, many years before, watching the same cleric walk down a street in one of our busy cities. Dressed as a priest, he stopped quietly and sat down on the pavement to chat with a group of men who were drinking methylated spirits. He made his approach look natural, and they received it that way. He was on his way to preach at a service, but he didn't appear to be in a hurry. Such meetings were obviously already a habit. He knew, from long experience, how to speak calmly and wisely with people of whom most others would be afraid. By the time it came to that great service, fifteen or more years later, the habit of faith, love, and courage had long been fully formed. And when the moment came, he didn't have to think about it. Second nature kicked in. He knew, authentically, what to do and how to do it. I have learned many things from that man, but this one stands out. His name is Rowan Williams.

FIVE

Examples come to us from all over, but they come within a context. That context is—and I know how trivialized this word has become— the *community* of the people of God. It will have become clear to readers that the vocation to be a royal priesthood, the challenge to develop the Christian virtues which constitute us as genuine, God-reflecting human beings, is a vocation and challenge that we receive not merely as individuals but as communities. Aristotle saw the person of virtue as taking a key role within the *polis,* the city, the basic political unit of his day. Christian virtue, though it generates great leaders, does so in order that the whole body of Christ may function with the same learned, habitual virtue. Following examples thus leads us around the circle to the point where we must recognize that one of the primary locations where, and means by which, any of us learns the habits of the Christian heart and life is what we loosely call the church.

This is not the place for a discussion of the nature of the church. That is a large and complex subject for another occasion. But when I say "church" here, I mean at least three interlocking things. I note this in order both to demystify the concept for people who find it impossibly fuzzy and to bring it within reach once more for people who have found it alienating.

First, I mean the whole and entire company of the people of God, from Abraham in the distant past to the child I baptized a few days ago: a great multitude which nobody could possibly count, from every nation and culture under the sun. A large number of these Christians have gone on before us to rest with Jesus Christ, awaiting the final resurrection. (They may be the majority, but since there are more human beings alive today than in most of the rest of history put together, and since the church has expanded enormously in recent decades, it is possible that this balance may have shifted.) Christians who have died are still part of the family, still members of Christ's people, and we still learn from them and celebrate their fellowship at those moments when heaven and earth come together—as we pray, as we read scripture, as we celebrate the sacraments, and as we serve the needs of God's world and especially the poor. Equally important, a large number of the Christian family live in places very different to our own, with local customs and expectations that look very strange to us, as we do to them. In 2008, hosting guests from around the world at the Lambeth Conference, I was struck, as we all were, by just how different the represented cultures were. This wide context of the church across time and space is the overall setting within which Christians learn, individually and together, the habits which together constitute Christian virtue.

Second, I mean the actual living family and fellowship of which I am a part. In my tradition, this means the unit we call a diocese, overseen by a bishop. This unit functions as an extended family, with its own local culture and traditions, and its own ordering of its common life. This unit understands itself, not as an independent body owing no allegiance to the large unit we just looked at, but as one instantiation of it, as though that entire family across time and space were boiled down to just this group. Within this relatively local setting—dioceses differ considerably in size, even within my denomination, but the principle is the same—there is a more sharply focused context within which we are to learn how to be the royal priesthood. The habits of heart and mind here are rather more obviously *corporate* habits: this is how *we* have learned to behave. I learn to trust you as you learn to trust me, and together we learn to act with hope and love in this or that situation, building up communities in which faith, hope, and love, and the ninefold fruit of the Spirit, become not things to think about, try once in a while, and then stop implementing, but things to think about in order to practice them *together*.

Third, I mean the small group—it may be a parish church, it may be a neighborhood Bible study group, it may be a group that meets to plan strategy in relation to local social issues, whatever—where sharply focused learning can happen and where decisive action can be planned and taken. Here the habits are formed by Christian friends, neighbors, and colleagues working together, praying together, sharing one another's lives and sorrows and frustrations and excitements. Here is Jane, slowly thinking through the plan to meet women ex-offenders when they emerge from prison, to prevent them going back to the habits that got them there in the first place. Here is Jack, full of a new Bible study guide he's been reading, which he knows will open the group's eyes to vistas of truth previously unimagined. Here is Jeff, who has been talking to the local education authority about starting a preschool for the young children of single parents (of whom there are many in the area) who have nothing to do when Mom goes out. Here is Lisa, who has been writing some new music for use at the Sunday night service for which a motley crew of young people typically drifts in. The point of introducing you to this four, and the millions like them in small groups around the world, is that *they are learning the habits of heart and life together*. The point of "virtue" for them is not that any of them will become the kind of striking "leader" who will win awards, be recognized on the street, and appear on television chat shows. Nor is the point that they are all just like one another. They are not; they are very different characters, with different gifts and vocations and temperaments and social and cultural backgrounds. They are together contributing to a community that is practicing the arts of being a royal priesthood, a working and worshipping fellowship for whom faith, hope, and love are being learned and exercised in the service of God's kingdom. And part of the point is this. In order to work together, these four, and the others in their local fellowship, have to develop the fruit of the Spirit. If they don't have love, joy, peace, patience, kindness, generosity, faithfulness, gentleness, and self-control, they won't get very far. Their fellowship will fragment. Each one will go off and do his or her own thing, muttering about the lack of vision in the rest of the church. This is what I mean when I say that the church, the community of God's people, is the forum within which virtue is learned and practiced.

Of course, as is obvious to anyone who's been part of a church community for more than a day or two, since we all know that the fruit of the Spirit is important *we all learn to pretend*. ("Sincerity is what matters," said Bob Hope. "Once you can fake that, you've got it made.") A general culture of "niceness" (though with self-control notably lacking, at least behind the scenes) can then clog the wheels and get in the way of addressing the tough issues that need to be worked through. There are many ways of avoiding those issues, of maintaining appearances rather than cultivating substance, but they all come down to not making the effort to develop the corporate as well as individual muscles of faith, hope, and love. And the result will be neither truly royal nor truly a priesthood. "Pretending" isn't the same as "putting it on," which as we have seen is the early stage of the habit of virtue. Pretending is a way of not working at it. And working at it is what counts.

But, happily, there are also communities where these things are worked at and worked out. They are, in particular, communities where the royal priesthood is very much in evidence. Come with me to one such, on a rainy Wednesday morning. Eight or ten people are coming out of the church after an early eucharist service. They emerge onto a street where half the shops have been boarded up. Unemployment has risen again, people are spending less money, and the shopkeepers couldn't pay the rent any longer. As a result, the local bank has been forced to close as well. But the bank is now "under new management"—consisting, more or less, of the eight or ten people coming out of church and putting up umbrellas. They go down the street, unlock the old bank, and set about preparing it for another day's work. These busy people and their fellow parishioners, many with full-time jobs, also offer a mothers-and-toddlers group; a debt-counseling service aimed at helping people whose finances are in such bad shape that they're ashamed even to go into a post office; an old people's day-care center where folks who might otherwise be stuck by themselves in a small apartment can come together, learn handcrafts, play games, and enjoy one another's company; and a literacy training center complete with a computer room. The point in relating all this is quite simple. None of this would have happened if it hadn't been for people, already trained in the habits of Christian thinking, looking at their small main street turning into a wilderness and *knowing* what they had to do—and then having the varied skills and practiced virtues to do it, to make it happen. And, what's more, this project—a great example of corporate virtue, Christian virtue that doesn't draw attention to itself but just gets on with the job—has in turn been an example to others, a sign of what can be done, a stimulus to other Christians to think, and pray, and practice living the life of God's kingdom, living as the royal priesthood.

Or come with me to an old school that was taken over by people from another church, and turned into a center for people suffering from various mental and physical disabilities. Many things go on in that building, but there's one that I've always found particularly moving. It's a furniture repair shop. People bring broken chairs, damaged tables, cabinets with doors falling off, and other such items to the center. Under the unobtrusive guidance of one or two experts, the workers—human beings who are themselves broken, damaged, and hampered by bits of body and mind that don't work properly—mend the furniture and send it out whole and complete. Of course, projects like this are somebody's brainchild, and usually one or two people have given sterling leadership. But the point is that the habits of heart and mind which had been generated and sustained within the life of the church spurred people to seize the opportunity to do something which has the fingerprints of the gospel of Jesus Christ all over it.

Others have written eloquently of the way in which whole communities can exemplify Christian virtue, and I trust that the point has been sufficiently made. Faith, hope, love, and the ninefold fruit are things which demand to be practiced, learned, and made habitual *together*. Even if you're called to be a hermit on a desert island—in fact, *especially* if you're called to be a hermit on a desert island—you need to be part of a wider community with and for whom you're praying and who are, in all likelihood, taking some responsibility for you. The one body is the place where, and the means by which, the work of royal priesthood goes ahead.

Specific examples of the communal expression of the main three virtues stand out in my mind. I think of a church that was challenged by its minister to a serious venture of faith, going out on a limb to raise money for a badly needed new heating system. They kept each other to it, stirred up one another to believe and pray, and succeeded. I think of a church which refused to give up hope when the minister's teenage daughter disappeared while on vacation abroad. Their hope sustained one another, including the minister and his family, until at last the daughter was discovered, safe. I think of a church not far from my home where, in a small congregation, there is one young adult with severe mental problems and quite serious physical difficulties. The congregation has surrounded him with love, incorporated him into their life, and wouldn't now feel complete without him. And so we could go on. Trivial examples? No. Think of Jesus's parables: part of the point of the kingdom of God is that it plants small seeds wherever it can and trusts God to let them grow in whatever way he wants. This is how virtue happens: whole communities deciding together, as Hebrews says, "to stir up one another to love and good works" (10.24), and then working at it so that what might to begin with have seemed impossible (or at least very unnatural) becomes, remarkably quickly, second nature.

It is communities like this that form the next step on the way around the virtuous circle. But there is one final step, which will then lead us back to where we began.

SIX

The *practices* of the community are all-important. The very fact that we call them by that name gives a hint: these are the things through which the community *practices* the habits of mind and heart which develop those corporate virtues of which we have spoken.

Central to the practices of Christian faith, as I have said all along, is shared worship. I assume that all serious Christians worship and pray in private, day by day; certainly little growth in virtue, or anything else for that matter, is likely to happen without this. But I assume, too, that serious Christians will worship and pray *together*, and will learn, as communities, how to do that wisely and effectively. Just as the sheer act of opening the Bible says, in effect, "Here I am, Lord; speak, for your servant is listening," which is itself the beginning of the heart habit of being open to God, so the sheer act of coming together in worship, week by week, says in effect, "We, together, hope and intend to be part of God's royal priesthood, and we are here to draw wisdom and strength from Jesus himself." Thus, before a hymn has been sung or a word spoken, the habit of the heart is being formed: a community that together intends to work on faith, hope, and love.

(Of course, I know only too well that some communities are all habit and no virtue. That's the point at which we're back with the old dilemma: Would you prefer shallow spontaneity, because it's better than inauthentic virtue-practice, or bored habit, because at least you've got a liturgy whose roots run deep? Answer, of course: neither. But those of us who live in a land where churchgoing used to be a habit of the many and is now a hobby of the few should not scorn such habits as still remain.)

The practices of worship have centered, for two thousand years, on the meal Jesus gave us. This meal was itself part of a corporate habit well over a thousand years old: the habit of keeping the Passover to celebrate the Exodus from Egypt. This habit trained the hearts and minds of generations of the Jewish people, and trains them still, to think of themselves instinctively as God's freedom-people, in continuity with their far-flung ancestors and in continuity, also, with generations yet to come. Jesus took that meal and transformed it so that it spoke of his own death and resurrection, drawing to its climax that long history of a freedom-community and constituting his own followers in the same way. There is more to the eucharist than this, but not less.

Generations of wary Protestants, anxious about the hypocrisy of virtue and the dangers of ritualism and formalism, have often missed what's actually going on here. Yes, of course ritual and formality can become an end in themselves. That is one reason why the practices of Christian faith have always included not only the reading of scripture (now, you see, we have come full circle) but also the preaching of the word, so that the word which explains both scripture and sacrament may be fresh, challenging the congregation to make the event real for themselves yet again and to ponder its implications for their mission in the world.

The details of eucharistic practice vary from place to place and church to church, of course, but the central actions of taking and breaking bread, of pouring out wine, of some kind of Jesus-based storytelling (often, a gospel reading) beforehand, with prayer and confession of sin, speak powerfully by their very shape of a slow, steady formation both of the individuals present and of the community. We are becoming, unless we resist, people who are living the freedom-story: God's story with Israel and the world, God's story above all with and in Jesus. We are becoming, unless our hearts are hard (and the more you come to the eucharist without letting it have any effect on you, the harder your heart must be), people who know in their bones, by an increasingly clear second nature, that we are forgiven and so we forgive. (In churches that "share the peace," that's what this is supposed to signify before we gather at the Lord's table.) We are becoming consciously (in order to become unconsciously) a people who together and individually find new energy, as we find new bodily energy in food and drink, by feeding on Jesus himself and his death and resurrection. In and through all of this, we are becoming people who gather up the praises of the world and the needs of the world and present them before the God we know in Jesus. In and through all of this, we are being formed into a people who will find that they then discern, in fresh and often surprising ways, the tasks that they can perform within their own communities. These are to be the tasks which put into practice the "royal" bit of our primary vocation, just as the worship puts into practice the "priestly" bit.

Healthy worshipping communities may well not realize that all this is happening to them. They simply know that church is where they need to be, that prayer and scripture and eucharist are what they need to be doing, and that they wouldn't know quite who they were without those things. That, again, is utterly characteristic of Christian virtue. The habituated Christian doesn't say, on emerging from church, "Why, what a splendid person I am! I can feel myself growing ten feet tall now! I can take on the world!" Habituated Christians are probably too busy checking that the children in the nursery are all right, that the elderly man in a wheelchair has a ride back home, and that their name is on the rota for visiting at the hospice next Thursday. By these undramatic, apparently humdrum activities (those who love grand schemes and big designs may curl their lip, but think what life would be like if several million Christians suddenly stopped doing this kind of thing), the church of Jesus Christ is becoming that actual royal priesthood, practicing the humble virtues that genuinely anticipate God's new world.

Along with eucharist there goes, of course, baptism. Again, many Christians couldn't easily explain what happens in baptism or why they do it. That doesn't necessarily mean that the practice has become a mere bit of formal ritual (though that, too, does happen). It may well mean that, as with virtue itself, it has become second nature. This is how we join the family: by plunging into water and coming up again! By dying and rising with Jesus the Messiah! I sense that, at least in the churches I know best, baptism may in fact need more explanation, and more working through in terms of how its meaning becomes a living reality for the core congregation and also for those on the fringe who want their baby baptized but are far from clear why. But the regular practice of baptism says something to the congregation, something that should go deeper and deeper until it becomes second nature.

So what does it say to them? First, nobody drifts into the kingdom of God. Sooner or later there must be a dying and a rising. Christian living, "virtue" included, is never a matter simply of discovering what I feel like doing and seeing how to do it. No: "You have died, and your life is hidden with Christ in God" (Colossians 3.3). Baptism makes it crystal clear that all Christian life is a matter of being signed with the cross, of sharing in the cross, of taking up the cross and following Jesus. This needs emphasizing today in view of the extraordinary idea which has crept in to some churches that baptism simply means God's acceptance of everybody as is, with no need for repentance or for dying to self and rising to God in Christ.

Second, baptism is the same for everybody, marking out the church decisively as a single body. We don't have a different rite for adults and children, or for men and women, or for rich and poor, or for people from different nations, races, and cultures. Yes, there are different modes of baptism—some people don't think it's real baptism unless the person gets wet from head to toe, for example, while most of us think it's enough if a handful of water is splashed on the head (just as the eucharist is a real meal even if you have only a tiny bit of bread and a small sip of wine). But the point is that baptism, by being the same for everyone alike, reminds us at a deep level, informing the heart and mind of every Christian, that we are all brothers and sisters in Christ. There are, in that sense, no "special" Christians. Ordination, for those called to it, is simply a sub-branch of baptism, setting certain persons aside (as in Ephesians 4) so that, through their ministry, the whole baptized body of Christ may continue to function as such and grow together to maturity. Every Christian has a different calling. But all callings are marked with the same water, the same cross.

I have spoken already of prayer in connection with the eucharist, but of course prayer remains central to all Christian practice, both in public and in private. Prayer remains a mystery. It wouldn't be prayer if it weren't. But it remains a mystery whose shape we can discern, a mystery shaped for us by the coming together of heaven and earth in Jesus Christ and our sharing in that coming-togetherness by the Spirit. But again the very practice of prayer, before we even begin to think about the content, says in and of itself: we are people who live at the interface between God's world and the life of this present world. We are people who belong in that uncomfortable borderland. We are called to stay at this post even when we have no idea what's actually going on. And, once again, this obviously constitutes training in humility, patience, faith, and hope—and, if we are persistent, maybe even love. But it means that we come to prayer knowing that we're to reinforce the heart habits that make us, by second nature, who we are. And we rise from prayer with the heart formed that bit more securely in its settled second nature of trust and obedience.

The regular habit of giving money is a further practice which forms the hearts and lives of God's people. Once more, this can become a hollow ritual or can, even worse, transform itself into the settled habit of people's minds which thinks, "The church is always asking us for money" or "God owes me a favor because I've written him a check." Don't let the parodies put you off. The habit of giving, of giving generously, is not an extra option for keen Christians. It is absolutely obligatory on all—because our whole calling is to reflect God the creator, and the main thing we know about this true God is that his very nature is self-giving, generous love. The reason why "God loves a cheerful giver" (2 Corinthians 9.7) is that that's what God himself is like. Someone like that is a person after God's own heart. Making a regular, formal, and public practice of the giving of money is designed to generate the habit of heart which forms a key part of what Paul meant by *agapē,* love.

And, of course, one of the most central things that the community must do, at every level, is to read scripture together. This says, as clearly as anything can do, "We are not a random collection of people doing strange things because this is what our families and friends have always done, even though we've all forgotten why. We are members of the body of Christ, taking our place in the story of Jesus Christ, and the ongoing purposes of the God he called Father, finding ourselves called to learn the art of genuine humanness by worshipping him and working for his kingdom in the world." Like actors checking through the script again before going onstage, or like musicians scanning the score before walking on to take their place in the orchestra, we remind ourselves of key bits of the story, not simply to learn something new about those bits, though we may well do that, but because they remind us of the story as a whole and of where we fit into it. We will then be able to walk out of church and discern, by second nature, what needs doing down the street, or in the local city council, or in the global economy.

Scripture has a particular function in relation to the other four elements of the circle. Without scripture, and not least without regular preaching from scripture, the stories can fly off in different directions. Examples can be misconstrued, communities can take on a life of their own, and practices can become, as we've noted, empty or meaningless ritual. With scripture, all that changes. God works, by the Holy Spirit, through the reading, teaching, and preaching of scripture, to create new frameworks of ideas, to remind us of facets of the story we were in danger of forgetting, to correct imbalances, and above all to stir our hearts and minds with fresh visions of God's love. It is, after all, love that creates all the other virtues: God's love, to which all moral effort is merely an answering word of thanks, praise, and returned love. And scripture is nothing if not the story of God's love—God's love in creation, in Israel, in Jesus, by the Spirit, in *new* creation. The more we are people of the story, the examples, the community, and the practices, the more we will understand the scriptures, and vice versa. And the more we join them all together, the more we shall be formed into a community, locally, globally, and across time, in whose lives the Jesus habits of faith, hope, and love have become second nature.

This closes the circle—not to make it a charmed holy huddle where everything merely reinforces itself and nothing can break in or out, but to make it clear that wherever you begin in developing the habits of the Christian heart, it's vital to go on around the circle, and around again, until the circle itself becomes a habit of the heart, a second-nature thing. Only then, when you are suddenly faced with an emergency demanding a creative, reconciling act of healing and hope, will you be ready to perform it. Only then, when there is a choice between campaigning for justice for people being unfairly treated by the government and saving our popularity by turning a blind eye, will we have all our instincts tuned, not to what the newspapers say, but to what the gospel says. Only then, when faced with personal tragedy among its members, will the rest of the congregation know, by second nature, what to say and do. Only then will we know in our bones what we should be doing "after we believe."

Only then, when someone says, "Tell me about Jesus," will we truly know what to say. And only then will what we say make the sense that it should.

AFTERWORD: FURTHER READING

I have been conscious, in researching and writing this book, of three streams of thought with which I have been in fairly constant implicit dialogue. I wish I'd had time and space to develop my arguments in relation to all three, but that will have to wait for another occasion. What follows is not at all an exhaustive bibliography of those subjects, but simply an indication of where I have found particular stimulus (often by disagreement) and help. Many of these books have good bibliographies indicating where matters can be pursued further.

There are some excellent recent books on New Testament ethics, but as far as I can see they do not usually approach the subject with virtue in mind, or haven't developed it in the way I have done. That doesn't mean I haven't had anything to learn from them; rather, the reverse. Richard Burridge's *Imitating Jesus: An Inclusive Approach to New Testament Ethics* (Grand Rapids, MI: Eerdmans, 2007) is the most recent major study and refers to all significant predecessors. Despite his kind words about me in his preface, I remain in significant disagreement with him both in his arguments and in his conclusions, but I am grateful for his massive and important work as well as his friendship. Abraham J. Malherbe's collection of materials in *Moral Exhortation: A Greco-Roman Sourcebook* (Philadelphia: Westminster, 1986) and Wayne Meeks's two books *The Moral World of the First Christians* (Philadelphia: Westminster; London: SPCK, 1986) and *The Origins of Christian Morality: The First Two Centuries* (New Haven, CT: Yale University Press, 1993) remain basic and important studies not least of the background of moral discourse from within which early Christianity emerged. Malherbe suggests that the emphasis on the Trinity and knowing God meant that the early Christians left virtue to one side (p. 15), whereas in my view this theological framework recontextualized and transformed, but did not abandon, that theme. An important study of the Jewish context of Pauline ethics is that of Markus Bockmuehl, *Jewish Law in Gentile Churches: Halakah and the Beginning of Christian Public Ethics* (Edinburgh: T & T Clark, 2000). Towering over other works on New Testament ethics is Richard B. Hays's masterpiece, *The Moral Vision of the New Testament: A Contemporary Introduction to New Testament Ethics* (San Francisco: HarperSanFrancisco, 1996), though again not much is made of virtue. The room where I wrote most of the present book happens to have in it a framed photograph of Richard and myself, taken on holiday in the north of England. I am turning to smile at the camera while Richard, with binoculars to his eyes, is surveying the far horizon. That sums up reasonably well the difference between our two books. I am delighted that the original lecture which got me started on the present train of thought has metamorphosed into an article in Richard's *Festschrift:* "Faith, Virtue, Justification, and the Journey to Freedom" in *The Word Leaps the Gap: Essays on Scripture and Theology in Honor of Richard B. Hays,* ed. J. Ross Wagner, C. Kavin Rowe, and A. Katherine Grieb (Grand Rapids, MI: Eerdmans, 2008), 472–97. Two other recent books of biblical theology which are not directly concerned with ethics or virtue but which have been important for my thinking through these issues are J. Richard Middleton, *The Liberating Image: The* Imago Dei *in Genesis 1* (Grand Rapids, MI: Brazos, 2005), and G. K. Beale, *The Temple and the Church's Mission: A Biblical Theology of the Dwelling Place of God* (Downers Grove, IL: InterVarsity Press, 2004).

Just as most writers on New Testament ethics don't pay much attention to virtue, so most recent writers on virtue give little attention to the New Testament—thus leaving an apparent gap which the present book is suggesting should be filled. Three interesting exceptions to this, which are not, I think, very widely known, are Joseph J. Kotva Jr.,

The Christian Case for Virtue Ethics (Washington, DC: Georgetown University Press, 1996); Daniel J. Harrington and James F. Keenan, *Jesus and Virtue Ethics: Building Bridges between New Testament Studies and Moral Theology* (Lanham, MD: Sheed & Ward [Rowman and Littlefield], 2002); and Graham Tomlin, *Spiritual Fitness: Christian Character in a Consumer Society* (London: Continuum, 2006). The last named came to hand, as a gift from the author, late in the process of working on this book, and I was delighted to note considerable overlap in our work. He gives a more balanced and rounded picture of Martin Luther's position on virtue than I was able to do here.

In recent writing on Christian ethics, with particular relation to virtue, I was fortunate to be sent, at a late stage in my thinking, the magisterial work of Jennifer A. Herdt, *Putting on Virtue: The Legacy of the Splendid Vices* (Chicago: University of Chicago Press, 2008). Prior to that, like most others who have thought about these things, I was massively indebted to Alasdair MacIntyre's *After Virtue: A Study in Moral Theory,* 2nd ed. (1981; Notre Dame, IN: University of Notre Dame Press, 1984), and, in parallel, to Stanley Hauerwas, including such books as *Christians Among the Virtues: Theological Conversations with Ancient and Modern Ethics* (with Charles Pinches) (Notre Dame, IN: University of Notre Dame Press, 1997) and *A Community of Character* (Notre Dame, IN: University of Notre Dame Press, 1991). I have particularly enjoyed the work of Samuel Wells—for instance, his *Improvisation: The Drama of Christian Ethics* (Grand Rapids, MI: Brazos, 2004) and his *God's Companions: Reimagining Christian Ethics* (Oxford: Blackwell, 2006). As I was working on the present book, there came to hand a remarkable textbook which explores Christian ethics in terms of virtue and makes more use of the New Testament than many of those I have just listed. I don't (of course) always agree with David S. Cunningham, *Christian Ethics: The End of the Law* (London: Routledge, 2008), but his book, though much fuller than mine, is in many ways running on a parallel track. My wider reflections on Christian ethics have, like so much in my life and thought, been significantly influenced by Oliver O'Donovan, whose *Resurrection and*

Moral Order: An Outline for Evangelical Ethics (Leicester, UK: Inter-Varsity Press; Grand Rapids, MI: Eerdmans, 1986) set a new standard of reflection for many of us. I am very grateful to Oliver for some clear and sharp comments on an earlier draft of this book, which saved me from some at least of the errors and unclarities into which I was wandering. His successor in the Regius Chair at Oxford, Professor Nigel Biggar, also offered some helpful comments on an earlier outline. The errors, unclarities, and confusions that remain are, of course, my own.

The third stream of thought with which I have been in implicit dialogue is the enormous and many-sided world of non-Christian (and non-Jewish) ethical thinking. Much of this remains, as with Western philosophy in general, "footnotes to Plato and Aristotle," particularly in this case to Aristotle's great *Nicomachean Ethics*, one of the key texts on which I cut my intellectual teeth at Oxford forty years ago. For most readers the most accessible edition may well be that in the Loeb Classical Library, ed. H. Rackham (1926; Cambridge, MA: Harvard University Press, 1934), or the Penguin Classic, tr. J. A. K. Thomson (Harmondsworth, UK: Penguin, 1953). Three recent writers I have found stimulating, though obviously in sharp disagreement at many points (such as the existence of God), are Simon Blackburn—e.g., *Being Good: A Short Introduction to Ethics* (Oxford: Oxford University Press, 2001); A. C. Grayling—e.g., *Life, Sex, and Ideas: The Good Life Without God* (Oxford: Oxford University Press, 2003); and the remarkable work, which has become a bestseller in its native France, of André Comte-Sponville, *A Short Treatise on the Great Virtues: The Uses of Philosophy in Everyday Life* (2001; London: Vintage, 2003). I suspect, actually, that in the last of these the average reader will understand "virtue" more in terms of "value" than in the sense meant by Aristotle. But that is one of the thousand other issues to be left for another opportunity.

Three books which have helped me to think a little about neuroscience and its relevance for moral and spiritual life are John Medina, *Brain Rules: 12 Principles for Surviving and Thriving at Work, Home, and School* (Seattle: Pear Press, 2008); Malcolm Jeeves and Warren S. Brown, *Neuroscience, Psychology, and Religion: Illusions, Delusions,* and Realities about Human Nature (West Conshohocken, PA: Templeton Foundation Press, 2009); and Joel B. Green, *Body, Soul and Human Life: The Nature of Humanity in the Bible* (Grand Rapids, MI: Baker, 2008).

I have not referred to my own previous works in the course of the book, but of course what I've said here stands on the shoulders of several earlier efforts. In particular, we might list the following:

2009 *Justification: God's Plan and Paul's Vision*. London: SPCK; Downers Grove, IL: InterVarsity Press.

2007 *Surprised by Hope* / U.S. subtitle *Rethinking Heaven, Resurrection, and the Mission of the Church*. London: SPCK; San Francisco: HarperOne (2008).

2007 *The Cross and the Colliery* / U.S. title *Christians at the Cross*. London: SPCK; Ijamsville, MD: The Word Among Us Press.

2006 *Judas and the Gospel of Jesus*. London: SPCK; Grand Rapids, MI: Baker.

2006 *Evil and the Justice of God*. London: SPCK; Downers Grove, IL: InterVarsity Press.

2006 *Simply Christian*. London: SPCK; San Francisco: HarperSanFrancisco.

2005 *Paul: Fresh Perspectives* / U.S. title *Paul in Fresh Perspective*. London: SPCK; Minneapolis: Fortress.

2005 *Scripture and the Authority of God* / U.S. title *The Last Word: Beyond the Bible Wars to a New Understanding of the Authority of Scripture*. London: SPCK; San Francisco: HarperSanFrancisco.

2003 *The Resurrection of the Son of God*. Volume 3 of *Christian Origins and the Question of God*. London: SPCK; Minneapolis: Fortress.

1999 *The Challenge of Jesus*. Downers Grove, IL: InterVarsity Press; London: SPCK.

1999   *The Millennium Myth* / British title *The Myth of the Millen-nium*. Louisville: Westminster; London: SPCK.

1997   *What St. Paul Really Said.* Oxford: Lion; Grand Rapids, MI: Eerdmans.

1996   *Jesus and the Victory of God.* Volume 2 of *Christian Origins and the Question of God.* London: SPCK; Minneapolis: Fortress.

1992   *The New Testament and the People of God.* Volume 1 of *Christian Origins and the Question of God.* London: SPCK; Minneapolis: Fortress.

NOTES

2. THE TRANSFORMATION OF CHARACTER

1. John Medina, *Brain Rules* (Seattle: Pear Press, 2008), 58, 61, 62.

2. See http://www.pnas.org/content/97/8/4398.abstract or http://en.scientificcommons.org/e_a_maguire.

3. C. S. Lewis, *Surprised by Joy: The Shape of My Early Life* (1955; London: Fontana, 1959), 115.

4. Simon Blackburn, *Oxford Dictionary of Philosophy,* 2nd ed., rev. (1994; Oxford: Oxford University Press, 2008), 319.

5. From his Foreword to the new edition of Charles C. Brown, *Niebuhr and His Age: Reinhold Niebuhr's Prophetic Role and Legacy* (1992; Harrisburg, PA: Trinity Press International, 2002), viii–ix.

4. THE KINGDOM COMING AND THE PEOPLE PREPARED

1. Bernard of Clairvaux, "Jesu, the Very Thought of Thee," tr. E. Caswall, in *Hymns Ancient and Modern (New Standard),* 14th ed. (Norwich, England: Hymns A&M Ltd., 1990), no. 120.

2. Simon Blackburn, *Oxford Dictionary of Philosophy,* 2nd. ed., rev. (1994; Oxford: Oxford University Press, 2008), 381.

5. TRANSFORMED BY THE RENEWAL OF THE MIND

1. A somewhat similar line of thought, introducing complications which go beyond our present purposes, is found in Romans 2.12–16.

6. THREE VIRTUES, NINE VARIETIES OF FRUIT, AND ONE BODY

1. Christopher Wordsworth, "Gracious Spirit, Holy Ghost" tr. E. Caswell, in *Hymns Ancient and Modern (New Standard)*, 14th ed. (Norwich, England: Hymns A&M Ltd., 1990), no. 120.

7. VIRTUE IN ACTION: THE ROYAL PRIESTHOOD

1. Rodney Stark, *The Rise of Christianity: How the Obscure, Marginal Jesus Movement Became the Dominant Religious Force* (San Francisco: HarperSanFrancisco, 1977), chap. 4.

2. See Aristotle, *Nicomachean Ethics,* book 4. The Afterword to this present volume lists two possible editions.

3. C. S. Lewis, *Miracles* (1947; San Francisco: HarperSanFrancisco, 2001), 183.

8. THE VIRTUOUS CIRCLE

1. *The Book of Common Prayer* (Cambridge: Cambridge University Press, n.d.), pp. 97–98, 156.

SCRIPTURE INDEX

SUBJECT INDEX

Aaron, 80
Abraham, 84, 153–54, 265
accidence (word formation), 40
Adam, 87
adultery, 209–10, 250
agape (love): between spouses, 251; charity as expression of, 253–54; community held together by, 207–8; description of, 144, 147; entire Law centered on, 192, 198–99; family affection and, 178; as firstfruit of the Spirit, 217; great power and strength of, 254–55; as lasting Christian virtue, 181–85, 188, 189, 205; monetary offerings as habit of, 282–83; *philia* (friendship), 183. *See also* God's love
Airbus A320 emergency, 18–20, 21
American culture: impact of financial chaos (2008) on, 8; loss of character issue of modern, 9–12; September 11, 2001, impact on, 8–9. *See also* culture; Western thought
Aquinas (Thomas Aquinas), 60, 242
arete (strength/virtue), 34, 168
Aristotle: comparing Jesus's approach to transformation to, 35–36, 42–43, 118, 125, 239–40; *eudaimonia* (flourishing) concept of, 33, 82, 89, 103, 117, 185; "hero" vision of virtuous

person by, 70; moral thinking model of, 33–34, 35–36, 70; *Nicomachean Ethics* by, 231; *polis* (city-state) center of virtue by, 204; *teleios* (perfect) goal of, 181
ashre (blessedness), 103–4
"assisted suicide," 156
atonement: at the heart of the revolution of virtue, 114–18; "theology" of, 111
Augustine, 60, 242
Augustus, 248
authenticity: appeal to freedom of, 55–57, 233–34; Christian behavior and, 30, 240; Christian worship, 224–25; eschatological, 107–8; existentialist movement on, 50, 57

baptism, 125, 280–82
baruch (blessedness), 103–4
Baxter, Laura, 22–24, 210
Baxter, Mark, 22–24, 210
Beatitudes, 104–5, 147, 229–30. *See also* Sermon on the Mount
beauty, 232
"being true to yourself," 51–52, 54–55, 57
Betjeman, John, 54–55
biblical stories, 264–67
Blackburn, Simon, 131
Bonhoeffer, Dietrich, 115